(continued from front flap)

writers—who have lived and worked there for many years and who combine first-hand knowledge with a gift for creative presentation. Joyce Cary, Otto F. Raum, Elspeth Huxley, and many others offer acute and realistic observations on an Africa they knew and loved.

African Heritage is a book which digs beneath the political facts and fancies that fill our newspapers to capture in depth the Africa of yesterday and today. Far removed from the usual cinematic, journalistic, or tourist-eye views, it presents an intimate picture of a dark continent illuminated by tradition, imagination, artistry, and humor.

* * *

JACOB DRACHLER, a member of the African Studies Association, has pursued an active interest in African life and literature for many years. During World War II he served with the Air Force in Egypt, Libya, Tunisia, and Sicily. In 1945, he was with an armed forces educational institute in London, where he was able to make extensive use of several specialized libraries on Africa. Realizing that the postwar role of Africa would be increasingly important in world affairs, and sensing the need for a deeper understanding of African cultures, he began to seek out material that could make an authentic contribution to such an understanding. This research resulted in **African Heritage.**

A graduate of New York University, Mr. Drachler is a teacher and an artist.

African Heritage

Selected and Edited,
with an Introduction by

JACOB DRACHLER

African
Heritage

Intimate Views of the
Black Africans from Life,
Lore, and Literature

Preface by
MELVILLE J. HERSKOVITS
Director, Program of African Studies,
Northwestern University.

THE CROWELL-COLLIER PRESS

First Crowell-Collier Press Edition 1963

Library of Congress Catalog Card Number: 62-16139

Grateful acknowledgment for permission to reprint the selections in this volume is due to the following:

Peter Abrahams for NKRUMAH, KENYATTA AND THE OLD ORDER, a portion of his article first published in *Holiday* Magazine under the title, "The Blacks," Copyright © 1959 by The Curtis Publishing Company.

Africa South Magazine for LOVE SONG OF A XHOSA GIRL; and GREETING THE BRITISH PRINCE, an excerpt from a poem by S. E. K. Mqhayi.

American Society of African Culture for AFRICAN DANCE by Pearl Primus; THE POLITICAL ELITES AND AFRICA'S FUTURE from "Evaluation of African Societies" by St. Clair Drake; and THE BLACK POET'S SEARCH FOR IDENTITY from "Tendencies in African Poetry" by Samuel Allen, all in *Africa from the Point of View of American Negro Scholars.*

Appleton-Century-Crofts, an affiliate of Meredith Press, for THE SOOTHSAYER from *The Leopard Priestess* by R. S. Rattray. Copyright, 1935, D. Appleton-Century Co. Inc.

Jonathan Cape Ltd. and the author for THE "FREE WOMEN" of CONGO CITY from *The African Awakening* by Basil Davidson, where it appeared as a chapter entitled "By the Waters of Babylon."

The Clarendon Press for THREE ASHANTI TALES from *Akan-Ashanti Folk Tales* by Robert S. Rattray.

The John Day Company, Inc. and Victor Gollancz Ltd. for ABOARD AN AFRICAN TRAIN from *Road to Ghana* by Alfred Hutchinson, Copyright © 1960 by Alfred Hutchinson.

Editions du Seuil and Georges Borchardt for THREE POEMS BY LÉOPOLD S. SENGHOR: "Black Woman" ("Femme Noire") and "Night in Senegal" ("Nuit de Sine") from *Éthiopiques* and "The Hurricane" ("L'Ouragan") from *Chants D'Ombre.*

Editions du Seuil, Georges Borchardt and the author for the poem To AFRICA, by Aimé Cesaire.

4

Permissions

Faber & Faber Ltd. for EPILOGUE TO APARTHEID from *Down Second Avenue* by Ezekiel Mphahlele; BARBING DAY IN THE TOWN OF SHORT GHOSTS from *My Life in the Bush of Ghosts* by Amos Tutuola; THE GOLDEN AGE OF CHIEF NJEMANZE from *African Women* by Sylvia Leith-Ross; and THE BLIND SINGER from "The Story of Bwembya" (recorded by Audrey I. Richards) in *Ten Africans* edited by Margery Perham.

William Fagg and the British Broadcasting Corporation for his talk THE TRIBAL ARTIST which appeared in *The Listener* under the title "The Dilemma of African Art."

Farrar, Straus & Cudahy, Inc. and William Collins Sons & Co. Ltd. for THE MYSTERIES OF MY FATHER'S WORKSHOP from *The Dark Child* by Camara Laye. Copyright 1954 by Camara Laye.

Fasquelle and Georges Borchardt for THE STORIES WHICH CRADLED MY CHILDHOOD and BREATHS from *Les Contes d'Amadou Koumba* by Birago Diop.

The Golden Cockerel Press for SONG OF A MOTHER TO HER FIRST-BORN from *Initiation* (Translations from Poems of the Didinga and Lango Tribes) by Jack H. Driberg.

Harper & Brothers and Michael Joseph Ltd. for MISTER JOHNSON from *Mister Johnson* by Joyce Cary.

Mrs. Frances S. Herskovits and *The New Republic* for two "Songs for the Dead"; Mrs. Herskovits and *The Yale Review* for "To Destiny," copyright Yale University Press; Mrs. Herskovits and *Poetry* Magazine for "To the Sun God," "For the Earth God," and "Song for the Dead" in SIX SONGS FROM DAHOMEY.

Thomas Hodgkin and the British Broadcasting Corporation for his talk THE AFRICAN RENAISSANCE, which was reprinted in *The Listener*.

Lutterworth Press for WAR AND PEACE IN OLD KENYA from *My People of the Kikuyu* by Jomo Kenyatta.

William Morrow and Company, Inc. and Chatto & Windus Ltd. for CHANGES ON THE LAND IN KENYA and ALL THE KAMBA ARE MY CHILDREN from *A New Earth* by Elspeth Huxley. Copyright © by Elspeth Huxley 1960.

The New York Times for THE DIGNITY OF MAN by Albert Luthuli.

Abioseh Nicol for his poem THE MEANING OF AFRICA.

Northwestern University Press and the authors for CREATIVE IMPULSES IN DAHOMEAN POETRY from *Dahomean Narrative* by Melville J. and Frances S. Herskovits (1958).

Oxford University Press and the International African Institute for FOUR TALES FROM TOGOLAND from *Tales Told in Togoland* by A. W. Cardinall; TEN PROVERBS FROM LIBERIA from *Jabo*

5

6

To Rose and Nina with love

"What's past is prologue."
—Shakespeare, *The Tempest*

Preface

MORE AND MORE, African modes of creative expression are receiving attention as we seek to understand the thinking of Africans who are responsible for and support developments in the continent. The African, long regarded as a lay figure in the African scene, whose role was to be manipulated by those of presumed superior culture and proved superior power, has suddenly come to life. The dynamic quality of his traditions, the subtlety of his skill in ordering human relations, and his adaptability to change, are increasingly being recognized. These remain matters for debate only among those who, because of ignorance or prejudice, will not see what is self-evident for those who view Africa realistically.

The present book derives its importance from this reorientation. Mr. Drachler, in his selection of materials, gives us a needed view of the human element in changing African life as reflected in what has been written about it by Africans and those who, though not Africans, know about it. He does what few writing about Africa do when they use the word "Africa" in the titles of their works. Unlike them, he ranges the entire Subsaharan continent, sampling the literary productivity of the writers in different parts of it, and works concerning these parts by non-Africans.

It is particularly to the point that he gives full weight to the writings of the Africans who use French as their vehicle. So few Americans interested in Africa control French—to say nothing of Portuguese—that scholarly work and popular writing alike have been overweighted by the attention given those parts of the continent where English is spoken. Yet French is the second language, and the official means of communication, in vast areas—all of what was French West and Equatorial Africa, and the great reaches of the Congo.

9

The African contributions range from recordings of oral tradition, translated from the aboriginal languages in which, as yet, a minimum of written literary forms have been produced, to poetry written in English and French, framed by Euroamerican conventions of prosody. These oral traditions make us aware of both the literary resources and literary potential of African cultures. Our view has long been befogged by our culture-bound conception of what is literature. Once free of the ambiguities implicit when we designate narrative and other forms designed for oral presentation as "folklore," we see aboriginal oral art for what it is, a valid expression of the creative imagination, channeled by a sophisticated assessment of man and his relation to the world in which he lives. The poetry cast in the Euroamerican model likewise has a value for us that goes beyond its aesthetic quality. For it demonstrates, here as in so many other manifestations of African capacities, the ability to adapt earlier conventions so as to take advantage of new forms of expression.

A substantial proportion of the African writing included in this book was published before the "year of Africa," which dramatized the penultimate phase of the colonial system by bringing most of the continent to self-government. What strikes us as we read these writings is how the colonial powers could have disregarded the clear evidence of living, passionate protest against the status of dependency given by them or, in the face of the psychological subtleties in the tales recounted by the peoples they governed, how they could have ever conceived the notion that they were dealing with a child race. In some measure, of course, this failure to grasp the realities must be assigned to the nature of administrative routine. Colonial officials were too pressed by problems of the moment, such as those of local government, economic development, industrialization and social change, to give the time and attention needed if they were to digest the meaning of the African oral narrative, the African poet's protest, the African writer's plea, or even the analysis of African thought by non-Africans.

There was another reason, too, for their disregard; one that arose out of some of the deepest values in European as in American culture. This is touched on by Mr. Drachler in his

Introduction, where he discusses the concept of underdevelopment. He quite correctly stresses the limited applicability of the term which treats man, as he tellingly puts it, "in his having and not in his being." The poetry, the tales, and the other manifestations of the African creative drive were disregarded because they were held to be of secondary importance when such matters as technological development, the needs of a changing economic system or the problem of adjustment to an urban setting called for attention. And this point of view continues to be dominant. It is apparent in the nature of "aid" programs, which are devoted almost entirely to providing material needs. Except for furthering education, which is held to be an essential part of the infrastructure of an economically viable present day society, the writers, the artists, the musicians are left to shift for themselves. Perhaps, as far as they are concerned, this is as it should be. But we cannot afford to neglect what they produce.

Their work is significant in another dimension. Because of the orientation of this book, it gives less attention to certain revealing concepts of importance in African thought than would otherwise be the case. One such concept is *négritude,* discussed in the following essays by Samuel Allen and Thomas Hodgkin. This concept, like that of "the African personality," represents profound reaction to the denigration of the African and his culture that marked the colonial period, and which brought many of the Africans to the psychologically perilous position of questioning the basic values by which they had been taught to live. Protest was the first move to reestablish these values—protest against the down-grading of Africans and their ways to which they had been consistently and increasingly exposed as they came to have more intimate contact with currents of thought among Europeans.

Overemphasis on the values they were convinced lay in their heritage, an obvious reaction of indignation and protest, is now being succeeded by analysis. The questions being raised reveal the nature of African thinking. What, in essence, is *négritude?* Wherein lies "the African personality"? What values are hidden in the manifestations of an African genius they imply; how can the values that the African feels are lodged in his traditional heritage be reestablished? In their writings, Africans are debating these questions, and it is through these writings that we can glimpse the answers toward which they are reaching. This is why we must have a care that these writings be not submerged in attention paid to the "practical" issues of Africa. For it is in the answers that the Africans reach today that the future of the African peoples will lie.

MELVILLE J. HERSKOVITS

Northwestern University
June 27, 1962

Introduction:

TOWARD TRUE DIALOGUE WITH AFRICA

What are Africans really like?

This question is not one bit easier to answer than a similar one about Europeans would be. We speak of European civilization, even though we are aware of the many significant differences between, say, Russians and Englishmen, Spaniards and Germans, or Italians and Frenchmen. As for the American transplant of the European tree, how remarkably new and different have been its fruits. Nevertheless, serious inquiry does not hesitate to trace the main streams of the European heritage to their sources, nor to seek the common cultural ground on which Western men stand.

So too there are great diversities among Negro African cultures. The search for common elements among them is still in its beginnings, however. One great difficulty here is the absence until the last hundred years of a written literature by Negro Africans. This lack has now begun to be supplied by the new African writers and thinkers. The literature *about* Africa, of course, is already vast. It is the purpose of this anthology to make readily available some of the best and most readable writings by and about the black Africans.

While there has been much valid and interesting material available, people have too often neglected this wealth of information because of prejudice and ignorance. A primary source of error has been the distorted conception of the "primitive" and the "savage." As Professor Herskovits points out in his book, *Man and His Works,* "Evidence is vast that the portrayal of the savage as a creature living in anarchism, without moral restraint, without sensibilities, is a vulgar caricature."

A more genteel caricature—but nonetheless a caricature—

13

is imbedded in the now popular term, the "underdeveloped" society. The implication here is that the more *things* a society has, the more "developed" it is. To this way of thinking, an African with a bicycle or a motorcar is like any other man with a cycle or a car. His possessions define him—or his lack of them. There is indeed a truth in this materialism. The fellow-feeling of cyclists or motorists the world over can be real and warm. Mutual understanding likewise can be fostered by sharing the benefits of electric generators, antibiotics, printing presses—the things of "developed" societies.

But the basic trouble with the well-intentioned concept of "underdevelopment" is that it tends to ignore the deeper, more moving concerns of life: attitudes toward work, play, love, children; responses to nature and death; use of traditions and wisdom. "Underdevelopment" tells us nothing about laughter, poetry, wonder, worship. In short, it treats man in his having and not in his being. *African Heritage,* on the contrary, aims to present the African in his being, as he is involved with these moving concerns of life.

This anthology, therefore, does not deal primarily with economics or politics (although their importance is undoubtedly great and calls forth a continuous flood of books). We seek rather to take the reader behind the headlines, behind the ever shifting and complicated political developments of Black Africa, to reveal the people in the essential patterns of personal existence. While the selections represent in generous measure recent African culture and social development, they also place a major emphasis on picturing the old ways of the African clan and tribe, for until we do justice to the full human stature of tribal man, we cannot meet him, or his de-tribalized compatriots, in fruitful dialogue.

A sort of mutilated dialogue has been going on between Negro Africa and the outside world for about five centuries. But slavery, coercion, and exploitation are hardly fit mediums for human conversation. Nevertheless, there have been thousands of individuals who, transcending institutions of over-lordship, have met Africans—and been met by them—as human beings. Healers, scholars, teachers—both black and white—have over the years built reservoirs of good will, of disinterested knowledge and understanding, which it has been the aim of this collection to draw upon.

But it is only in mid-twentieth century that a truer dialogue between Africa and the world has begun, for true dialogue can only flourish in an atmosphere of equality. That equality, signaled by the dramatic upsurge of nationalist movements and independent states, is now in the air we breathe. For the human meaning of that equality, we need to go deeper than the political facts and fancies that fill our daily news media. We have to seek more basic knowledge of the African: What does he believe? What are the ruling forms of his imagination? What underlying values guide his life, whether of the old Africa or the new? In short, what is the African heritage, and in what ways does it survive the onslaughts of change?

It is questions of this sort that will sound the most significant themes in the world dialogue. The same questions the Africans will likewise ask of the other cultures, each side listening, learning, and more truly defining itself.

Within this broader dialogue, a more particular and poignant interchange emerges—that between the Africans and the Afro-Americans, the new-world Negroes whose ancestors were so tragically torn from their native lands. In the United States, the Carribean area, and South America there are probably over forty million people of African descent. It has been strikingly shown by Herskovits and others that African cultural traits have survived in varying degrees among these Negroes of the western hemisphere. However, until quite recently very few Afro-Americans have chosen to identify themselves consciously and positively with their African background. Over the years, only a handful of Negro scholars, such as Carter G. Woodson, applied themselves to research and writing about the African heritage. This situation is now changing radically.

Today, twenty million Americans of African descent move impressively forward in their own struggles for equality, with a new sense of dignity and identity inspired in part by the phenomenal rise of the Negro nations of Africa and their growing importance on the world scene. Evidences multiply that a new interest in the African identity has taken deep root among Afro-American intellectuals.

In Part II of this collection, Afro-American Responses, we

present a varied group of selections from several poets, a novelist, a creative scholar of the dance, and a sociologist to illustrate the many ways in which these cultural leaders are seriously involved with their African background.

One of these, René Maran, author of the novel, *Batouala,* from which we reprint a chapter, was the first Negro writer to make Africa the subject of a notable literary work, and his influence has been widespread. Born in Martinique, he spent ten years in French Africa as an administrator, and raised a literary storm in Paris because of his novel's passionate identification with the grievances of the Africans.

Naturally, the Africans themselves contribute the major part of this anthology, whether they are gifted storytellers known only in their own localities, or the writers of books read in places far from Africa. Part I, African Voices, starts with the oral literature,—the tales, songs, and proverbs which are the prime repository for the wit and wisdom of the people. For Africans, they are evening theater and daytime school. For us, also, they are both entertainment and instruction. From them we can learn something of the forms of feeling and imagination that are in the grain of African culture. The influence of the oral literature is likely to persist, not only because tribal and rural life will not soon be finished in Africa, but because new generations of African writers will probably continue to refresh themselves at this source, no matter how many springs of world literature they choose to drink from.

About the turn of the century, the first noteworthy creators of written African literature began to emerge heroically from obscurity. Encouraged to write in their native languages under missionary tutelage, they were in an extraordinarily difficult situation for writers. They had few or no African antecedents whom they could follow in what they were trying to do. And what was perhaps a greater disadvantage, they had very small audiences of fellow Africans who could read their works.

Under such conditions, Thomas Mofolo of Basutoland produced the first African historical novel, *Chaka,* about the dreaded Zulu king whose Genghis-like career is treated by the author as a Macbeth story. In marked contrast with this is another of Mofolo's books, the mystical tale, *The Traveller of the East.* Excerpts from both of these books are given not

merely as examples of literary expression, but as authentic
pictures of phases of the African heritage.

During the same period in a remote part of Nigeria, Akiga,
the first of the Tiv tribe to receive a missionary education,
spent twenty years of his life in a labor of love, an exhaustive
study of the folkways of his people combined with autobiography. Our excerpts from *Akiga's Story* reveal a person
of great charm and intelligence, who, while he embraced the
"new knowledge" of Christianity, clung all the more to his
tribal heritage.

Another of the literary "forerunners" was B. W. Vilakazi,
who wrote noteworthy poetry in the Zulu language. His
brooding poem, "In the Gold Mines," pictures the terrible
toll of African lives taken by the white men's underground
Moloch.

The note of protest against white domination was not
absent from other early African literary work, as can be seen
from our selection by another pioneer of African writing,
S.E.K. Mqhayi, the trenchantly ironical praise-poem, "Greeting the British Prince."

The tide of the new generation of African intellectuals
began to rise during the period of World War II and after.
Most of these men were educated at the universities of
France, England, and the United States. All of them wrote in
English or French rather than in their native vernaculars.
They became the political leaders, scholars, poets, teachers,
and journalists of their countries. Selections from their
writings account for the longest chapter in this volume. While
they all favor developing and modernizing Africa, it is interesting to note in how many of their stories, essays, and poems
the theme of the old Africa looms large. Whether it is the
important and controversial political leader, Jomo Kenyatta,
making an excursion into the early history of his tribe, or the
sociologist, K. A. Busia, discussing African religious concepts,
the sense of the heritage is strongly present.

One is not likely to forget Camara Laye's beautiful account
of his father practicing the mysteries of the goldsmith's craft.
Is the aura of poetry we find there to be identified with sentimental nostalgia? Or isn't it more likely to flow from the
durable conviction that some essence of African selfhood is

at stake in the poetry of the older ways? In French-writing Africans, such as Diop, Laye, Dadié, and Senghor, poetic feeling and form seem most natural. Is this perhaps the result of the strong literary bias of French education and the artistic ambience of a place like Paris? Or is the African heritage— with its religion, its music, its dancing, its songs, and stories— the basic school of poetry which French training does less to negate?

At any rate, the virtues of the English-speaking Africans are not usually of the poetic sort. Our outstanding examples here—Hutchinson, Mphahlele, Abrahams (all, by the way, exiles from an impossible-to-live-with South African regime)—write a vivid, dramatic prose. They tend to share a rational rebellion against white oppression and a rationalist distrust of the old tribal order. The African dignity they envision seems to be oriented toward the future without very strong emotional ties to the past. But even Peter Abrahams, whose intimate account shows us how keenly such important Africans as Kenyatta and Nkrumah feel the tensions between the old and the new, concludes that there are some things in the African heritage worth saving: "If the men inaugurating the new ways have the sense and the patience to preserve the finer qualities of the old ways and fuse these with the new, then we can expect something magnificently new out of Africa."

Thus the third dialogue illuminated in this book is that between western-educated Africans and their pre-European heritage.

Since the aim of *African Heritage* is to let Africans be seen close up and understood in depth, we cannot neglect the abundant resources of interpretation by non-Africans. In Part III, Through the Eyes of Others, we have selected writings by white scholars who have lived and worked with Africans, often for many years, and who combine deep knowledge with a gift for interesting presentation. Here again it is the African person who is the center of our focus. Narratives, anecdotes, reminiscences, portraits, dialogue, quotations—these are the preferred forms of material to ensure that the information is presented in its personal dimensions.

Two unusual selections are chapters taken from novels written by anthropologists. In R. S. Rattray's *The Leopard Priestess* and J. H. Driberg's *People of the Small Arrow,* we have profound knowledge of tribal cultures cast in vivid fictional form. We are thus able in the one case to be present at a seance where a soothsayer searches out the "guilt" that brought about a lion's attack on a village. In the other case, we witness the beautiful New Year's ritual for bringing good crops to a clan's gardens, and hear the prayers, the songs, and jests of the people.

If an anthropologist can turn novelist, something like the reverse is also possible, as in the delightful excerpt from *Mister Johnson* by Joyce Cary. Joyce Cary happens to have had long experience in Africa and wrote several novels with African backgrounds. We are fortunate to have African characterizations from the pen of this fine artist.

It would be difficult to find any piece of writing more heart-wrenching than the little vignette of the blinded singer recorded by Dr. Audrey I. Richards; or glimpses of children at play more captivating than those afforded us by Dr. Otto F. Raum; or portraits of people more inspiring than Elspeth Huxley's picture of the redoubtable, obscure old woman in Kenya who generaled the building of a dam because, as she said, "All the Kamba are my children"; or domestic contretemps more diverting than the anecdote of a family quarrel, again reported by Dr. Richards.

In our final chapter, "Roots of the Future," we offer four penetrating views of aspects of the cultural heritage. Will African culture—poetry, art, literature, philosophy—find the resources to enter the stream of world culture without being swept away and losing its identity? What part will resilient African character and traditions play? What part will be played by the thousands of young Africans now studying in universities throughout the world?

Answers to these questions—though, of course, not definitive ones—are suggested throughout *African Heritage* and particularly in the last chapter.

Will the new intellectuals find the traditional oral literature usable? The creative vigor of Dahomean oral poetry, for example, is thoroughly documented by M. J. and F. S.

Herskovits. In Dahomey, poetry originates in all sorts of sacred and secular contexts and is truly an everyday matter; it is composed by ordinary men and women as well as by professional verse makers—where can one find a livelier cultural situation than this? But can it be preserved when sacred and secular customs are destroyed by modernizing forces?

William Fagg, a leading authority on African art, poses the same question with reference to the plastic arts. Outside commercial influences on tribal art, as Mr. Fagg shows, can be lethal and absurd. They tend to replace good art with nonart.

T. L. Hodgkin's brilliant discussion of a pioneering international Negro conference in 1956 demonstrates that the Negro intellectuals of Africa and elsewhere may not have the answers but are acutely aware of the issues involved in preserving or creating African initiative, individuality, and self-confidence in the field of culture.

Bantu Philosophy, a small book by the Franciscan missionary Placied Tempels, has already had a very large influence since it was published in the Belgian Congo in 1945. Here a man with a long and intimate knowledge of Africans shows that a subtle, humane, and coherent system of thought does exist among Africans, not written down by them but implicit in custom, ritual, act, and comment.

In fact, *African Heritage* in its entirety may be seen to project the Africans' full human spectrum of feeling and wisdom, of ethical concern and esthetic expression.

For the prologue and epilogue of this book (and also under "Afro-American Responses") we have used sections of Melvin B. Tolson's long poem, *Libretto for the Republic of Liberia,* which, in our opinion, is the greatest poem thus far written on the theme of Africa. Simply as poetry, subject aside, it is a superb modern work. Tolson, an American Negro poet, was commissioned to write it to help celebrate, in 1947, the centennial of the founding of the Liberian republic, the oldest Negro republic in Africa. But the subject of *The Libretto* is not Liberia alone but Africa and the whole gamut of Negro experience as part of the human story, "a moment of the conscience of mankind." It has been well said that *"The Libretto,* christened for a historic occasion, voyages beyond this time and that place—voyages into the world of all times and all men."

African culture itself is embarked on this voyage.

JACOB DRACHLER

Acknowledgments

I wish to thank the following people for all they have done to make this book possible: the authors of the selections, both African and non-African, who are the prime makers of the book; Bruno Fischer, Executive Editor of Collier Books, who brought it to the light of day; Melville J. Herskovits and Frances S. Herskovits, who gave me many valuable suggestions, but, of course, are not responsible for my editorial judgments; my wife Rose for all sorts of help, particularly in preliminary screening of a vast literature; my sister, Mrs. Sophie Schwartz, for faithful typing of selections; Anne Atik for her fine translations from the French; and also Dr. Meyer Fortes, Samuel Allen, Hugh Tracey, Ronald Segal and Dr. A. C. Jordan for their generous help. The facilities and co-operation of the following organizations were invaluable: the International African Institute, London; Présence Africaine, Paris; and the American Society of African Culture, New York.

J. D.

Contents

Chapter 2 Forerunners: Written Literature in African Languages

Chapter 3 The New Generation: African Literature in European Languages

PART TWO · AFRO-AMERICAN RESPONSES

Chapter 4   Affirmations: The New-World Negro and His Heritage

PART THREE · THROUGH THE EYES OF OTHERS

Chapter 5   The Old Order: Personality in the Matrix of Tradition

Chapter 6   **Between The Old and The New:**
Ways of Life in Transition

Chapter 7   **Roots Of The Future:**   **Aspects of**
the Cultural Heritage

Epilogue

African Heritage

Prologue

FROM LIBRETTO FOR THE REPUBLIC OF LIBERIA

M. B. Tolson

Liberia?
No micro-footnote in a bunioned book
Homed by a pedant
With a gelded look:
You are
The ladder of survival dawn men saw
In the quicksilver sparrow that slips
The eagle's claw!

Liberia?
No side-show barker's bio-accident,
No corpse of a soul's errand
To the Dark Continent:
You are
The lightning rod of Europe, Canaan's key,
The rope across the abyss,
Mehr licht for the Africa-To-Be!

Liberia?
No haply black man's X
Fixed to a Magna Charta without a magic-square
By Helon's leprous hand, to haunt and vex:
You are
The Orient of Colors everywhere,
The oasis of Tahoua, the salt bar of Harrar,
To trekkers in saharas, in sierras, with Despair!

Liberia?
No oil-boiled Barabas,
No Darwin's bulldog for ermined flesh,

No braggart Lamech, no bema's Ananias:
                    You are
Libertas[1] flayed and naked by the road
To Jericho, for a people's five score years
Of bones for manna, for balm an alien goad!

                    Liberia?
No pimple on the chin of Africa,
No brass-lipped cicerone of Big Top democracy,
No lamb to tame a lion with a baa:
                    You are
Black Lazarus risen from the White Man's grave,
Without a road to Downing Street,
Without a hemidemisemiquaver in an Oxford stave!

                    Liberia?
No Cobra Pirate of the Question Mark,
No caricature with a mimic flag
And golden joys to fat the shark:
                    You are
American genius uncrowned in Europe's charnel-house.
Leave fleshpots for the dogs and apes; for Man
The books whose head is golden espouse!

                    Liberia?
No waste land yet, nor yet a destooled [2] elite,
No merry-andrew, an Ed-dehebi[3] at heart,
With St. Paul's root and Breughel's cheat:
                    You are
The iron nerve of lame and halt and blind,
                    Liberia and not Liberia,
A moment of the conscience of mankind!

[1] The motto of Liberia: "The love of liberty brought us here."
[2] On the Gold Coast the stool is the symbol of the soul of the
nation, its Magna Charta. In 1900 Sir Frederick Hodgson, Gov-
nor of the Gold Coast, demanded that the Ashantis surrender
their "stool." They immediately declared war. "Destooling" is a
veto exercised by the sovereign people over unpopular rulers.
[3] "The Master of Gold." He was the conqueror of Songhai with
its fabulous gold mines.

PART ONE
AFRICAN VOICES

Chapter 1

At the Source:
The Oral Literature of the People

FOUR TALES FROM TOGOLAND

In one of the following tales, "The Eye of the Giant," Death is momentarily killed by men. At the roots of his hair they find a magical substance with which they restore Death's victims. But ironically, the same substance, sprinkled by a curious youth, restores Death himself. This ambivalence—actually a profound realism—is to be found over and over again not only in the stories, but in the proverbs, songs, and other oral literature of Africa.

One might call "The Eye of the Giant" simply a *Just So* story intended to account for the origin of death. It has that effect, certainly. But it goes beyond didacticism; it touches off a shudder of recognition: death and life are inseparable.

A shudder of the conscience is the theme of "The Hunter Who Hunts No More." Here also we have a paradox: that which is sanctioned and indeed essential to life (hunting) is also brought under a ban, at least for this particular hunter.

In the Ashanti tale about the origin of divorce, the hunter is granted the magic knowledge of the language of all creatures. This knowledge gets him into serious trouble with his mother-in-law, but the same gift also presents him with his solution. The word which effects a divorce is a "forbidden" word, but it comes to be permitted by the Sky-god. A permitted forbidden word—what better definition for divorce? And with all this, we get the irresistible earthy humor about the hens and the cock.

Humor—whether of the Rabelaisian or Machiavellian sort

—seasons the famous Anansi stories. Anansi is the trickster hero who is sometimes tricked himself (as in "The Singing Cloak"). He is the hero and villain of countless stories that celebrate the triumph of the underdog, the superiority of cunning over power. The trickery is often delightfully devious and sometimes of a nursery nastiness that is not unknown in polite society elsewhere.

Needless to say, the four tales from Togoland and the three Ashanti tales which are presented in the following pages are only a small sampling of the wealth and range of African stories.

The Eye of the Giant

LONG, LONG AGO there was a great famine in the world, and a certain young man whilst wandering in search of food strayed into a part of the bush where he had never been before. Presently he perceived a strange mass lying on the ground. He approached and saw that it was the body of a giant whose hair resembled that of white men in that it was silky rather than woolly. It was of an incredible length and stretched as far as from Krachi to Salaga. The young man was properly awed at the spectacle, and wished to withdraw, but the giant noticing him asked what he wanted.

The young man explained and begged the giant to give him some food. The latter agreed on condition that the youth would serve him for a while. This matter having been arranged, the giant said his name was Owuo or Death, and then gave the boy some meat.

Never before had the latter tasted such fine food, and he was well pleased with his bargain. He served his master for a long time and received plenty of meat, but one day he grew homesick, and begged his master to give him a short holiday. The latter agreed if the youth would promise to bring another boy in his place. So the youth returned to his village and there persuaded his brother to go with him into the bush and gave him to Owuo.

In course of time the youth got hungry again and longed for the meat which Owuo had taught him to like so much.

So one day he made up his mind to return to his master, and leaving the village made his way back to the giant's abode. The latter asked him what he wanted, and when the youth told him that he wanted to taste once more of the good meat, the giant told him to enter the hut and take as much as he liked, but he would have to work for him again.

The youth agreed and entered the hut. He ate as much as he could, and set to at the task his master set him. The work continued for a long time and the boy ate his fill every day. But to his surprise he never saw anything of his brother, and whenever he asked about him the giant told him that the lad was away on his business.

Once more the youth grew homesick and asked for leave to return to his village. The giant agreed on condition that he would bring a girl for him, Owuo, to wed. So the youth went home and there persuaded his sister to go into the bush and marry the giant. The girl agreed, and took with her a slave companion, and they all repaired to the giant's abode. There the youth left the two girls and went back to the village.

It was not very long after that he again grew hungry and longed for the taste of the meat. So he made his way once more into the bush and found the giant. The giant did not seem overpleased to see the boy and grumbled at being bothered a fourth time. However, he told the boy to go into the inner chamber of his hut and take what he wanted. The youth did so and took up a bone which he began to devour. To his horror he recognized it at once as being the bone of his sister. He looked around at all the rest of the meat and saw that it was that of his sister and her slave girl.

Thoroughly frightened he escaped from the house and ran back into the village. There he told the elders what he had done and the awful thing he had seen. At once the alarm was sounded and all the people went out into the bush to see for themselves the dread thing they had heard about. When they drew near to the giant, they grew afraid at the sight of so evil a monster. They went back to the village and consulted among themselves what best they should do. At last it was agreed to go to Salaga where the giant's hair finished and set light to it. This was done, and when the hair was burning well, they returned to the bush and watched the giant.

Presently the latter began to toss about and sweat. It was quite evident that he was beginning to feel the heat. The nearer the flames advanced the more he tossed and grumbled. At last the fire reached his head, and for the moment the giant was dead.

The villagers approached him cautiously, and the young man noticed "medicine" which had been concealed in the roots of the giant's hair. He took it and called the others to come and see what he had found. No one could say what power this medicine might have, but an old man suggested that no harm would be done if they took some and sprinkled it on the bones and meat in the hut. This idea was carried out, and to the surprise of every one, the girls and the boy returned to life at once.

The youth who had still some of the medicine left proposed to put it on the giant. But at this there was a great uproar, as the people feared Owuo might come to life again. The boy therefore by way of compromise sprinkled it into the eye of the dead giant. At once the eye opened and the people all fled away in terror. But it is from that eye that death comes; for every time that Owuo shuts that eye a man dies, and unfortunately for us he is for ever blinking and winking.

The Singing Cloak

ANANSI AND THE Chameleon used to live in the same town. Anansi was a rich man and had plenty of children to help him with his farming, but the Chameleon was only a poor man and alone had to till his farm. Now it chanced that one year the rain fell only on the Chameleon's farm, and on Anansi's there was a complete drought. Thus the spider's farm did not come up at all, and the Chameleon's was already well up and a good harvest promised.

This annoyed Anansi, and one day he called on the Chameleon and asked him if he would sell him his farm, but the Chameleon said he would not, because if he did he would not be able to get any food during the dry season. Then Anansi was even angrier than before, and swore he would have revenge on the Chameleon.

Now it happens that chameleons do not make any roads as others do. They like to walk over the grass and bushes. Thus there was no path leading from the Chameleon's house to his farm. So that night, Anansi called all his children together and told them to clean and make a good path from his compound to the Chameleon's farm. At first, they begged their father not to do this, but as he insisted they obeyed him, and in the morning there was finished a clean road and a well-used one leading from Anansi's house to the farm.

Anansi at once went to the farm and began to pull up some cassava. Presently the Chameleon came along and saw Anansi taking his cassava and called out: "Hi! Anansi, what are you doing in my farm?" Anansi at once replied: "Go away and do not vex me. Can you not see that I am busy working in my farm?"

"Your farm," cried the Chameleon, "why, it is my farm, and every one knows that." "Do not be silly; go away," answered the Spider, "or I shall get angry and kill you."

So the Chameleon went away and laid a complaint before the chief. Anansi was sent for, and when both had told him how the farm was theirs, the chief asked for proofs. Then Anansi said: "That is easy. I have a path from my house straight to the farm, which the Chameleon is falsely claiming. He has no path."

The chief saw that if Anansi was speaking true then verily the farm must be his. So he sent his messenger to see and the man came back and said that it was so. Then the Chameleon was asked what he had to say, and he said that he did not know anything about the path, that he always used to go there over the bushes and grass. This made the chief laugh, and he at once gave the farm to Anansi, who took all his children with him and gathered the crops.

The Chameleon did not know what to do. He was very poor and had but little food left to keep him alive. So he went to his house and shut the door and refused to see any one.

For many days he remained thus thinking over his wrongs and wondering how to get revenge. Then he began to dig a hole. He dug and dug and dug and made an immense well. It went far down. No man had ever seen such a well. When the

Chameleon thought he had made it large enough he made some mud and began to roof the well so that soon only a very small hole was left.

Then the Chameleon went out to see Anansi. He came to the latter's house and greeted him: "Master, I am only a poor man. May I go to your farm and glean what you have left there?" And Anansi was pleased at the Chameleon's humility and told him he could. But there was little in the farm to gather. Then the Chameleon, who had deceived the spider into thinking that he was properly humbled, again sat alone in his house. This time he amused himself in catching hundreds and hundreds of that great fly which makes so big a buzzing noise. These he tied to some dried yam vines which he had brought back from the farm.

One day, the chief sent messengers to all the land to call his people together, and from every place people came into town. Then the Chameleon arose and covered himself with the dried yam vines and walked slowly like a proud and rich man to the chief's compound, and as he went he kept swinging his strange costume and the flies, being shaken, buzzed. This was wonderful, and as he drew near the chief, swinging his dress, which buzzed more and more, every one admired it and the chief himself asked to buy it. But the Chameleon refused and went home. Now Anansi was late for the meeting, and when he did arrive every one was talking about this wonderful costume. The chief told Anansi that the Chameleon had refused to sell it, and Anansi said that was nothing, and that he would buy it and would bring it to the chief.

He went and called on the Chameleon. "Friend," he said, I hear you have a most wonderful cloak, which wherever you walk sings to you. Is this so?" The Chameleon answered that it was so, and then Anansi asked him if he would sell it.

The Chameleon at first refused, but after a time did agree to sell it if Anansi would give him some food. Anansi asked how much food he would want, and the Chameleon said that he did not require a great deal, merely enough to fill the hole which Anansi himself could see. Then Anansi laughed and said that he would willingly do that, and to show that he bore him no grudge, would give him twice as much.

Then Anansi went to his own house and called his children

and told them to come with him and each to carry a little food. They all went to the Chameleon's house and began to fill the hole with food they had brought. But that hole could not be filled. All the family of Anansi worked, and for many days they carried the corn and other food to fill that hole and always the Chameleon reminded Anansi that he had promised twice the amount.

Anansi did not know what to do. He had finished all the food that there had been stored in his own bins and granaries and he had sent out in all directions to buy food. But still the hole was not filled. He sold his sheep and his cows and everything that he had, for he knew that when he did get the cloak the chief would repay him. But he could not fill the hole.

Then when the Chameleon saw that Anansi was no longer a rich man and that he had no food left for himself, he called him and said: "Friend, you have not paid me the agreed price. But I am not a hard man and I will now forgive you the rest of the debt. Here is the cloak."

Saying this he took out the cloak from its box and put it over the shoulders of Anansi.

But the cloak had been a long time in the box and the strings which held the flies were all rotted. This Anansi did not know, and when he went outside and began to swing the robe the flies all buzzed, but suddenly there came a strong blast of wind and shook the cloak too much. All the flies were released and flew away and left Anansi dressed only in the dried vine stalks of the yams.

Then all the town laughed, and Anansi grew so ashamed that he began to hide himself from that day away from the sight of man, and does not walk in the streets.

The Hunter Who Hunts No More

This is a story of the Kulparga, a race of pixies described by all the tribes in Togoland as being naked hairy folk with long noses, and feet turned the wrong way, who talk in twitterings like birds. This story is told by a certain famous hunter. The number of the heads of animals outside his com-

*pound was beyond reckoning. He was always in the bush
hunting. But one day he returned after killing a roan and
from that time he never went hunting again; and this is the
story he would tell to any young man whom he might have
noticed as likely to become a good hunter.*

As YOU KNOW, I have killed many animals. Do you not see
the heads of all I have killed at my door? But I do not go
into the bush now to hunt, for I have seen a fearsome thing.
All men who hunt learn strange things, but this is more fearful than any other I have seen or heard.

I had killed a large roan. When I shot it, it ran away and
I followed the blood trail. This led me to a great baobab tree
and there the trail finished and I could see no more marks. I
looked and looked everywhere, but I could see nothing. I
grew tired and I sat down by a tree to rest, and as I was sitting there I saw an old man coming along.

He was carrying on his head a part of a white ants' nest
for his fowls. When he came up he asked me what I was
doing, and I told him how I had shot the large roan and how
the trail had finished at the large baobab. He told me that
was what one might have expected, and that if I followed him
he would show me things.

He told me to leave my gun behind against the tree and
then took me into the tree through a long dark hole. We
came out into a wonderful village which I knew at once to
be the village of the Kulparga. It was a very rich place and
the houses were much larger than ours and cleaner, and the
people had rich clothes. But as we drew near, we heard the
noise of much weeping, and we learned that the eldest son of
the chief was dying.

We went to the house of the chief and there saw the young
man. He was a very fine man to look at, but he had been
wounded in the chest and his life was certainly near its end.
I asked how the accident had occurred and I was told that
there was a certain hunter in my own village who was always
killing the young men of this fairy township and that they
were very much afraid of him. They told me that they did not
understand why he was always doing this as they had never
done him any ill thing. I knew then that they spoke of me.

At last the young man died and my friend the old man told me to come away. We went back the road we had come and passed through the baobab tree. Then the old man left me. And as I came out, there at the foot of the tree lay my roan shot through the chest.

From that day to this I have never hunted. And you will hear that many other hunters have seen the same thing which I have just told you.

The Gourd Full of Wisdom

THE SPIDER NOTICED one day how other people than himself were beginning to use wisdom. This did not suit him at all, as he wanted to keep all the wisdom for himself. So he collected it all and put it into a large gourd that he had hollowed out for the purpose. He then hung the gourd up on the wall of his house. But his fears were not allayed and he decided to hide it right away in the bush where no man could find it. Therefore on the following morning he took down the gourd from the wall, and accompanied by his son went forth into the bush. Presently they came to a tall palm tree, and it seemed to the spider that if he put the gourd at the top among the foliage it would be quite safe. So he began to climb the palm tree. But the gourd was a large one and the spider had slung it in front of him. So he could not make any progress. Always the gourd got in his way. Now the son of the spider had been watching his father's efforts and at last cried out: "Father, why not sling the gourd over your back?"

And Anansi the spider answered: "My son, you are right: but your words show to me that it is better for many people to have wisdom rather than one. For alone I should not have thought of that." So speaking, he opened the gourd and scattered the wisdom all over the ground so that he who may want it can gather what he will.

TWO SONGS FROM SOUTHERN RHODESIA

These two songs were chosen from the many that have been collected and translated by Hugh Tracey, director of the International Library of African Music at Johannesburg. Each song deals with a poignant situation in a manner that is pure poetry.

The Refusal

She went with an elder down to the stream,
And left him where she threw him aside into the rushes.
"Why cast me into these reeds, woman?" he said.
"Should I climb a dead tree stump it would fall,
And knifelike, stab me to the heart," she replied.

On the Death of a Child

Alas, the lonely one weeps.
For whom do you lament?

He mourns for his child—the father—
And cries as he digs the grave.

Who is it wields this spade?
I wield this spade, his father.

Why does the mother weep?
She is weeping over the shroud.

Who is it brought this death?
Who brought this death?—it is God.

TEN PROVERBS FROM LIBERIA

The proverbs of other nations are always intriguing. However, to use them as valuable clues to ways of thinking and feeling, we must know how they are employed, in what situations and with what intent.

We have therefore extracted the following proverbs, together with commentaries from the excellent volume, *Jabo Proverbs from Liberia,* by George Herzog and Charles G. Blooah, because the authors give very interesting concrete examples of how these proverbs are used. Dr. Herzog was, for many years, an anthropologist at the University of Indiana. His collaborator, Mr. Blooah, is a native of Liberia, educated in America, who has acted as informant and interpreter for Dr. Herzog and other anthropologists. Most of the explanations given with these sayings were supplied by Mr. Blooah.

When it rains, the roof always drips the same way.

This is a comment on the immutability of certain laws. Whenever there is rain, the roof will drip, and always drip downward, no matter how the roof is placed or from what direction the rain is hitting it. The proverb also has implications like our "As ye sow, so shall ye reap." The following illustration was given: "We and the people of Fishtown agreed that we would not fight any more. In making this agreement we called upon God. If one of the parties breaks an agreement like this, he is bound to lose. The Fishtown people broke the agreement and so we won the war."

We climb the hill before we recognize the land.

This is used also as an honorary title on the horn. The title belonged to a public speaker of Nimiah, now dead. The office of the speaker is to set the matter before the assembly as objectively as he can, introducing the arguments of both sides without taking a stand of his own. His penetration and elocution elevate the average man to a clear, broad view of the issue, such as a person gains by climbing a hill.

One doesn't throw the stick after the snake has gone.

This can be applied to suggest that a passing opportunity may not return; quick action and decision are often imperative.

Whenever a snake is found to be in a Jabo village, the village seems to become transformed into a disturbed ant heap; everybody shouts and runs, but nobody is overanxious to get close to the spot where the snake is supposed to be hiding. Some men finally gather courage and begin to beat about the place, usually hitting anything but the snake, which is most likely to have disappeared by that time. Still, as the hopes of killing it diminish, the number of our dauntless hunters increases, while the women pour forth a generous supply of mocking and teasing remarks until the affair finally dissolves amid general laughter.

You kill the snake with whatever may be in your hand.

This was applied in a rather characteristic manner. On one occasion three men came to visit the house, and as they prepared to leave they were presented with a leaf of tobacco. Two of the visitors felt that one leaf was hardly enough for three people, but the third guest had more discretion and evinced it by quoting the proverb.

He acts like a dog who drives the flies away from food it has spurned.

The proverb embodies a criticism of hypocrisy. It is used in questioning the sincerity of some one who seems too particular about something for which he professes to care nothing. For example, if a mother scolds a child of about six or seven years of age about something, the child may become very angry and wish to make his mother feel the intensity of his anger by refusing disdainfully whatever she offers him. But should the child interfere when his brother or another member of the family accepts the offer, the proverb is appropriate.

If some one says he dislikes a certain girl and yet watches her constantly, the girl herself or any other person who suspects him of dissembling may say to him, "You behave like a dog who drives the flies away from the food it has spurned."

A man may have publicly divorced his wife but object to her going with another man. The woman may rebuke her former husband with the proverb.

A man may openly declare that he is not connected with a project which other men are about to undertake. At the same time he appears quite anxious to give advice. Those who question his attitude will say to him, "Why do you act like a dog who drives the flies away from food it has spurned?"

The proverb is also used in law proceedings. If two tribes enter a dispute, one of them may be made to cede its rights to a tract of land in favour of the other. The land offered may not seem fully satisfactory to the second tribe, which would definitely refuse it. The court, however, would make it understood that no further land is forthcoming, that it must accept what is offered and make the best of it. If the tribe still would not touch the land but would not let any one else touch it either, the proverb could be quoted.

The dog's nose is cold.

The proverb conjures an image often seen in West Africa: the man reclining comfortably in his low chair. Suddenly the dog comes up to him unnoticed and, nudging him, touches his body with its cold nose. The man yells at it, but he has had his unpleasant shock. The proverb serves to express ill bodings or as a warning against the doubtful wisdom of a plan. It may point out that a person in trouble should have foreseen the effects of his ill-advised action. It was recorded as a title praising a man on the horn. The title praises the warrior for his undaunted bravery. Or it may sound a warning to the hero who does not consider any risk. Finally, the cold shock at the touch of the dog's nose is symbolic of the uncomfortable feelings arising in the warrior's enemies whenever they think of him or confront him.

There is no wealth where there are no children.

There is true happiness only where there are children. But children are not only a source of happiness. They are also a great help to their parents. When parents become too old to provide for themselves, they pass into the care of their children and are provided for by them. Thus, children are a source of wealth to the parents and a valuable investment.

In the native community, married people are most unhappy if they should have no children of their own, and steps are taken to correct the situation. If, upon examination, it is thought that the husband is sterile, another man is substituted until a child is born to the woman. If the woman is thought sterile, the misfortune is not so great since the husband's other wives may bear him children. If everything should fail, the couple try to adopt children.

If a person boasts copiously of the great things he has done for which the whole tribe praises him, some of his fellows may become annoyed. In their jealousy they would rebuke him, saying, "Keep quiet, you are worrying us too much for what little you have accomplished!" The man could reply in self-defence, "Yes, but there is no wealth where there are no children." In other words, "I have good reason to be proud, for I have done something."

Again, if a person is accused of witchcraft, he is given sass-wood poison to prove his innocence. If, after a hard struggle, he expels the poison from his system and is given the freedom to celebrate his liberation, some unsympathetic individual may remark with sarcasm on the exuberance with which the man enjoys his release. A more sympathetic individual may reply with the proverb.

Children are the wisdom of the nation.

In travelling from village to village the native visitor will almost invariably make it his business to ask the children whom he is certain to find playing below the village, "Well, children, what is the news in the city?" Without any suspicion or fear the children will tell him the most important of the latest news. If the stranger should find it not expedient to enter the village because the news indicates that his tribe had become involved in some trouble with it, he would turn back at once. The children would calmly resume their play with the feeling that they had done their duty by giving the man the information he desired. The lives of many who were wise enough to trust the knowledge of children have been saved in this way. Thus the proverb recognizes that children generally know some facts, and, if properly approached, will tell the truth to any one who should desire it; they are frank, trusting and friendly.

The proverb is, in the first place, applicable if the testimony of a child is needed badly, and there are still some who tend to make light of the validity of such testimony. In that case, anybody who favours the testimony of the child may say to the objectors, "Do not worry, for children are the wisdom of the nation."

The mother of a child may become imbued with the fear that the child is growing too imaginative in his world of fancies to be depended upon for telling the truth. If she wishes to impress upon the child the danger of becoming an habitual liar, and how detestable a creature a liar is, she will say to him, "Son, it seems you cannot tell the truth about anything lately! You must stop this practice, for it is often said that children are the wisdom of the nation. Let it be said of you too that you belong to the group which really constitutes the wisdom of this nation."

A child saw a war that destroyed a city.

The implication being that even a child has had experience and has seen events. The proverb may have originated from a story. It was quoted when the people of Upper Nimiah discussed the grave illness of a boy in Lower Nimiah. Like any other case of illness or death, this was supposed to have been caused by witchcraft. The consensus of opinion in Upper Nimiah was that the people of Lower Nimiah did not act with sufficient zeal to trace the witch in good time. In this matter, as in many others, the upper town felt that the lower town did not always use good judgment. The lower town, situated on the seashore, on the road between civilized Liberian towns, was more exposed to Western influences. More used to confronting unforeseen situations, it represented the less conservative element of the tribe. It did not always feel that it had at its disposal the time necessary to observe the formalities prescribed by tradition. The more conservative upper town regarded this laxity as childish, hasty, and haphazard. 'Nevertheless," to quote the comments of the Upper Nimiah people on the sickness, "although the people of Lower Nimiah are like children, we look upon them with hopes since we could not accomplish anything without them." Then the proverb was quoted. The inhabitants of the lower town are looked upon and referred to as children of the upper town because their settlement is more recent.

One who loves the children of his fellow will surely love his own children.

Perhaps the truest test of love is to love sincerely that which is not one's own, whereas it is common and easy for a man to love or value the things that are closely related to him or are actually his own. Thus, a father who has love for another father's children will surely be able to love his own. Furthermore, through his experience with other children he will be better equipped to take care of his own.

The question may arise in the assembly whether one's tribe should treat another tribe with toleration. If opinion seems to be divided, the side which is for toleration may quote the proverb to plead for indulgence. People who are unkind to children are often rebuked with the proverb.

People may object bitterly if members of another tribe come to hunt in the forest owned by their tribe. If some one thinks that the objection is ungenerous, he will quote the proverb.

SONG OF A MOTHER TO HER FIRST-BORN

Jack H. Driberg, who translated this Sudanese mother's song, spent fourteen years (1912-1926) living with and studying various peoples in Uganda and the Sudan. (See other note on page 208.)

The overflowing joy of the mother here celebrates not only her love and her pride, but the role of the child as the incarnation of a dead ancestor and as his father's "redemption from the dead."

Speak to me, child of my heart.
Speak to me with your eyes, your round laughing eyes,
Wet and shining as Lupeyo's bull-calf.

Speak to me little one,
Clutching my breast with your hand,
So strong and firm for all its littleness.
It will be the hand of a warrior, my son,
A hand that will gladden your father.
See how eagerly it fastens on me:
It thinks already of a spear.
O son, you will have a warrior's name and be a leader of
   men.
And your sons, and your sons' sons, will remember you long
   after you have slipped into darkness.
But I, I shall always remember your hand clutching me so.
I shall recall how you lay in my arms,

And looked at me so, and so,
And how your tiny hands played with my bosom.
And when they name you great warrior, then will my eyes
be wet with remembering.

And how shall we name you, little warrior?
See, let us play at naming.
It will not be a name of despisal, for you are my first-born.
Not as Nawal's son is named will you be named.
Our gods will be kinder to you than theirs.
Must we call you "Insolence" or "Worthless One"?

Shall you be named, like a child of ill fortune, after the dung
of cattle?
Our gods need no cheating, my child:
They wish you no ill.
They have washed your body and clothed it with beauty.
They have set a fire in your eyes.
And the little puckering ridges of your brows—
Are they not the seal of their finger-prints when they fash-
ioned you?
They have given you beauty and strength, child of my heart,
And wisdom is already shining in your eyes,
And laughter.

So how shall we name you, little one?
Are you your father's father, or his brother, or yet another?
Whose spirit is it that is in you, little warrior?
Whose spear-hand tightens round my breast?
Who lives in you and quickens to life, like last year's melon
seed?
Are you silent, then?
But your eyes are thinking, thinking, and glowing like the
eyes of a leopard in a thicket.
Well, let be.
At the day of the naming you will tell us.

O my child, now indeed I am happy.
Now indeed I am a wife—
No more a bride, but a Mother-of-one.
Be splendid and magnificent, child of desire.
Be proud as I am proud.

Be happy as I am happy.
Be loved as now I am loved.
Child, child, child, love I have had from my man.
But now, only now, have I the fullness of love.
Now, only now, am I his wife and the mother of his first-born.
His soul is safe in your keeping, my child, and it was I, I, I
    who have made you.

Therefore am I loved.
Therefore am I happy.
Therefore am I a wife.
Therefore have I great honor.

You will tend his shrine when he is gone.
With sacrifice and oblation you will recall his name year by
    year.
He will live in your prayers, my child,
And there will be no more death for him, but everlasting life
    springing from your loins.
You are his shield and his spear, his hope and redemption
    from the dead.
Through you he will be reborn, as the saplings in the Spring.
And I, I am the mother of his first-born.
Sleep, child of beauty and courage and fulfilment, sleep.
I am content.

THREE ASHANTI TALES

These Ashanti tales were collected and translated by the
famous ethnologist, Robert S. Rattray, who spent many years
among the Ashanti as a District Commissioner in the British
colonial service. (See also notes on pages 35 and 203.)

How Divorce Came into the Tribe

A CERTAIN HUNTER, who was called Kwasi Gyaba, and his wife
once went to reside in a camp in order to hunt. When Kwasi
Gyaba went to the bush, he did not bring any meat. He never
brought back any meat. Now, one day his wife questioned

him, saying, "I believe, when you kill meat, you sell it, and eat the proceeds or else you give it away in presents; so today, if you go to the forest, and do not return with meat, I am going off to my mother yonder, for I am sick of living on rats, and fish, and snails, and such-like."

The hunter, Kwasi Gyaba, set out for the bush. He saw a Duyker going past. He said to himself, "Duyker, where you sleep, there shall I rest with you." The Duyker went and stood beneath a tree. He, the hunter, raised the gun, pam!

A Python—where it came from goodness only knows—landed on the Duyker, and a Leopard, too, leaped upon it. The hunter remained hidden and silent. He said to himself, "Alas! what misfortune I have beheld."

The Python said, "Father hunter, come, what one head is thinking, another head has sometimes heard, so, hunter, come hither, and let us go to our village and let us share this Duyker, for we will not do you any harm."

The hunter took his gun and followed them. They went and shared up the meat. The Python said, "Father hunter, I like you, so sleep here today, and I shall give you medicine; now this medicine, when you put it in your ears, you will hear the voice of the leaves, of the trees, and of rivers, and the speech of all animals. Therefore this night go and sleep, but do not breathe."

The hunter went to sleep; he left off breathing. The Python took medicine and put it in his ears. Next morning, when things became visible, the hunter understood the language of all things. He set out, and came to his village. When he came, he heard that his mother-in-law had come to her daughter's house. Now his mother-in-law was blind in her right eye. The hunter went and sat down in the room. Now, I forgot to mention, that when he met his mother-in-law, she was pounding corn. The hunter sat there in silence, and two fowls who were there began to talk. One asked the other, saying, "How do you manage to get the corn, while, when I go to pick it up, I get chased away by her?" The other replied, "Why, have you not noticed that she is blind in her right eye, so when you want to pick up corn, if you pass by the damaged one, she can't see you?"

Kwasi Gyaba heard this; he threw himself on his back and

laughed, twe! twe! twe! His mother-in-law said, "Ah, my
son-in-law, why are you laughing at me like this?" But Kwasi
Gyaba lay on the ground laughing, and he kept on laughing.
There and then, his mother-in-law uttered the forbidden word
of the Sky-god upon him, saying that Kwasi Gyaba should
show the cause of his laughter before the face of the Sky-god.
The Sky-god sent messengers to bring Kwasi Gyaba. When
he reached the end of the town he lifted up his song:

"Now I am going to speak and die, Kwasi Gyaba e!
I am going to speak and die, when this happens you
        must not weep for me.
Kwasi Mpuroko Gyaba, he is going,
When this happens you must not weep for me."

The Sky-god's elders said, "Listen to the prisoner's song."
They took Kwasi Gyaba before the Sky-god. The Okycame
spokesman rose up and said, "Kwasi Gyaba, did you really
laugh at your mother-in-law, or is she lying?" Kwasi Gyaba
replied, "Sire, owing to certain medicine, under the influence
of which I am, if I reveal the reason of my laughter I shall
die." The Sky-god said, "Because you are my hunter, I shall
not allow you to die."

His mother-in-law said, "Sire, he is lying, he was just laughing at me, so I shall be content with nothing else but an
explanation." The spokesman said, "Kwasi Gyaba, have you
heard?" Kwasi Gyaba replied, "Then I beg for a grave, and
when I am dead, lay me in it."

No sooner had his mouth stood still, than a Cock and a
Hen came by; and the Cock said to the Hen, "Stand still
and let me mount you." The Hen said, "What, in front of
these people?" The Cock said, "If you don't stand still there,
I shall speak the forbidden word to the effect that you can
take yourself off."

Now Kwasi Gyaba heard that. Immediately he said, "Sire,
Sky-god, let them stop digging a grave, for I have something
to say." The Sky-god said, "Speak."

Kwasi Gyaba said, "I speak the forbidden word, that my
mother-in-law may take her child away." All the elders said,
"That is true, that is true, the case is finished." There and

then the Sky-god made a law to the effect that, "any one, even your friend, if he troubles you, speak the forbidden word upon him, or if it be your wife who does so, speak the forbidden word and divorce her." Thus it came about that divorce came into the tribe. It is the Cock we copied.

This, my story, which I have related, if it be sweet, or if it be not sweet, take some elsewhere, and let some come back to me.

Sleeping Mat Confidences

THEY SAY THAT ONCE upon a time Nyankonpon Kwame, the Sky-god, had cleared a very large plantation, and had planted okras, onions, beans, garden eggs, peppers, and pumpkins. The weeds in the garden became thick and nettles grew up. The Sky-god then made a proclamation by gong-gong to the effect that his plantation was overgrown with weeds, and that any one who could weed it, without scratching himself, might come forward and take his daughter, Abena Nkroma, i.e. Abena the ninth child, in marriage.

This one, when he went to try, scratched himself where the nettles tickled, and they hooted at him; that one went and was also hooted; all men went and tried; they failed.

Now Kwaku Ananse said, "As for me, I am able." Now the Sky-god's plantation was situated on the side of the path, and that path was the one people used to take, going to the market every Friday. Now the Spider, because he knew this fact, used only to go and clear the weeds every Friday. For when he was hoeing, and the people who were passing by used to greet him with, "Hail to you at your work, Father Spider!" he used to answer, "Thank you, Aku." They continued, "A plantation, which no one has been able to clear, do you mean to say you are weeding it?" The Spider would answer, "Ah, it's all because of one girl that I am wearing myself out like this. Her single arm is like this." And he would slap and rub his arm where it was tickling him, and when he did so, would get relief from the irritation. Some one else would pass again and hail him at his work; and he would take his hand and slap the place that was itching. For example, if his thigh, he would say, "That single girl, they say her thigh is like this," slapping and rubbing his own.

In this manner he finished clearing the plantation. Then he went off to tell the Sky-god how he had finished the weeding of his farm. The Sky-god asked the messenger, saying, "Has he really finished?" The messenger said, "Yes." The Sky-god asked him, "Did he scratch himself?" He said, "No, he did not scratch himself." The Sky-god took Abena Nkroma and gave her to Ananse in marriage.

One night Ananse and his bride went to rest, and the bride questioned him, saying, "However was it that you of all people were able to clear father's plantation of weeds, a plantation such that, whosoever went on it, turned back, but which you were able to clear?"

Then the Spider said, "Do you suppose that I am a fool? I used to hoe, and when any one passed by, and asked me, saying, 'Ananse, are you clearing this farm which no one else has ever been able to clear?' thereupon, I would slap with my hand any place on my skin that was tickling me, and scratch it, and declare to the person that, for example, your thigh was like the thigh of a buffalo, and that it was beautiful and polished. That is how it came about that I was able to weed it."

Thereupon Abena, the ninth child, said, "Then tomorrow I shall tell father that you scratched yourself after all." The Spider spoke to her saying, "You must not mention it, this is a sleeping-mat confidence." Abena, the ninth child, said, "I know nothing whatever about sleeping-mat confidences, and I shall speak." Abena Nkroma took her sleeping-mat away from beside Ananse and went and lay down at the other end of the room.

Now Ananse's eyes grew red, (i.e. sorrowful,) and he went and took his musical bow, and he struck the strings and sang:

"Abena, the ninth child, this is not a matter about which
    to quarrel.
Let us treat it as a sleeping-mat confidence.
'No,' she says.
She has a case against me, but some one else has a case
    which is already walking down the path."

Then the Spider got up, and went and lay down. After Ananse had lain there for some time, then he rose up. He said, "Abena Nkroma"—not a sound save the noise of the cicada chirping *dinn!* Ananse said, "I've got you." He took a little gourd cup and splashed it full with water, and poured it over Abena Nkroma's sleeping-mat. Then Ananse went and lay down.

After he had lain down a while, he said, "Ko! Abena Nkroma, whatever is this? You have wet the sleeping-mat, you shameless creature, surely you are not at all nice; when things become visible, I shall tell every one. It was true, then what they all said, that when any one went to that plantation, he used to say, 'A girl who wets . . .! I am not going to clear a nettle plantation for such a person.'

Then Abena said to him, "I implore you, desist, and let the matter drop." The Spider said, "I will not leave it, my case came first; you said you would tell your father; I said, 'Desist'; you said, 'No.' Because of that I will not drop the case."

And Abena, the ninth child, said, "Leave my case, and your case, too, about which I spoke, I shall drop it; for if you do not leave mine, my eyes will die for shame." Then Ananse said, "I have heard; since you so desire, let it be a sleeping-mat confidence, so the matter ends there." That is how the elders came to say that "Sleeping-mat confidences are not repeated."

This, my story, which I have related, if it be sweet, or if it be not sweet, some you may take as true, and the rest you may praise me for telling of it.

If Someone Does Good to You

THEY SAY THERE once was an Eagle, and in her wandering she went and met a certain old woman who had a sore on her leg. And the Eagle said, "Gracious me! This is a sore in a class by itself; with one like this, however hard you try, are you able to walk?" The old woman said, "Oh, just a very little."

The Eagle said, "You people, nowadays, if I were to do something good for you today, tomorrow you would take something bad to thank me." The old woman said, "Oh, I could not do that."

The Eagle said, "If you cannot behave like that, I have heard." She said, "Shut your eyes and open them." And the old woman shut her eyes and opened them. The Eagle said, "Look at your sore." And when the old woman came to look —not a vestige of it.

Then she made her close her eyes again; she opened them, and she saw that all the land had been cleared. She said, "Close them again." She closed them, and she opened them, and houses stood there, firmly. And she made her close them again. She opened them to see a town this size; there it was— huge. The Eagle said, "Old woman, it's yours." The old woman said, "Thanks I give to you." Then the old woman said, "What must I take to thank you?"

The Eagle said, "I do not want even a trifling thing, as for me, all I desire is this silk-cotton tree that stands there." The old woman said, "This thing you ask for what of it, take it." Then the Eagle flew off, and alighted on it, and wove a nest, and laid two eggs, depositing them in it. And she hatched the two eggs, and went off to seek something for her children to eat.

The old woman's grandchild, who lived with her, began to whimper, "Ehe! Ehe!" The old woman said, "What's the matter?"

She said, "Let me chew an Eagle's children." The old woman said, "Where am I to get an Eagle's children?" The small grandchild commenced again, whimper! whimper! The old woman said, "What's the matter?"

The child said, "Let me chew an Eagle's children, for if I don't get some to chew, I shall die." The old woman said, "Ah! must this, my grandchild die for want of an Eagle's children to chew? Up you get, take axes and go and strike the silk-cotton tree and bring me an Eagle's children."

The village folk went there, the axes sounded, Pinpin! Pinpin! Pinpin! It was as if the tree was going down, when the elder of the Eagle's children jumped up, and came and stood on the edge of the nest, and raised a cry; she called the mother, saying:

Sango, the bird e!
Sango, the bird, the Eagle's child!
Sango, the bird e!
Sango, if she went to eat, come back!
Sango, the bird e!
Sango, o! o!

The mother heard that her child was crying; she rose up, and the sound of her wings flapping was, fa! She came; she said, "Sanguri," and that tree which was nearly severed came together again, and all the people who had been striking it, were swallowed up. Then she took the food which she had brought and gave to her children. Then she bade them good-by, saying, "I am going, if the old woman comes to take you away, let her take you." And the old woman said, "Go and strike the tree and bring the creatures for my grandchild to chew." And they went there a second time, Pinpin! Pinpin! Pinpin! It was as if the tree was to go to the ground, when the Eagle's child came out and came and stood on the edge of the nest, and called its mother, saying:

Sango, the bird e!
Sango, the bird, the Eagle's child!
Sango, the bird e!
Sango, if she went to eat, come back!
Sango, the bird e!
Sango, o! o!

She called her mother, and called, and called, and called—no answer—and now the tree spoke as it hit the ground; "Brim!" it said. They took away the Eagle's children; they gave one to the old woman, but one that remained flew away and alighted on a Wawa-tree. One, they roasted, and gave it to the old woman's grandchild, who added it to the roasted plantain she was eating.

Not long after, the Eagle came. When she reached the tree which they had felled, she saw one of her children sitting there; she asked her what had happened, and she told her all the news. The Eagle set off for the old woman's village. When she went there, the old woman's grandchild was eating one of her children. She said, "Old woman, I congratulate you."

She came out from the old woman's house and commenced her magic at the outskirts of the town. She said, "Sanguri," and every person disappeared, and again she said, "Sanguri," and every house broke up at once and not a dwelling remained. "Sanguri," the village once again became the forest. "Sanguri," and the old woman's sore came back. And she said, "Old woman, you have seen, that is why the elders say, if some does good to you, thank him by doing good to him and do not take evil to thank him."

This, my story, which I have related, if it be sweet, or if it be not sweet, some you may take as true, and the rest you may praise me for the telling of it.

SIX SONGS FROM DAHOMEY

These six songs deal with somber themes: death, bereavement, hunger, harsh fate. While Dahomeans highly value realism and resilience, these laments, these prayers for the lightening of burdens, show that they are far from an unheeding stoicism. Dahomeans know that song is a precious outlet for the groaning spirit: "Great our need to sing." As Dr. and Mrs. Herskovits point out in their book, *Dahomean Narrative,* the song seems to be the only literary form in which Dahomeans permit themselves to express a tragic theme. In traditional spoken stories this is not done.

The third "Song for the Dead," however, transforms mourning into a celebration of life: "Come, then, dance all the colors of life for a lover of pleasure now dead."

The beauty, power, and dignity of these poems can be enjoyed, even without a detailed knowledge of the Dahomean world. (See other note on page 249.)

To the Sun-God

Softly, softly, Lisa—o
Softly, O Sun-God,
Do not ravish the world.
Ram pawing the earth with hooves of flame,

Ram pounding the earth with horns of fire,
Do not ravish the world,
Do not destroy us.

For the Earth God

Thy need is great
And great our need to sing,
For days of trouble are upon us.
The bullock of Abomey
Says to him in Cana,
It is the day of our trouble;
The carrier of grain
Says to the bearer of salt,
Thy load is heavy, brother.
And this is the day for carrying;
The bearer of the dead
Says to the carrier of ladders,
It is the day for carrying loads,
It is the day of trouble.

To Destiny

Bear down lightly,
O my load,
Bear down lightly
As the boat touches the water;
Bear down lightly,
O my load
For my boat is near to sinking;
Bear lightly,
And I will make offerings
To the Master of Destiny.

Song for the Dead, I

I came to drink with my friend,
And find him I could not.
O Death, who taketh away Life

And giveth no day at court,
A day will come and I shall see him again.
Aye, I shall see him . . .
For I too am going toward death.

Song for the Dead, II

The planter gathers his peppers,
And the pepper bird weeps,
And weeping, sings
"Alas, Life has given us an evil portion,
For hunger is our lot, and death."

Song for the Dead, III

I see it,
There is no enjoying beyond Death,
And I say to all of you say,
That which your senses taste of Life,
Goes with you.

I say to you say
The wives you have,
The passion you know of them
Goes with you.

I say to you say
The drinks you drink,
The pleasure of them
Goes with you.

I say to you say
The meats you eat,
The relish you have of them
Goes with you.

I say to you say
The pipes you smoke,
The quiet they bring
Goes with you.

Come, then
Dance all the colors of Life
For a lover of pleasure
Now dead.

Translated by Frances S. Herskovits

LOVE SONG OF A XHOSA GIRL

The far-off mountains hide you from me
While the nearer ones overhang me.
Would that I had a heavy sledge
To crush the mountains near me;
Would that I had wings like a bird
To fly over those farther away.

Translated by A. C. Jordan

Chapter 2

Forerunners:
Written Literature in African Languages

CHAKA, CHILD OF SIN

Thomas Mofolo

Chaka was probably the bloodiest tyrant in African history. At the beginning of the nineteenth century he swept like a Genghis Khan over a vast area of southern Africa. A conqueror of insatiable cruelty and ambition, he stopped at nothing, annihilating enemies, sacrificing his own soldiers by the thousands, and finally even murdering friends and closest kin. He met his end at the hands of his own brothers.

Out of this sensational material, Thomas Mofolo created his interpretation of Chaka's life. Mofolo, born in Basutoland about 1875, got a missionary education, and wrote three books in Sesuto. His novel, *Chaka,* is not only a fusion of history and imagination; it also combines a Christian orientation with a faithful and graphic portrayal of indigenous customs.

Mofolo conceives Chaka's career as the working out of a nemesis born in sin. Child of an unsanctioned union, and finally cast out by his father, the boy Chaka, in the following excerpt, begins to emerge from his alienation as one dedicated to domination and terror. Tempered in the fires of witchcraft and counterwitchcraft he takes to violence as to meat and drink.

THE CIRCUMSTANCES of Chaka's birth were not publicly known, for very few knew that Nandi was pregnant when she was married, and these few would not disclose the secret for fear of the consequences. Some, perhaps, who had given thought to the matter had noticed that the period of her pregnancy was shorter than that of other women.

As Senzangakona still loved Chaka and his mother dearly the other wives became very vexed and said that Senzangakona should declare publicly the order of seniority of his children so that they and the tribe might know it; but Senzangakona refused. The wives discussed the question for a long time among themselves, and finally told the councillors to advise the chief to make matters regular with regard to his children. However, when the councillors broached the matter, Senzangakona became very angry and told them to leave his private life alone; their function was a public one only. Then the wives sent for a witch doctor to turn Senzangakona's heart away from Nandi, so that whenever he intended visiting her his conscience would trouble him and he would come back again.

Nandi returned to her home at Qube for her second confinement, and as soon as she had gone the wives appeared before Senzangakona and with bitter feeling declared that Nandi must never come back again to Nobamba. Senzangakona tried to refuse his consent, but the women said: "Do thou think well before thou speakest: as for us our patience is gone. Thou didst refuse to tell the people as we bade thee that though Chaka is the first born the heir is Mfokazana, and after him Dingana and then Mhlangana. Now today thou refusest thy consent when we say that Nandi must not return to this place. We will not suffer ourselves to be shamed by a dog like Nandi, who came to thee already pregnant, while we were married to thee as virgins without spot or stain. We have borne thee children and have filled thy huts, and the cattle will come here in great numbers and the kraals will soon be full. Further we have borne thee boy children. If there had been no sons of ours, then we could understand. Today we will tell thy story and Nandi's and will bring the matter before the great chief, Jobe."

When Senzangakona heard this he was much frightened and trembled, for he saw that his shame and Nandi's would now become known. Nandi and her companions would be

put to death and he as well, since although he was the chief
he had set the people a bad example. He therefore begged
his wives to let the matter go no further and told them that
Mfokazana and not Chaka would succeed him as chief, and
he promised also that Nandi should not set foot in Nobamba
again. But his wives said that to satisfy them it was necessary that Nandi together with her child Chaka should be
driven away from Qube to her home at Langeni. And Senzangakona did drive her away, but afterwards he persuaded
his wives to allow her to return to Qube. But the wives of
Senzangakona in their folly did not see to it that Senzangakona explained to Jobe the seniority of his sons, and therefore
Jobe still continued to regard Chaka alone as the heir.

We cannot describe the grief which Senzangakona felt at
having to part with his son Chaka and his wife Nandi, for
he had great love for them. But he was in a panic about his
affair with Nandi and did not wish people to hear a single
whisper of it. He therefore thought it better to give up Nandi
and her son and regard them as lost to him for ever. Besides
he saw that unless he gave up Chaka, not only would Nandi
and her companions be put to death but his little kingdom
also would be torn to pieces when his sons grew up. So he
closed his eyes, accepted his fate, and gave up his wife and
her boy child.

There is a proverb, "Scandal is not like bread: there is
never any shortage," and though Senzangakona had hidden
so carefully his affair with Nandi yet it was certainly known,
and although it was not common knowledge, all the same
people knew of it and alluded to it. And as soon as men
heard of the charge they hated Chaka and Nandi with a fearful hatred and agreed with Senzangakona's wives that Mfokazana was the heir, and they even wanted Chaka to be killed
as being born of sin: he was only a child, but he was illegiti-
mate.

Chaka was terribly ill-treated when he went herding the
calves; the other herdboys persecuted and tormented him all
day and every day for no reason. One day when they were
herding they sent him to head off the calves, and when he
came back he heard one of them say, "Seize him." They
seized and beat him until they were tired and then they

desisted. He tried to ask why he was being beaten, but got no answer and he saw that the question merely made them beat him the more. The herdboys persecuted Chaka because they heard people say that it would be a good thing if they killed him. Once during these daily fights Chaka knocked out a boy's eye. The next day the boy's father seized Chaka and gave him a severe beating, wounding him terribly.

This incessant fighting taught Chaka how to use a stick, how to parry the many blows directed at him at one and the same time, and how to strike while keeping his head guarded, also it taught him swiftness and how to escape by running. He was quite fearless when fighting, because he had become accustomed to it, nor was he short of breath when he took to flight. He learnt to parry quickly, to stoop, to dodge, to give ground, and then leap up and strike home at the right time.

Chaka's grandmother was distressed at the hard life which Chaka was leading when herding calves; and when he was beaten by the injured boy's father she took him away and put him to scare birds from the fields of kafir corn. For this he had to get up early in the morning when it was still dark, keeping alight the wisp of tinder-grass which burnt his fingers before he reached his field. He had to walk through the chilly dew and arrive at his place too cold to be able to scare the birds. The other bird-scarers did not beat him, but they mocked him, spat when they spoke to him, made faces at him and generally caused him to look ridiculous. Chaka did not know what crime he had committed or how he had transgressed to deserve all this. Truly there never was a child who grew up under such hardships as Chaka did; it is indeed distressing for any one to be deserted by his father.

The herdboys now became much disgusted at having nothing to do, for previously they had been able to use Chaka to relieve the tedium of their days; so they went to fetch Chaka from the fields where he was. While Chaka was sitting resting he saw a gang of boys suddenly appear quite close to him, some in the ploughed field, some in the thick grass and some all around him. He looked this way and that but there was nowhere he could flee, and worst of all his stick was some distance away at his shelterplace. They seized and beat him till he fainted and then threw him into a deep hole in the long grass and left him for dead. A woman who had gone to look at the fields was watching them from a distance, and when she reached the spot where they had thrown him she found Chaka not dead but unconscious. She poured water over him and placed him in the shade where it was cool, and Chaka soon recovered. However, he was too weak to stand, so the good woman went and told his relations who came and carried him home on an ox hide.

This was too much for Nandi and she told Senzangakona what a hard life Chaka was leading, but he did not reply to her. Though his heart also was sore and he controlled his feelings with difficulty, yet he knew that if he spoke he would be giving other people the chance to speak also. His wives, who saw the messenger, told Senzangakona to cease sending cattle and goats as food for Chaka, and much against his will he obeyed them in order to keep his shame concealed. How bitter is the fruit of sin. Here was Senzangakona parted from the wife he loved and whom he had married with fifty-five head of cattle, and parted from his child Chaka, the first son he had ever had, and worst of all forced to persecute them as well.

From now on Chaka's grandmother forbade him to herd or even to scare birds and Chaka became a laughingstock and a stay-at-home.

When Chaka became a youth Nandi took him to her witch doctor to be treated with medicines, which would protect him from people who wished to take his life. The witch doctor took a little powder and mixed it with other medicines and gave it to them saying, "When the moon is about to go into darkness Chaka must get up early and go to the river as before. When he has finished bathing and is still at the river he must inoculate himself with this medicine and then come home and smear his head with the medicine which I gave you before. The result will be that even if people surround him in a mob they will not be able to hold him in; he will scatter them with ease; he will kill, but will not be killed. Moreover, I confirm what I said before that this child will receive blessings innumerable. Hast thou ever seen aught at the river when thou wast bathing?" Chaka said he had not. Then the woman took him by the hand and felt his pulse and said: "Of great import are the happenings which will take place in the life of this child. I will hasten and will return from Zwide's village whither I have been called, and if it is possible I shall be with you here on the tenth day from now. If the tenth day pass by, ye must know that my work delays me and I will send one to inquire for me how things are, since I know that Chaka will go early to the river tomorrow, for that is his day."

On the road it occurred to the witch doctor that Chaka must not be a timid person or it would spoil the effect of her medicines. So she sent him medicines of two kinds—one for drinking and one for inoculation—that he might become brave and warlike, that he might be stouthearted and without fear. Among the ingredients were the liver of a lion, the liver of a leopard, and the liver of a man who had been a great warrior in his lifetime. The liquid potion was sprinkled upon Chaka's food and she ordered him to be inoculated by a woman who had just borne a child, and moreover a first-born child.

The messenger brought the medicines and Chaka was inoculated in his presence, after which the messenger returned. From that time Chaka had a wonderful love for fighting—either with the club or the spear. When he slept at night he dreamt of it, and in the daytime while awake he dreamt of it. When he saw a man with a stick or spear in his hand his whole body itched to come into contact with him. He dreamt that tribe after tribe was attacking him, and he saw himself scattering them singlehanded with none of his people to help him. The only conversation he enjoyed was about fighting. Even before this, Chaka was a great fighter, but he was never the challenger or the aggressor; but now these medicines excited him and he went forth to the veld in spite of his grandmother's orders.

As soon as he arrived there the herdboys all attacked him, but he gave them such terrible bleeding wounds that they scattered in flight. And very soon they let him alone and he became their leader. At the pools his cattle drank first, and the best grass was their grazing place. At the end of any fight he was full of joy and felt pleasantly refreshed, like the venomous snake which after biting a man falls ill until the man dies and then casts its skin and begins once more to move about again. Chaka soon noticed that he did not tire even when he was fighting for a long while; he only felt tired when he had finished his enemies. During the fight his stick struck home and with such force that his enemies were sent spinning to the ground; but their sticks touched him lightly as if they were stalks of grass.

Translated from the Basuto by F. H. Dutton

FEKISI'S FAREWELL

THOMAS MOFOLO

The Traveller of the East by Thomas Mofolo is a romance about a mystical herdboy who leaves his home in ancient Basutoland to search for God. Fekisi, the hero, loves his cattle and is loved by his fellows, but is weighed down by the envy and fear which divide his people, the drunkenness, the cruelty of man to man. As he is about to set forth on his pilgrimage, he takes fond leave of his cattle. Fekisi's whispered farewell to the "god with the wet nose" is really a moving pastoral poem, expressing the affection and reverence that the cattle-raising peoples of Africa must feel toward their herds, which play such a central part in their social system.

WHEN HE HAD FINISHED making his preparations, but in less time than we take writing about them, he went outside. He stood there, quite still. His heart said he should tell his family his plan, but he was afraid they might forbid him and say he was mad. He thought he would tell that old man, his friend. Even then he said there is no knowing, he might perhaps say something, or tell people, and then they would stop him. He went out secretly, no man seeing him, no man knowing his intention and his plan.

Before he left, while he was still standing there wondering what he could do, the grey cow lowed; it lowed softly, softly. When it lowed a second time the white-faced cow lowed with

it. They lowed softly, softly, as if they wanted him only to
hear. They lowed, they lowed for a long time. As soon as
they were quiet, the oxen, the fat cows and all the cattle
stood up together, and looked at him. His heart failed him,
he went to the kraal to greet them and to praise them for the
last time. When he came near the kraal, he found the hard-
horned cattle were clashing their horns together. The big
oxen were by now excited, it was as if a stick cracked away
in the pastures. They smelt him, they smelt him; they came
crowding towards where he was. He whispered to them, he
praised them one by one. He spoke to the white-faced cow,
he said:

White faced Tsemeli, finest of the herd,
In the greenness of spring it throws off the herd boys,
The oxen are casting the long hair of winter.
Where the grass has been burned graze the cattle,
And black are the faces and eyes of their herd boys.
If you should get lost, child of peace!
What herd boys are those who will find you?
Sweet smelling Tsemeli, cow of Rakhatoe.
When sweet-smelling Tsemeli is perfumed,
She is perfumed by girls in the pastures.
What do the girls when they cover themselves with white clay?
It goes and it goes not, it goes not and goes.
Far away on the high ground, the girls dance and sing,
Here the chief herd cooks the first milk.
Beware boys, take heed that you scratch not,
Lest the milk should be spoiled, and the great one should fall.
We, the poor ones, have bitten our fingers,
We have wagered the kids of our goats
When you vanquished the gambler Kholoane.
Kholoane who boasted those cattle of his
Which are with Tsoanyane and Mochesi
Do not run, but they fly!
And there where you meet with the bones of diviners
The high places of people are silent together.
Tsemeli, with white on your forehead
Whose lowing begins at the sun's going down
And reaches the heart and o'erwhelms it,

Which rings through the village while yet
The cattle are still far away;
Tsemeli, you imitate whom
With your lowing so loud and so long?
What say the men of the chief
At the court when they hear?
They will say: 'Tis not fitting, Tsemeli,
For a cow so to low in a village.
The cow of my father reminds me
Of the days and the cattle of old.
In the enemy's hands were they lost
And no man knows where they are.
Your lowing, Tsemeli, is heard,
Is heard by the Zulus afar.

To the grey cow, he said:
Cow of the herd boys, with horns upstanding,
Cow of the spring of 'Malekoatla,
Cow with the dewlap of silver and grey,
Which shines like the shield of the warriors of old!
O black cow, leader of herd boys,
You run not, you trot not,
But filled with high pride you pace by in anger.
Sad cheats are the Sefikeng herd boys
They capture the wagtail I hit,
And with a loud roar falls the rock,
It falls on those Sefikeng herds.
O grey one, blue crane so beloved of the men!
No more drinks the cow of the poor man's clear water,
But stands all forlorn in the mud of the marshes.
O mother of beauty, revealer of truth!
O Tsoelia, cow of the chief, with your horns
Downward sweeping, disturb not our rest with your lowing
Which causes the tears to spring to men's eyes.
The grey cow, the mother of silence,
Long time is she silent refusing to speak,
Her silence is that of a daughter-in-law
When the mother rebukes her in anger.
Listen, O black Tsoelia, to the singing of clever Tsemeli.
Long did she lead you in singing, answer her now,

Tsoelia is one who won't hurry unduly,
She joins in the singing on nearing her home
And at her singing sit silent the men.
In the forecourts the women stop short in their grinding
And even the praisers stop short in their praises;
At the sound of that wonderful singing,
The song of the God,
The God with the wet nose.

When he had finished praising these he praised them all in a common praise.

But he was praising them thus in a hurry, and in a whisper, so that no one might perchance hear him. And it was as if the cattle knew; they were quite, quite quiet; there was none that poked with its horns, none that chewed the cud, none that looked away from him. The eyes of all were on him, it was as if they knew they were seeing him for the last time. Swiftly he left those cattle of his, he left the home of his father, he left his father and his mother, his sisters, and all the people of the village. He went away treading on tiptoe through the village, he went noiselessly. He went away secretly, not a dog barked, none raised the alarm, all was silent and still.

Translated from the Sesuto by H. Ashton

WHY I WRITE OF THE TIV

AKIGA

The Tiv, a tribe in West Central Nigeria numbering over half a million people, first came in contact with the white man early in this century. Akiga was the first of his tribe to be educated by missionaries. Intensely loyal to his people, although no longer sharing their old beliefs, he dedicated twenty years of his life to recording their history and traditions. The resulting volume, *Akiga's Story*, translated by his mentor, Rupert East, represents an original piece of research carried out by a person without technical training or models. It is the work of an insatiable, tolerant, inquiring mind which is determined that the pre-European heritage shall not pass away without a memorial. Since writing *Akiga's Story*, B. Akiga Sai has been editor of a Tiv newspaper and an elected member of the Northern Nigeria House of Assembly.

IT IS NOW NEARLY twenty years ago that I began to set my heart on writing this book. For at the time when the missionaries first brought the Word of God to the Tiv country, and came to settle at my father's house, my father took me and gave me to them, and I remained with them in the care of Mr. Zimmerman, of the Dutch Reformed Church Mission, who was the first to come and live among the Tiv. This was in the year 1911, and I was about thirteen years old at the time. After some years I also believed, and became a Christian. So they taught me the knowledge of God and of the world. And it was while I was wandering round through every part of Tivland, preaching the Gospel of Jesus Christ, and at the same time seeing and hearing the things of Tiv, that the idea of this "history" took shape in my mind. So I began to ask and to look, and to delve into everything concerning the Tiv people. Whenever I sat talking with my father, or with the other elders, it was always about these things that I questioned them, for my father, Sai, was a man well known amongst the Tiv.

So it has been my constant prayer that God would help me to write this book, in order that the new generation of Tiv, which is beginning to learn this New Knowledge, should also know the things of the fathers as well as those of the present generation. For everything that belongs to the Tiv is passing away, and the old people, who should tell us about these things, will soon all be dead. It makes me sad to think that our heritage is being lost, and that there will be none to remember it.

It is not every elder who is well versed in Tiv lore. Some know, others do not. It is the men of mature years who know best; of the very old men only one or two are wise, the ignorant are in the majority. Moreover if you wish to ask them about something, and do not go about it the right way, you will never get the truth from them. They will think that you have been sent by the white man, and give you no information of any value. As for the chiefs, if you ask one about his district or about his chieftainship, he will be afraid to give you the true facts of the case, lest you go and tell the European, who will depose him and give the office to whom it rightly belongs. Moreover some of the old men still believe that the white man will soon be going, so why should they tell him about these things, in order that he may take them away from them, or forbid them their use? Others think, when you ask them something and they see you write it down, that you are making a report to give to a government official, who will increase their tax.

*　　*　　*

As for myself, I am known by a large number of the tribe, and they understand me. There is no chief today who does not know me well. I am favored, too, by Providence in my relations with them, in that they never fear to tell me what I ask them; while I, on the other hand, am careful not to put questions to them in such a way that they will not answer. But I take no credit to myself for this.

I praise God who inspired me with the desire to write this book, and has not left me with it still unfinished. For who am I, with the knowledge that I have, to write a work of any value?

This book fulfils a father's duty to all Tiv who have a care for that which concerns their own tribe. You, then, my Tiv brothers of the new generation that can read, read it and tell others, who cannot, of the things of our ancestors; so that, whether we have learnt to read or not, we all may still know something of our fathers who have gone before us. And do you, however great your knowledge may be, remember that you are a Tiv, remain a Tiv, and know the things of Tiv; for therein lies your pride. Let us take heart. The old mushroom rots, another springs up, but the mushroom tribe lives on.

HOTTER THAN RED PEPPER

AKIGA

In our second excerpt from *Akiga's Story* we learn a little about the mystifying matter of *tsav*. Akiga devotes a lengthy chapter to this, and anthropologists have made intensive studies of it without arriving at a basic agreement. *Tsav* can be variously translated. One of its meanings is witchcraft power, but it may also mean personality, charm, talent, charisma. Rupert East says, "It is that indefinable something which enables a man to impose his will on others and succeed in whatever he undertakes."

Akiga's father, Sai, was himself a man of *tsav;* for he was a leader in the tribe, a skillful practitioner of the magic craft of the blacksmith. (See the selection by Camara Laye in the next chapter.)

The boy Akiga, because he had lost an eye and had a deformed foot would be regarded as somewhat uncanny. His constant attendance at his father's smithy could only add to that impression. But the amusing incidents which he relates below show us how such a reputation can grow, and give us some fascinating glimpses into the minds of the Tiv of that time, to whom this witchery was as intimate as dreams, and as palpable as little black pigs.

MANY YEARS AGO, when I lived in close companionship with my father, Sai, all my group said that I was *tsav,* but there was never any truth in it. My reputation for *tsav* was acquired in this way. My mother left me when I was a child, and my life was a very hard one. But my father took great care of me, and did all he could to find means to feed me. For this reason he used to perform the rites of the *akombo* of the crops in the farm of his chief wife, the daughter of Turan, called El. The *akombo* was in the field at the foot of a shea tree, and *iyandegh* had been planted round it. Whenever the time came to perform the rites my father woke me at cock-crow, before it was light, caught a cock and gave it to Hilekaan, his eldest son, to carry, filled a gourd of water for me to take, and he himself carried the fire. Then we went out to the farm. My father carried out the *akombo* rites, we killed and ate the chicken, and returned to the village in the early morning. Seeing this, people said, "Hilekaan and Akiga are *tsav* beyond all measure. There is no one in these parts to be compared with them. They are eating human flesh with their father." But for my part, I knew that it was not so; my father was only seeking an opportunity to give me something

to eat. Yet when I heard that people interpreted the affair in
this way, and that it seemed to them the work of the *mbatsav*,[1] I was content to let the matter rest there, but did everything I could to play up to my reputation for *tsav,* in order
to attract attention to myself and make people afraid of me.

There was another incident. An agent of the firm of John
Holt at Ibi gave my father a large iron box. This was very
highly prized, for at that time iron boxes in Tivland were
rare. The key was kept by Hilekaan, and he alone used to
open the box; no one else touched it. At the time when the
daughter of Buriya, one of my father's chief wives, was being
brought home as a bride, and the marriage dance was in
progress, I went into the house of the daughter of Adamu,
where the box was kept, this being also the house into which
the bride had been taken.[2] I sat down on a bed, on which
were several boxes, including the iron box in question, and
began to play about with it for amusement. While I was engaged in this, I noticed that the iron hasp into which the
padlock fits was raised, by which I knew that it was unlocked.
So I went out and told my father that Hilekaan had opened
the box, and had forgotten to lock it again. My father asked
me how I knew this, and I told him that I saw that the hasp
was pointing upwards. So he called Hilekaan and questioned
him. Hilekaan replied that he had locked it quite securely,
and that I had opened it by *tsav.*

Thereupon my father seized hold of me, and undoing the
girdles round his waist, set about beating me. To everyone
who came to stop him he said, "No, leave me alone. Akiga's
tsav has passed all bounds. Look at my iron box that he has
opened by *tsav* in order to see the *imborivungu*[3] inside!"

When the other heard this he was seized with fear and
backed away, saying, "Beat him! If so small a child has this
much *tsav* in him, what will he not do with it when he grows
up?"

My father beat me till my body was covered with sores. In

[1] *Mbatsav:* witches.
[2] The bridal chamber is filled with drummers, etc., for several days.
[3] A charm "for setting right the land." It is dangerous for one
man to see another man's *imborivungu.* R. East.

the end I broke loose from him, and ran away and hid. But
for the love which he had for me he sought me out, and when
he had found me in the house of the daughter of Adzande,
he took me in his arms and soothed me.

The next morning my name was in every one's mouth.
They all spoke of my *tsav,* and many things were invented
to add to the story. Some said that yesterday I had opened
the box and put my head and shoulders inside, so that the
sweat poured from me. Others said that I had taken out the
imborivungu, and was looking at it, when Hilekaan found
me and went to tell Sai, who came and caught me with it in
my hand, and beat me. "With this sort of *tsav,*" they said,
"Akiga, when he grows up, will surpass Hilekaan." When I
realized that every one admired me for my *tsav,* I was much
flattered, and began to tell people all sorts of lies about the
mbatsav. In this, moreover, I was never contradicted. They
said I was so full of *tsav* that anything I said about the
mbatsav was not to be doubted. I was delighted at this and
henceforth set my whole heart on *tsav,* so that people came
to marvel at me. And I was only a very small boy.

There was another reason why people called me *tsav.* In
those days, when I was still a child, I used to follow my
father about like his shadow. Day and night I never left him;
only when he went on a long journey did we part company.
So it happened that being always with him I had the chance
to see and hear much. For he was a man of high standing,
and the head of his group. Now he had many wives, and in
the house of whichever wife he was spending the night I
would sleep, too. And if in the night I felt the need to relieve
nature, I went outside to do it; I was never afraid of darkness
like other children. Moreover, it was a case of necessity; I
was afraid to make water in the house, lest, if I did so, the
wife to whom it belonged would rate my father on the
morrow for having brought me in to make a mess in her
house, and when she came to cook the meal she would
refuse to give me any.[4]

[4] It is not only unnatural for a child not to be afraid of the dark, but
definitely sinister, in view of the connection between witchcraft
and darkness. He is already well on the way to become one of the
"People of the Night." R. East.

One night when I had gone out, according to my usual
custom, I saw two little black pigs which scampered away
from me, one this way and one that. Now there were two
people who owned pigs in our village: Akure, my father's
sister, and Gata, his wife, and as each of their pigs had litters
I concluded that the young pigs belonged to them.

When I went back into the house my father was awake,
so I told him about it. "When I went out just now," I said,
"I saw two little black pigs. I wonder who has left his pigs
out like this for a hyena to take?" My father asked me
whether they were both black or whether one was white, and
I answered that in the darkness they both seemed to be black.[5]

The next morning he told Hilekaan. Hilekaan called me
and asked me what I saw when I went out in the night, and
I told him that I had seen two little pigs. When I said this
Hilekaan answered angrily that I was to stop lying and tell
him exactly what happened, otherwise he would give me a
thrashing. Even so I did not at first understand what he
wished to hear, and so when he asked me again I repeated
exactly what I told him the first time. Thereupon he picked
up a stick to beat me for not telling him the truth. I had not
the least idea what to do, and the thought passed quickly
through my mind, "I have told the truth, and Hilekaan is
not satisfied. I will tell him a lie and see whether he will
believe it." So I turned round the story as though it were the
work of the *mbatsav*.

"I will tell you the truth," I said, "What I saw last night
were the owls of the *mbatsav*. There were two of them, and
they had indigo clothes wrapped about their bodies. When
I came out they scuttled away along the ground flapping their
wings."

Hilekaan said, "Ah, now you have told me the truth!"

When the story got round, my reputation for *tsav* was
much enhanced. "Last night," they said, "The *mbatsav* appeared in Sai's village, and Akiga came out and drove them
off."

For many days people talked of nothing else. Koho, a kins-

---

[5] Black is the color associated with witchcraft, and white with the
"People of the Day." R. East.

man of my father, gave me the name of Ipemke, a name connected with the *mbatsav,* which means a pepper that is
different from all other peppers; that is to say, the *mbatsav*
were hot as red pepper, but I was hotter than they, and had
driven them off. The people at my home still remember this
name, but I do not like to be called by it now.

IN THE GOLD MINES

B. W. VILAKAZI

The first generation of Africans who were lured or forced into
the mines of South Africa must have experienced a special
horror going beyond the fear of physical destruction. ("You
eat away the joints of our bodies," says the African miner in
Vilakazi's poem.) But those huge, screaming, fire-breathing
machines of the white men were alien monsters; against them,
how helpless was a "black rock-rabbit" or a "black field-mouse
with mind all wrapped in darkness." This poem's rugged, plain-
spoken style—with metaphors growing most naturally out of
the harsh facts—achieves an overwhelming pathos.

But in a later part of the poem, which unfortunately we
cannot print in full, Vilakazi goes beyond this pathos to strike
a note of revolt:

> "Wait just a while, for feeble as I seem,
> From these same little arms one day
> There flew some fierce, long-bladed spears
> Which I hurled till the sun was darkened. . . .
> I was robbed
> But still I go on dreaming, son of Iron,
> Dreaming that the land of my fathers' fathers
> Comes back to the hands of the homeless Blacks."

Benedict W. Vilakazi, who died in 1947, was a linguist on
the staff of the Witwatersrand University, Johannesburg. An
award in his memory was established at the University. He had
published two volumes of verse in the Zulu language. The
translation here is by Dr. A. C. Jordan who teaches at the
School of African Studies, University of Capetown. He has

written many articles on the history of African literature, and
done much translating from African languages.

Thunder away, machines of the mines,
Thunder away from dawn till sunset;
I will get up soon: do not pester me;
Thunder away, machines. Heed not
The groans of the black labourers
Writhing with the pains of their bodily wounds,
The air close and suffocating
With the dirt and sweat of their bodies
As they drain their hips till nothing is left.

Call aloud, old boy. It is far,
It is far away where you were moulded,
Where you roasted in the fire till you were strong;
The coal remained; you were sent away,
And we saw you cross the waters of the sea;
You were borne overland by the engines of fire
That puffed and glided to Goli here;
You screamed one day, and all at once there appeared,
There came rock-rabbits from all sides.

Those black rock-rabbits without tails
You caught and stowed away in holes
To own and milk as yielding cows.
Whirl round and round, you wheels of iron;
It was for us they brought you here;
You were tied together against your will;
Today you thunder and strain unceasingly;
See how some of your kind, now rusty and old,
Have been cast away on the rubbish dumps.

As I pass along the road
I turn around and watch,
Wondering if you will ever give birth,
Perchance increase. But no!
Your brothers too go rusty
Within the mine compounds;
Their lungs go rusty and rusty,

And they cough and they lie down and they die.
But you irons, you never cough. I note and wonder why.

I have heard it said that in the hole
There are tribes and tribes of the Black One;
It is they who raise the great white mounds
That astonish their black forbears.
I have heard it said that on a certain day
A siren shrieked, and a black field-mouse
With mind all wrapped in darkness came;
He was caught and changed into a mole,
And he burrowed the earth and I saw the gold.

O yes, they burrowed, those burrowing moles,
And the great white mounds appeared.
Swelling from the ground and climbing and climbing
Till to-day they top Isandlwana Mountain.
I labour to the top, I wipe off the sweat,
And from on high I see the piles
Of fine white dust, fine dust arising
From below my feet. I look around
And I note that the piles block the earth around.

Thunder away, machines of the mines,
Thunder loud and loud,
Deafen with noise that we may not be heard
Though we cry out aloud and groan
As you eat away the joints of our bodies;
Giggle and snigger, you old machines;
It is well that you laugh and scorn our rage,
For great is your power and fearful;
You may do as you please: we succumb.

GREETING THE BRITISH PRINCE

S. E. KRUNE MQHAYI

According to his translator, S.E.K. Mqhayi "dominated the
Xhosa literary field" in the early part of this century as a
journalist, poet, novelist, biographer, essayist, and translator.

The present selection is part of a poem that Mqhayi wrote when the Prince of Wales visited South Africa in 1925. It achieves a sledgehammer irony by using the style of the traditional praise-poem, in effect using a garland as a hangman's noose.

Ah Britain! Great Britain!
Great Britain of the endless sunshine!
She has conquered the oceans and laid them low;
She has drained the little rivers and lapped them dry;
She has swept the little nations and wiped them away;
And now she is making for the open skies.
She sent us the preacher, she sent us the bottle,
She sent us the Bible, and barrels of brandy,
She sent us the breechloader, she sent us cannon.
O Roaring Britain! Which must we embrace?
You sent us the truth, denied us the truth;
You sent us the life, deprived us of the life;
You sent us the light, we sit in the dark,
Shivering, benighted, in the bright noonday sun.

Translated from the Xhosa by A. C. Jordan

Chapter 3

The New Generation:
African Literature in European Languages

WAR AND PEACE IN OLD KENYA

JOMO KENYATTA

Jomo Kenyatta, one of Africa's outstanding leaders, was released in 1961 after long confinement for his alleged leadership of the Mau-Mau terrorist organization. His influence was
considered crucial in the developments toward an autonomous
state in Kenya.

We cannot here attempt to assess the degree of Kenyatta's
involvement in Mau-Mau. Our present interest is in his attitudes toward his African heritage. A man who spent some
sixteen years in England, acquiring wide-ranging cultural interests and social contacts there, Kenyatta has nevertheless
strikingly affirmed his interest in that heritage. Until the age
of ten, when as an orphan he ran away to a mission school, he
had received the traditional tribal education. Indeed, his
grandfather was an influential witch doctor of the Kikuyu
tribe, who had taught his grandson something of the diviner's
craft. Later, after his mission education, Kenyatta became an
aggressive and talented political leader. He spent his years in
England getting further education and doing spadework for
pan-Africanism among the overseas Africans. After studying
anthropology in London he published a notable study of his
people entitled *Facing Mount Kenya*. Interestingly enough, as
a frontispiece for this scholarly work, Kenyatta supplied a
studio photograph of himself wearing a leopard skin and carrying a spear. This was apparently his way of saying that he did

85

not choose to turn his back on the old Africa. It would be difficult to say whether political calculation entered into this posture to any great degree. Peter Abrahams, describing a meeting with Kenyatta years later in Africa, suggests that the political motivation was strong. (See the selection by Abrahams later in this chapter.) Be that as it may, in the following pages from Kenyatta's little volume, *My People of the Kikuyu,* which celebrates the history and traditions of his people, he gives us a romantic reconstruction of a bit of the past of the tribe—telling of one of the perennial wars between the Kikuyu and the Masai, and of the talents for war-making and peace-making of the legendary leader, Wangombe.

WANGOMBE LED his regiment along the riverside until they came to a sacred grove, under which several bulls had been slaughtered and their blood collected in raw hides spread in a basin-like hole in the ground. The ceremonial place was well hidden from view by the high banks of the river and the thick forest above; only those who knew the secret passages through the giant rocks could find their way down to it. Scouts were stationed along the ridge to give warning if they saw any stranger approaching the secret entrances.

When the warriors arrived at the sacred grove, Wangombe called a halt. At his command they lined up in fours. Standing in front of them, his eyes glaring as though he were about to attack, he lifted up his long spear and raised his shield above his shoulder. Without a word he trotted rhythmically towards the warm bull's blood, and kneeling down he took a long draught of the beverage, which the war doctor was stirring with a forked twig.

In a few seconds he jumped to his feet like a disturbed lion, and with a powerful and fierce voice he burst into a song of command: "Hio-ho-o-o-o; itimo-nango-ho-o-o, na-ro-hio-hio-ho-o-o-o.

"Brave warriors, lift up your sharp spears; hio-ho-o-o-o. Fix your eyes on the foe like hungry eagles swooping upon their prey; io-ho-o-o-o.

"Vultures are floating above waiting for you to feed them: hio-ho-o-o-o.

"Is there anyone here who is afraid and trembles? Hio-ho-o-o-o. If there is, let him go home and wear his mother's skirt and front apron: hio-ho-o-o-o.

"Let brave warriors lift up their spears and hold shields above their shoulders: hio-ho-o-o-o.

"Let them advance and sip the warm bull's blood, vowing that they will fight to the last drop of their blood: hio-ho-o-o-o."

He concluded his recitation with a high-pitched note: "Hio-ho-o-o-o; ho-ra-re-yo-o-o-ho-o-o-o!"

The warriors, who stood erect tossing their heads in a war-like manner, now advanced, and following their leader's example each drank. Then, shaking their plumed headgears frantically, they answered in unison:

"Hio-ho-o-o-o; ho-ra-re-yo-o-o-ho-o-o-o! We go forward to win the battle or die in the attempt: hio-ho-o-o. We will crush our enemies like a black ants' nest: hio-ho-o-o-o. Like the sting of the bee, we will thrust our sharp spears into their flesh: hio-ho-o-o-o; ho-ra-re-yo-o-o-ho-o-o-o."

When the ceremony was over, Wangombe ordered his comrades to rest and refresh themselves with meat which had been roasted on an open fire. On the ridge above, at the edge of the forest, there were several cattle kraals which the fierce Masai warriors had planned to raid. It was now about sunset; the council of war was discussing a plan for deceiving the enemy, and it was decided that the cattle should be brought ostentatiously into the kraals, and that after dark they should be secretly driven away to places of safety, leaving behind only a few inferior ones whose mooing would entice the invading Masai.

Messengers were sent to the herdsmen to inform them what the Njama had decided and to instruct them to act accordingly. Spies, some disguised as Masai warriors and others as Ndorobo, had been sent into the enemy's camps, and had brought information that the Masai were determined to raid the kraals early in the morning, and that their scouts had informed them about the festivities which were going on in the Kikuyu country, in which the warriors were thought to be busily engaged. With this conviction, the Masai warriors did not expect to meet with a strong resistance. The spies reported that they had heard them say boastfully: "The tillers of the soil love their dancing too much; they dance and dance, and then drink their dirty millet gruel in which their womenfolk have dipped their defiled hands, and then with their bellies hanging like calabashes they go to sleep like old women. What do they know about cattle? Their profession is to dig the land, and to drink polluted beverage. How can they fight with us who never let a woman touch our meat or come near us when we are feasting? E-Ngai[1] has given us the right to possess large flocks and herds. But these tillers of the soil have no right to own them. Cattle are our heritage and it is our duty to take them into our care. Tomorrow before these slumberers recover from their dancing fatigue we will be driving their cattle towards our sacred plains of Laikipia, for that is where they belong."

The Kikuyu warriors listened to the report in silence, and then with fury they said to one another: "We will show these impudent thieves that we can till the land and fight as well!" In the dead of the night the Kikuyu warriors, marshalled by Wangombe, rose and went stealthily with their rattles covered with dried banana leaves, and hid themselves in the bush around the almost empty kraals. There they waited excitedly for the enemy. Early in the morning, when in the northeast the reflection of the rising sun brightened the sky like a polished sword and the morning stars were throwing their fading lights over the crest of mighty Kere-Nyaga, word was passed on to warn the warriors to be ready and await the signal from the scouts.

The Masai, unaware of the preparation which the Kikuyu had made for the defence of their cattle, marched boldly towards the kraals, determined to kill anyone who came in their way, and to drive off their booty. On reaching a ford where several paths leading to various kraals met, they halted to prepare themselves for the attack. At the command of their leader they lifted up their spears and held their shields in position. With a yell, they dashed forward like hungry leopards springing to their prey; like a gust of wind they sped

[1] E-Ngai: the High God. The name, Kenya, is derived from *Kere-Nyaga* the mountain of mystery, or the abode of Nyaga or Ngai, the High God.

over the slope and in a short time surrounded the kraals and were wildly pulling away the thorny branches blocking the entrances.

When they were thus engaged a warning horn was sounded. Like lightning the bowmen who were stationed on a little hill nearby sent a volley of poisoned arrows which fell on the Masai like a swarm of bees; the men with slings followed with a shower of stones. In a twinkling Wangombe's regiment closed with the Masai. First the club throwers hurled their war clubs, and there was a sound of thunder as they crashed down on thick rows of upraised shields. Some struck with terrific force not on the shields but on heads, and the unfortunate Masai warriors dropped to the ground with their skulls split open. But their comrades never wavered though taken by surprise; they closed their ranks and advanced with yells of fury.

The club throwers stood upright and drew their swords, while the spearmen advanced a step forward. The warriors of both sides now came together, fighting hand to hand in a raging mass. Swords and spears in practised hands were dancing like reeds in the water. Spearmen crouched on the ground and thrust their spears upward at their enemies' legs, ribs, and faces; others crippled suddenly in full charge, spun round with quivering weapons until they toppled over; others, with arrows sticking deep in their flesh, went on thrusting and hewing until the poison overcame them and their fingers would no longer close over their sword hilts.

The Masai fought like mad dogs, but the first shower of poisoned arrows had weakened their ranks. Many of them were lying still, or squirming in a death agony, and their blood was running in streams down the hillocks and collecting in little pools on the ground. Suddenly, finding the force against them too strong, they bolted in a great panic. Fiercely the Kikuyu warriors followed them down the slopes. When the Masai warriors reached the ford which a short while ago they had crossed without meeting any resistance, they were met by Wamahio's regiment which had gone to cut them off at the rear. They tried to force their way through but were overpowered.

Wangombe, who was at their heels, pressed forward, with

his spear aiming at a tall warrior whose lion's mane headgear he longed to carry home as a war trophy. He was about to thrust his spear into the enemy's flesh, when suddenly he heard a beseeching cry: *"Ole yoyo, tapala,"* meaning "Brother, stop!" At once he looked intently, but he could hardly believe his eyes that he was face to face with an old playmate, who as a young boy had gone to Masailand with his Kikuyu mother who was married to a Masai elder.

In order to avoid annihilation of the Masai and to save his playfellow, who was at the head of the enemy's regiment, Wangombe shouted for a halt; and speaking in the Masai language he called on the Masai warriors to surrender. With dignity those who were left put down their weapons, and each held a handful of Nyarageta grass in his right hand as a sign of peace. Immediately a lamb was sent for, and slaughtered on the spot. There and then a treaty of friendship was entered into. The warriors of both sides rubbed their feet with the contents of the lamb's stomach to cool down their fighting spirit. Each promised the other not to have any more raids on their friends' territory, and that in future if they wished to raid other territories they would act as allies. The wounded were tended and the dead left on the battlefield to feed the hyenas and vultures, and at the same time to fertilize the soil.

From that time on the two sections remained friends, and the friendship was later strengthened when a cattle disease devastated both Masai and Kikuyu cattle. The Masai, who depend entirely on the milk, meat and blood from their cattle, experienced great hardship and thousands of them died of starvation. But the section which had established friendship with the Kikuyu were saved, for during this time trading relations were established and marketing centers were set up.

In the markets, or sometimes in the homesteads, the Kikuyu women brought grain, yams, flour, sweet potatoes, and bananas, which the Masai women bought with sheep, skins, or hides. The Masai warriors, who hitherto had regarded the cultivated crops as things cursed by the E-Ngai, now ate garden produce ravenously and comforted themselves with the excuse that *"Ciatura ngoyo ireaga ngumo,"* that is, "When there is only one article there is no choice."

THE STORIES WHICH CRADLED MY CHILDHOOD

BIRAGO DIOP

Birago Diop was born in Dakar in 1906. As in the case of many middle-class Senegalese, M. Diop's ancestry derives from several African peoples. He has been chief of veterinary service for the Upper Volta, devoting part of his leisure to the production of stories and poems. His stories, as he tells in the brief memoir given here, owe their source and inspiration to Amadou, son of Koumba, the *griot* of his own family. (A *griot* is a story-teller, singer, genealogist, and custodian of oral traditions.)

"BAKE, ARE you sleeping?"

"Yes, grandmother!"

So long as I answered so, grandmother would know that I wasn't sleeping, and that, trembling with fear, I was listening with all of my ears and closed eyes to the terrifying tales in which the Genies, the Goblins, and the long-haired Kouss intervened; or that, as full of joy as the grownups who were also listening, I was following the cunning and prank-playing Leuk the Hare in his interminable adventures, through the course of which he ridiculed animals and people, in the village as in the bush, even so far as the King's residence.

When I wouldn't answer grandmother's questions, or when I would begin to deny that I was sleeping, my mother would say, "We must put him to sleep," and grandmother would raise me from the mat which had been growing cold in the night air and would put me to bed after I had made her promise, in my sleepy voice, to tell me the rest the following night, because in a black country one must only tell stories when the night comes.

Grandmother dead, I had other old people around me, and, in growing up at their side, "I drank of the infusion of rind and of the decoction of roots, I climbed on the baobab." As a child, I drank plentifully at the source, I heard many wise words, I have retained some of them.

I saw and heard the last *M'Bandakatts* (singing and dancing clowns); I heard the *Ritikatts* on their one-stringed violin, which was only a gourd tautened by a lizard skin, able to make a horse bristle talk, laugh, and cry. I heard the *Lavankatts* recite the entire Koran at one stretch, and to refresh themselves from their exploit, mix satire in with the sacred verses, to the detriment of ugly young girls and stingy old women.

Later, under other skies, when the weather was dull and the sun ill, I often closed my eyes, and from my lips rose the *Kassaks* which one sang in "The Men's Hut"; I heard my mother and above all grandmother, who was still telling of the disappointments of the cowardly and vain Bouki the Hyena, the misfortunes of the orphan Khary Gaye, the wiles of Djabou N'daw, *enfant terrible,* the triumphs of Samba Seytane, and the misadventures of Amary the Devout.

This fugitive return into the recent past tempered the exile, softened for a while the tenacious nostalgia, and brought back the bright and hot hours which one only learns to appreciate once one is far away.

When I returned to the country, having forgotten almost nothing of that which I had learned as a child, I had the great happiness of meeting, on my long road, the old Amadou Koumba, the Griot of my family. Amadou Koumba told me, on certain nights—and sometimes by day, I confess—the same stories which had cradled my childhood. He told me others which he embellished with maxims and apophthegms containing the wisdom of the ancestors.

These same stories and these same legends—with certain variations—I also heard in the course of my rambles on the banks of the Niger and in the plains of the Sudan, far from Senegal. Other children, similar to the child that I had been, and other grown-ups, similar to my elders, listened to them with the same eagerness sculpted on their faces by the high-flaming faggots. Other old women, other Griots told them, and the songs which interrupted them and which all took up again in chorus were often made rhythmic by the rolling of the tam-tam or scanned on an overturned gourd. The very same fright entered the audience with the breathing of the brush and the same gaiety brought forth the laughter as well as the fear and gaiety palpitating at the same hours in all the African villages enveloped in the vast night.

If I have not been able to reproduce, in what I set down, the atmosphere in which I had luxuriated as a young listener, nor describe those attentive, quivering, contemplative people about me, it is because I have become a man, therefore an incomplete child, and being thus reduced, am incapable of re-creating the marvelous. It is especially because I lack the voice, the verve, and the art of mimicry of my old Griot.

In the sturdy woof of his tales and his aphorisms availing me of a warp without seams, I wanted, unskillful weaver that I am with a faltering weaver's shuttle, to put together a few strips so grandmother, if she returned, would find the thread which she was the first to spin; and where Amadou Koumba would recognize the colors, much less vivid, no doubt, of the beautiful fabrics which he wove for me but lately.

Translated by Anne Atik

TWO POEMS

Birago Diop

A sharp, almost excruciating, sense of the past sings in the two poems reproduced below. In "Breaths," "the great pact which binds" is M. Diop's epithet for the compelling importance of ancestors in African cultures. All nature is alive with the presence of the dead. In "Vanity," we hear the poignant note of a separation, a breach between the living and the dead, anguished intimations of a betrayal.

Vanity

If we say, then, gently, gently
All we'll one day have to say,
Who'll hear our voices without laughing,
Gloomy, whining beggars' voices
Really hear them without laughing?

If harshly we cry our torments

Ever mounting layer by layer,
What eyes will gaze at our ample mouths
Made of grown-up children's guffaws,
What eyes will gaze at our ample mouths?

What heart will hear our vast clamors?
What ear our paltry wraths
That remain in us like tumors
In our plaintive throats' black depths?

When our dead came with their dead
And spoke to us in their dull voices,
How deaf our ears were
To their cries, to their strongest appeals
How deaf our ears were!

They have left their cries on earth,
In the air, on the water, they have traced their signs
For us, blind, deaf, unworthy sons
Who see nothing at all of what they have placed
In the air, on the water, where their signs are traced.

And since our dead are beyond our grasp,
Since we never hear their cries
If we lament softly, softly
If we cry out our torments harshly
What heart will hear our vast clamors
What ear the sobs in our hearts?

Breaths

Listen more often
To things than to beings;
The fire's voice is heard,
Hear the voice of water.
Hear in the wind
The bush sob:
It is the ancestors' breath.

Those who died have never left,

They are in the brightening shadow
And in the thickening shadow;
The dead are not under earth,
They are in the rustling tree,
They are in the groaning woods,
They are in the flowing water,
They are in the still water,
They are in the hut, they are in the crowd:
The dead are not dead.

Listen more often
To things than to beings;
The fire's voice is heard,
Hear the voice of water.
Hear in the wind
The bush sob:
It is the ancestor's breath.
The breath of dead ancestors
Who have not left,
Who are not under earth,
Who are not dead.
Those who died have never left,
They are in the woman's breast,
They are in the wailing child
And in the kindling firebrand.
The dead are not under earth,
They are in the fire dying down,
They are in the moaning rock,
They are in the crying grass,
They are in the forest, they are in the home:
The dead are not dead.

Listen more often
To things than to beings,
The fire's voice is heard,
Hear the voice of water.
Hear in the wind
The bush sob:
It is the ancestors' breath.
Each day it repeats the pact,

The great pact which binds,
Which binds our fate to the law;
Acts, to stronger breaths
The fate of our dead not dead;
The heavy pact which ties us to life,
The heavy law which binds us to acts
Breaths dying
In bed and on river banks,
Breaths which stir
In the moaning rock and crying grass.
Breaths which lodge
In the shadow brightening or thickening,
In the rustling tree, in the groaning woods,
And in the flowing water, and in the still water,
Breaths much stronger,
Breaths which have taken
The breath of the dead not dead,
The dead who have not left,
The dead no longer under earth.

Listen more often
To things than to beings;
The fire's voice is heard,
Hear the voice of water.
Hear in the wind
The bush sob:
It is the ancestors' breath.

Translated by Anne Atik

THE MYSTERIES OF MY FATHER'S WORKSHOP

CAMARA LAYE

Artist, magician, priest, celebrant—the goldsmith here described is all of these. And the son of the goldsmith, Guinean author Camara Laye, is no less of an artist-magician in his own craft. In a beautiful and deservedly famous book, *The Dark Child* (translated from the French by the poet, James Kirkup), Camara Laye tells the story of his early life in

Guinea, carrying it to the painful time when he has to separate himself from his loved ones and go off to college in France. In a fresh, direct, poetic style, M. Laye reveals a people of great grace and character. His family combine Moslem religious practices with the older tribal culture of the Malinké people. There is no sense of strain between Camara Laye and his heritage: he carries it within himself quite happily. In addition to *The Dark Child,* he has written a strange allegorical novel, *The Radiance of the King.*

OF ALL THE DIFFERENT kinds of work my father performed, none fascinated me so much as his skill with gold. No other occupation was so noble, no other needed such a delicate touch; and, moreover, this sort of work was always a kind of festival: it was a real festival that broke the monotony of ordinary working days.

So if a woman, accompanied by a go-between, crossed the threshold of the workshop, I would follow her in at once. I knew what she wanted: she had brought some gold and wanted to ask my father to transform it into a trinket. The woman would have collected the gold in the placers of Siguiri, where, for months on end, she would have crouched over the river, washing the mud and patiently extracting from it the grains of gold. These women never came alone: they were well aware that my father had other things to do than to make trinkets for all and sundry; and even if the making of jewellery had been his main occupation, they would have realized that they were not his first or his only customers, and that their wants could not be immediately attended to.

Generally these women required the trinket for a certain date, either for the festival of Ramadan or for the Tabaski; or for some other family festivity, or for a dance ceremony.

Thereupon, to better their chance of being quickly served, and the more easily to persuade my father to interrupt the work he had in hand, they would request the services of an official praise-singer, a go-between, and would arrange with him in advance what fee they would pay for his good offices.

The praise-singer would install himself in the workshop, tune up his cora, which is our harp, and would begin to sing my father's praises. This was always a great event for me. I would hear recalled the lofty deeds of my father's ancestors, and the names of these ancestors from the earliest times; as the couplets were reeled off, it was like watching the growth of a great genealogical tree that spread its branches far and wide and flourished its boughs and twigs before my mind's eye. The harp played an accompaniment to this vast utterance of names, expanding it and punctuating it with notes that were now soft, now shrill. Where did the praise-singer get his information from? He must certainly have developed a very retentive memory stored with facts handed down to him by his predecessors, for this is the basis of all our oral traditions. Did he embellish the truth? It is very likely: flattery is the praise-singer's stock in trade! Nevertheless, he was not allowed to take too many liberties with tradition, for it is part of the praise-singer's task to preserve it. But in those days such considerations did not enter my head, which I would hold high and proud; for I used to feel quite drunk with so much praise, which seemed to reflect some of its effulgence upon my own small person.

I could tell that my father's vanity was being inflamed, and I already knew that after having sipped this milk-and-honey he would lend a favourable ear to the woman's request. But I was not alone in my knowledge; the woman also had seen my father's eyes gleaming with contented pride; and she would hold out her grains of gold as if the whole thing were settled: my father, taking up his scales, would weigh the gold.

"What sort of trinket do you desire?" he would ask.

"I want . . ."

And often it would happen that the woman did not know really what she wanted, because she would be so torn by desire, because she would have liked to have many, many trinkets, all out of the same small quantity of gold: but she would have had to have much more than she had brought with her to satisfy such a desire, and eventually she would have to content herself with some more modest wish.

"When do you want it for?" my father would ask.

And she would always want it at once.

"Why are you in such a hurry? How do you expect me to find the time?"

"It's very urgent, I can assure you," the woman would reply.

"That's what all women say, when they want an ornament. Well, I'll see what I can do. Now are you happy?"

Then he would take the clay pot that was kept specially for the smelting of gold and pour in the grains; thereupon he would cover the gold with powdered charcoal, a charcoal which he obtained by the use of plant juices of exceptional purity; finally he would place a large lump of the same kind of charcoal over the whole thing.

Then, having seen the work duly undertaken, the woman, by now quite satisfied. would go back to her household tasks, leaving her go-between to carry on with the praise-singing which had already proved so advantageous to her.

On a sign from my father, the apprentices would start working the two pairs of sheep-skin bellows which were placed on the ground at each side of the forge and linked to it by earthen pipes. These apprentices remained seated all the time, with crossed legs, in front of the bellows; at least the younger did, for the elder would sometimes be allowed to take part in the craftsmen's work and the younger—in those days it was Sidafa—only had to work the bellows and watch the proceedings while awaiting his turn to be elevated to less rudimentary tasks. For a whole hour they would both be working the levers of the bellows till the fire in the forge leapt into flame, becoming a living thing, a lively and merciless spirit.

Then my father, using long pincers, would lift the clay pot and place it on the flames.

Immediately all work would more or less stop in the workshop: actually while the gold is being melted and while it is cooling all work with copper or aluminium is supposed to stop, for fear that some fraction of these less noble metals might fall among the gold. It is only steel that can still be worked at such times. But workmen who had some piece of steel work in hand would either hasten to finish it or would openly stop work to join the other apprentices gathered round the forge. In fact, there were often so many of them at these times pressing round my father that I, the smallest, would have to get up and push my way in among them, so as not to miss any of the operation.

It might happen that, feeling he had too little room to work in, my father would make his apprentices stand well away from him. He would merely raise his hand in a simple gesture: at that particular moment he would never utter a word, and no one else would, no one was allowed to utter a word, even the go-between's voice would no longer be raised in song; the silence would be broken only by the panting of the bellows and by the faint hissing of the gold. But if my father never used to utter actual words at this time, I know that he was uttering them in his mind; I could see it by his lips that kept working while he bent over the pot and kept stirring the gold and the charcoal with a bit of wood that would keep bursting into flame, and so had to be constantly replaced by a fresh bit.

What were the words my father's lips were forming? I do not know; I do not know for certain: I was never told what they were. But what else could they have been, if not magical incantations? Were they not the spirits of fire and gold, of fire and air, air breathed through the earthen pipes, of fire born of air, of gold married with fire—were not these the spirits he was invoking? Was it not their help and their friendship he was calling upon in this marriage of elemental things? Yes, it was almost certainly those spirits he was calling upon, for they are the most elemental of all spirits, and their presence is essential at the melting of gold.

The operation that was going on before my eyes was simply the smelting of gold; but it was something more than that: a magical operation that the guiding spirits could look upon with favour or disfavour; and that is why there would be all round my father that absolute silence and that anxious expectancy. I could understand, though I was just a child, that there was no craft greater than the goldsmith's. I expected a ceremony, I had come to be present at a ceremony, and it really was one, though very protracted. I was still too young to be able to understand why it was so protracted; nevertheless, I had an inkling, beholding the almost religious concentration of all those present as they watched the mixing process.

When finally the gold began to melt, I used to feel like shouting, and perhaps we would all have shouted if we had not been forbidden to make a sound: I would be trembling, and certainly everyone else would be trembling as we sat watching my father stirring the mixture, still a heavy paste in which the charcoal was gradually being consumed. The next stage followed swiftly; the gold now had the fluidity of water. The guiding spirits had smiled on the operation!

"Bring me the brick!" my father would say, thus lifting the ban that until then had kept us all silent.

The brick, which an apprentice would place beside the fire, was hollowed out, generously greased with Galam butter. My father would take the pot off the fire, tilt it carefully, and I would watch the gold flowing into the brick, flowing like liquid fire. True, it was only a very sparse trickle of fire, but oh, how vivid, how brilliant! As the gold flowed into the brick, the grease would splutter and flame and give off a thick smoke that caught in the throat and stung the eyes, leaving us all weeping and coughing.

It occurred to me later on that my father could easily have relinquished all the work of smelting the gold to one or other of his assistants: they were not without experience in these matters; they had taken part hundreds of times in the same preparations and they would certainly have brought the work to a successful conclusion. But as I have told you, my father kept moving his lips! We could not hear those words, those secret words, those incantations which he addressed to powers that we should not, that we could not hear or see: this was essential. Only my father was versed in the science of conjuring the spirits of fire, air and gold, and conjuring evil spirits, and that is why he alone conducted the whole operation.

By now the gold would have cooled in the hollow of the brick, and my father would begin to hammer and stretch it. This was the moment when his work as a goldsmith really began. I noticed that before embarking on it he never failed to stroke stealthily the little snake coiled up under the sheepskin; one can only assume that this was his way of gathering strength for what remained to be done, and which was the most difficult.

But was it not extraordinary, was it not miraculous that on these occasions the little black serpent always coiled up under the sheepskin? He was not always there, he did not visit my father every day, but he was always present whenever there was gold to be worked.

Moreover, it is our custom to keep apart from the working of gold all influences outside those of the jeweller himself. And indeed it is precisely because the jeweller alone possesses the secret of his incantations; but also because the working of gold, besides being a task of the greatest skill, is a matter of confidence, of conscience, a task which is not undertaken excepting after due reflection and experiment. Finally, I do not think that any jeweller would renounce the opportunity of performing such a task—I ought to say, such a spectacle!— in which he can display his abilities with a virtuosity that his work as a blacksmith or a mechanic or even as a sculptor is never invested with; even though in these more humble tasks his skill is no less wonderful, even though the statues which he carves in wood with his adze are not insignificant works!

The snake's presence came as no surprise to me; ever since that evening when my father had talked to me about the guiding spirit of our race, it had ceased to surprise me; it was quite natural that the snake should be there: he had knowledge of the future. Did he impart any of that knowledge to my father? It seemed to me quite obvious that he did: did he not always warn him of what was going to happen? But I had another reason for believing implicitly in the powers of the little snake.

The craftsman who works in gold must first of all purify himself, that is, he must wash himself all over and, of course, abstain from all sexual relationships during the whole time. Great respecter of ceremony as he was, it would have been impossible for my father to ignore these rules. Now I never saw him make these preparations. I would see him address himself to his work without any apparent preliminaries. But from that moment it was obvious that, forewarned by his black guiding spirit in a dream of the task that would await him in the morning, my father must have prepared for it as

soon as he arose, and had entered his workshop in a state of
purity, his body smeared with the magical substances hidden
in his numerous pots full of secret potions. So I believe my
father never entered his workshop except in a state of ritual
purity; and that is not because I want to make him out as
being better than he is—he is a man like any other, and has
a man's weaknesses—but always when it was a matter of
ritual he was uncompromisingly strict.

The woman for whom the trinket was being made, and
who would often have looked in to see how the work was
getting on, would come for the final time, not wanting to miss
anything of the marvellous sight as the gold wire, which my
father had succeeded in spinning, was transformed into a
trinket. She was here now, devouring with her eyes the fragile
golden wire, following its tranquil and inevitable spirals round
the little metal cone which gave the trinket its shape. My
father would be watching her out of the corner of his eye,
and sometimes I would see the corners of his mouth twitch
into a smile: the woman's avid attentiveness amused him.

"Are you trembling?" he would say to her.

"*Am* I trembling?" she would ask.

And we would all burst out laughing at her. For she *was*
trembling! She was trembling with covetousness for the spiral
pyramid in which my father was inserting, among the con-
volutions, tiny grains of gold. When finally he terminated the
work by placing at the summit the largest grain of gold, the
woman would jump excitedly to her feet.

Then, while my father was slowly turning the trinket round
in his fingers, smoothing it into perfect shape, no one could
have displayed such utter happiness as the native woman,
not even the praise-singer, whose trade it was to do so, and
who, during the whole process of transformation, had kept
on singing his praises, accelerating his rhythm, increasing his
flatteries as the trinket took shape, and praising my father's
talents to the skies.

Indeed, the praise-singer participated in a curious—I was
going to say direct, effective—way in the work. He, too, was
intoxicated with the joy of creation; he declaimed his rapture,
and plucked his harp like a man inspired; he warmed to the
task as if he had been the craftsman himself, as if the trinket

had been made by his own hands. He was no longer a paid thurifer; he was no longer just the man whose services each and anyone could hire: he had become a man who creates his song under the influence of some very personal, interior necessity.

When my father, after having soldered the large grain of gold that crowned the summit, held out his work to be admired, the go-between would no longer be able to contain himself, and would intone the douga—the great chant which is only sung for celebrated men, and which is danced to only for them.

But the douga is a tremendous chant, a provocative chant, a chant that the go-between would not venture to sing, and that the man for whom it is sung would not venture to dance to, without certain precautions.

My father, forewarned in a dream, had been able to take these precautions as soon as he got up; the praise-singer had taken them as a matter of course when he had made his bargain with the woman. Just as my father had done, he had smeared his body with magic lotions and so had rendered himself invulnerable to the bad spirits which the douga would undoubtedly stir into activity, invulnerable also even to his fellow praise-singers who, jealous perhaps, were only waiting to hear the chant, the note of exaltation and the loss of control which that exaltation entails, to cast their evil spells upon him.

At the first notes of the douga, my father would rise and utter a cry in which happiness and triumph were equally mingled; and brandishing in his right hand the hammer that was the symbol of his profession, and in his left a ram's horn filled with magic substances, he would dance the glorious dance.

No sooner had he finished than workmen and apprentices, friends and customers in their turn, not forgetting the woman for whom the trinket had been created, would flock round him, congratulating him, showering praises on him, and complimenting at the same time the go-between, who found himself laden with gifts, gifts that are almost the only resources he has in his wandering life, that he leads after the fashion of the troubadours of old. Beaming, aglow with dancing and the praises he had received, my father would offer kola nuts, that small change of Guinean civility.

All that now remained to be done was to redden the trinket in a little water mixed with chlorine and seasalt. I could go now: the ceremony was over! But often, as I was leaving the workshop, my mother, who might be in the yard pounding millet or rice, would call me.

"Where have you been?" she would ask, although she knew very well where I had been.

"In the workshop."

"Oh, yes, your father was making something out of gold. Gold! It's always gold!"

And she would pound furiously the helpless bowl of rice or millet. "Your father's ruining his health! You see what he's doing."

"He's been dancing the douga," I would reply.

"The douga! The douga won't stop him ruining his eyesight! And you would be better off playing here in the yard instead of going and breathing the dust and smoke in the workshop!"

My mother did not like my father to work with gold. She knew how harmful the soldering of gold can be: a jeweller can wear his lungs out, puffing at his blowpipe, and his eyes suffer by being so close to the intense heat of the forge; and even more perhaps from the microscopic delicacy of the work. But even if there had been no danger in it, my mother still would have disliked this sort of work: she held it in suspicion, for you cannot solder gold without the help of other metals, and my mother used to think that it was not strictly honest to keep the gold which was saved by its alloys, although this was the accepted thing; and she, too, was quite prepared, whenever she took cotton to be woven, to receive in return a piece of cloth of only half the original weight.

TWO POEMS

DAVID DIOP

David Diop was born in France; his father was Senegalese, his mother from the Cameroons. He spent part of his child-

hood in France and part of it in Africa. His poems are deeply
felt and directly stated. They combine pathos with keen indignation at the historic martyrdom of Africans by white
colonialists.

In 1960, David Diop died with his wife in a tragic airplane
accident just off Dakar.

Africa

Africa my Africa
Africa of proud warriors in ancestral savannas
Africa of my grandmother's singing
Along the banks of her far-off river
I have never known you
But my gaze is charged with your blood
Your beautiful black blood spread abroad over the fields
The blood of your sweat
The sweat of your labor
The labor of your slavery
Slavery of your children.
Africa tell me Africa
Is it you, then, this back that bends
And sinks under the weight of humility
This trembling red-striped back
That says yes to the whip on the noonday roads?

Then gravely a voice answered me:
Impetuous son, that young and robust tree
That tree over there
Splendidly alone midst white faded flowers
It is Africa your Africa that springs up again
Springs up patiently obstinately
And whose fruits ripen with
The bitter flavor of freedom.

He Who Has Lost All

The sun shone in my hut
And my wives were fair and supple
Like the palms in the night breeze.

My children passed over the wide river
Deep as death
And my canoes vied with the crocodiles.
The motherly moon attended our dances
The wild and heavy rhythm of the tom-tom,
Tom-tom of joy, tom-tom of recklessness
        Midst fires of freedom.

Then one day, the Silence . . .
The sun's rays seemed to die out
In my hut empty of meaning.
My wives crushed their reddened mouths
Against the thin hard lips of steel-eyed conquerors
And my children left their calm nudity
For the uniform of iron and blood.
Your voice, too, died out.
The irons of slavery have rent my heart
Tom-toms of my nights, tom-toms of my fathers.

Translated from the French by Anne Atik

ABOARD AN AFRICAN TRAIN

Alfred Hutchinson

The author's maternal grandfather was a Swazi chief; his other grandfather was an Englishman; his grandmothers were both African. After getting his degree at Fort Hare University College, Alfred Hutchinson took up high school teaching in Johannesburg, and was on the national executive of the African National Congress. In 1956 he was arrested on charges of high treason. When the prosecution temporarily withdrew the indictment, Hutchinson left the country without a passport and headed overland for Ghana where his English fiancée was to follow him.

On a train puffing and swaying northward across the immense distances of southeast Africa, we live through the tensions and revelations of Alfred Hutchinson's secret flight from the South African "treason trials." In the train's microcosm, the Africa of recorded jazz, sewing machines, city slums, and political police is thrown together with the Africa of tribal ways and "medicines." Here is a glimpse at the social destruction visited on migrant labor in Africa, a destruction which is bound to increase as the needs of nation-building and industrialism force more and more people out of their traditional communities. We see through Mr. Hutchinson's horrified eyes the tragic confrontation of two armies of miners—the green troops headed for the mines, being cursed and cuffed by the veterans who are returning home from the front, embittered by years of separation from family and tribe.

Whether Hutchinson, with his undeniable gifts as a writer, will in the future belong to African literature, now that he has gone to live in England with his English wife, we do not know. But his book, *Road to Ghana,* does so belong, at least in its tensely rendered, compassionate involvement with the Africans, the broken ones and the resilient, unbreakable ones.

THE STATION WAS full of migrant miners returning home. Escorts taking the men home stood herding them. These were the men of the Mzilikazi (Witwatersrand Native Labour Association) who were returning home after their contracts in the mines. And the station belonged to them. They wore patchwork trousers and miner's hob-nailed boots and sombreros of all descriptions: yellow, orange, black, red. They tugged the hats down with knotty hands. They wore cheap wire spectacles or goggles, some on their noses others on their foreheads. Their socks were tattered, did not match, and some had tops only. Some wore battered khaki shorts and were barefoot, and one of them was on crutches. Loaves of bread were tied to bundles standing on the ground. They swaggered a bit and looked at us, the surface people, with contempt, and they looked at women with a terrible longing in their eyes.

"These can kill you," said the woman beside me reading the look.

I pulled out the fish and chips and the loaf of bread from my paper bags and asked the man from Salima to eat with me. We ate slowly and washed the food down with cold drinks. Railway policemen walked up and down the platform among the miners and stopped to chat with the escorts who had the W.N.L.A. brass letters on their caps glittering in the morning sun. The woman at my side chattered with a dry ecstasy in her voice about the terrible look the miners had in their eyes.

A man came pushing a wagon with various articles on it. He was selling. The man from Salima bought soap and razor blades, and I bought soap and razor blades too. But then I made the mistake of taking the articles from the wagon.

"Don't touch!" the man shouted at me. "Don't touch!" I said I was sorry. "Don't touch! Wait till you're given!"

A railway policeman wandered up to us. I made a profusion of apologies and the man from Salima made more on my behalf. I slunk back to the bench and buried myself in a newspaper.

A howl, a whoop, tore me from the newspaper. A train, laden with migrant workers was coming into the station headed for the mines. The windows were packed with black faces. An answering howl and whoop rose from the train as the train pulled to a stop. Then the men on the platform broke ranks and their boots crunched the ground as they swarmed to the windows of the train going to the mines. The whoop rose again and again, a terrifying jellying sound. It churned and boiled and twisted with a nameless agony—rejection, welcome, derision—bundled into one. The miners going home swaggered as they interrogated the newcomers. They cuffed them. And some of the men on the train returned blow for blow. At various points actual fights threatened and a railway policeman cuffed and clouted the returning miners where the cuffing and clouting had gone too far. The eyes were red and blank with a nameless agony. It was stupid, senseless, terrifying. What had been done to the poor people, I kept thinking in despair. And the whoop rose and fell, jellying and uncertain and crackling with the despair of fallen leaves. They swore and cursed. They cuffed and clouted and chatted a bit. And clouted and jeered.

The Bulawayo train pulled in at ten o'clock. The men from Mzilikazi lifted their bundles to their shoulders and heads and formed an Indian file. There was a fourth class on the train and the miners packed into the fourth-class carriages. We trooped into the third-class. I did not want to lose sight of the man from Salima. There were six of us in the compart-

ment; the man from Salima, an old man wearing wire spectacles, a sickly looking chap with an expensive green hat, a
boy in a shoddy green jacket and cheap grey hat, and a big,
black, old woman. It was an African train except for the
driver and the conductor.

The train swung westward. I wondered when we should
reach Francistown and how it would go at the nearby border
of the Union and Bechuanaland. I sat tense as the train swung
with slow looping movements, like an African woman playing
with her hips. We were swinging westward towards the desert.
The land grew dry and tedious and the grass and trees were
withered and coated with brown dust. There was no urgency
in that train: it swung and rocked and we swung and rocked
with it. We looked out of the window, glancing at each other's
faces as we did so. But no one spoke for a long time.

"Hai," said the sickly chap with the green hat, "the train
of Nyasaland!"

That began the conversation. We all began to complain
about the slowness of the train. The old man in the wire
spectacles said that he had been days on the train already.
He was from Cape Town and uttered a word or two in Xhosa
—the African language spoken in Cape Town. He was returning to Nyasaland and asked the others where they were
going. Except for the old black woman who was going to
Salisbury, we were all going to Nyasaland. Even the old
woman originally came from Salima, the home of my coal-
black friend.

"A person only works for train fare," said the old man
taking a pinch of snuff from a Royal Baking Powder tin.

We agreed that we only worked for the train fare back
home. But I thought that a single ticket from Johannesburg
to Salisbury for £2 13s. 11d. was very cheap, notwithstand-
ing the class we were travelling. The sickly man pursed his
singularly thin lips tightly as if fighting back pain. He had a
look of world-wiseness in his eyes which the others in the
compartment did not have. There was something knowing
and mocking in those eyes. They did not ask me what I was
going to do in Blantyre and that made me feel easy. But I
was thinking about the border and dreading what might happen. If the news of my escape had leaked, there I would

surely be arrested and turned back. The train swung easily like an African woman slowly swinging her hips.

In trepidation I waited for the border. The train swung on and on and on until surely we had crossed the border. There was no border post: no checking of passes or customs. I was in Bechuanaland. One hurdle had been jumped. Anything could still happen.

In the compartment next to ours a man was taking his Union wife and two children with him to Nyasaland. The woman and the children were a pitiful sight. The children were half blind with filth and dirty sores. Flies swarmed round their eyes and the woman, exhausted with hunger and neglect, did not even wave the flies from the children. The man sat. He too was prostrated by helplessness.

It grew hot on the train and the lavatory began to stink. Dirt began to pile in the corridors and flies buzzed. At the sidings desert women and children, insubstantial and wraith-like in their trailing, shapeless, dirty white dresses, came to sell homemade cold drinks in bottles, bottled tea, scones and hunks of dubious meat. The meat was too much for the price they asked and we asked why among ourselves and decided not to buy it. At intervals through the morning and afternoon a man in a guard's cap came to the door and pointed the spout of a kettle at us, stood silent for a long time and then went his way. He was selling tea, they said. But he did not utter a sound.

We swung throughout the day and the shadows of the thorn trees lengthened with the dipping western sun. Past Atloss, Artesia, Gaberones, Pilane. . . . At intervals the train stopped for a long time for no apparent reason, and the white driver got out and sat African-wise on a stone chatting to other whites, or made water on the bushes at the side of the rail-way. It was the all-African train. And then again we swung onward carrying miners and new blue Massey-Harris tractors and water tanks with us. I stood in the corridor a long time looking at the thirsty land, at the tedious thorn trees and bare hills.

A man came to lean against the window.

"Going to Nyasa?" he said. I nodded. "Going to fetch horse medicines?" I spread my hands dubiously and shrugged to say that perhaps I was fetching "medicines" of luck for horse racing. "Ah, don't deny it. Don't tell me—I know!" The man laughed. "In two months you'll have a shop and a motor car. The medicines of Nyasaland are strong," he said with pride, "but don't let them cheat you. You must get out of the towns. Not Blantyre—right out—away from the towns."

I winked an eye and he winked back. That meant he understood. It was the life. I had found an explanation for going to Nyasaland: I was going to buy horse-racing *mutis*. He would never know that I had never seen the inside of a race course and didn't gamble because I hadn't the nerve for it. The woman who had spoken about the look in the miners' eyes came to the window. She was going to Nyasaland, she told me, to her husband. She had been to visit her people in Orlando. She was itching for a flirtation and I hastily gave her trail. As the evening grew she stood in the corridor with a strong young Nyasa. She had hooked her man.

A chap speaking Xhosa collared me again and again for a cigarette. He was a Nyasa returning home but he wanted very much to be "Xhosa." He was full of city-talk and this frightened me off. I did not want to be identified with the city. There was a pretty young girl in the next compartment going home to Bulawayo. She was Zulu-breed, strong-thighed and solid—a descendant of Mzilikazi's, who had blazed a bloody trail north, fleeing the wrath of the Zulu monarch, Tshaka. She was thickly powdered and tortured the chaps of the train with her city ways and inaccessibility. She broke into a jive, there in the corridor, to one or both of the gramophones playing simultaneously in different compartments. And the men groaned listening to the gramophone records, and said it took them "back there"—meaning Johannesburg—which they had probably never seen.

I found the man from Salima adding sums of money with a stub of a pencil and some paper. He was adding £ 15 10s. plus £ 15 10s. The first time he got it wrong. The second time it was right. There was something strange about this man in the brown jacket frayed at the sleeves and the fawn trousers which were thin at the knees. He was solid, unequivocally honest, I thought, looking at him. He had a terrific self-containedness—like a man long used to living and relying on himself.

The sickly man was huddled in a corner.

"How's it?" I said to the sick man.

"That woman has finished me, S'bali (brother-in-law). She's killed me," he said, trying to smile through the pain, while carefully brushing the expensive green hat with the palm of his hand. "I've left her—left her with house, furniture, three children and all."

"Yours?" I said, meaning the children.

"Yes, S'bali, two boys and a girl."

The trouble had started, he said, when he spoke of going to Nyasaland for a time. The city woman would not hear of it, especially as she knew that he had two wives and children in Nyasaland. She didn't want to lose her "milch-cow." Nyasas were regarded as "milch-cows" by Johannesburg women, he explained. She had immediately procured *mutis* to stop him from going. And his illness had started. She had even confiscated his pass in order to stop his departure. He had told her to keep it if she wanted to: he was going. He thought he would get better in Nyasaland. I thought he was suffering from T.B.

"When did you leave Nyasaland, S'bali?" I said.

"Long ago, S'bali. In 1952."

"Six years ago!" I said. "That's a long time!"

The old man turned his wire spectacles to me.

"What do you say of me, S'bali," he said, calling me brother-in-law also. "Fourteen."

"Fourteen!"

"I left a baby boy, S'bali. He's a man now."

I turned to Moses Banda, the man from Salima. He had left home six years ago. Mweli, the sick man, six. Moyo, the youth, three. The old man, fourteen. These were long times to be away from home, especially from a wife and children.

"That's too long," I said.

"We can't help it, S'bali," said Mweli. "It's hard to get into the Union and the longer you stay the better."

"Blantyre?" said Granny looking at me. "That's just next door. He is from Salima—where I come from," she said, pointing at my friend. "You can take a good wife there," she added. I expressed interest. "Not Blantyre—no, no. The women are all crooks. They'll eat your money and when it's finished, leave you! Get to Salima and get a good Thonga girl. She'll look well after your things."

I told Granny that my grandmother had been a Thonga like her, and she promptly married me to someone—most likely a relation of hers. She invited me to spend a few days at her home in Salisbury. From the time of the "marriage" Granny referred to me respectfully as *Mkwenyana* (son-in-law).

Granny started scolding Moyo, the youth. The big hulking, ugly woman had a heart of gold. Granny, I thought, had been too long away from home and wanted to scold someone and had picked on Moyo because he was the youngest in the compartment.

"You'll get lost, you!" she said to the boy, who was adjusting his hat to a jaunty angle. That hat was the symbol of his manhood and throughout the day I watched him fuss over it.

"I won't. I know. I'll take a bus from Lusaka to Mzimba."

"This child is lost, Mkwenyana," said Granny, turning to me. "He doesn't know where he is going. He says he is going to Mzimba but here he is going to Lusaka."

"I'm not lost," said Moyo with dignity. "I know. I left that way."

Moses Banda, the man from Salima, was again adding sums of money. They looked like the same figures he had been adding all the time. Whenever he got tired of listening to us or looking out of the window, he pulled out his pocket book and pencil and the addition started. I turned from Banda to Moyo who had put on his wisest airs.

"Are you sure you won't get lost?" I said.

"He doesn't know anything," said Granny.

Moyo had left home in 1955 in a band of fourteen other boys. They had taken a bus from Mzima to Lusaka and from Lusaka a train to Bulawayo. In order to avoid the pass blitz at Plumtree they had walked in the bush from Bulawayo to Mafeking—a journey that took a month. Then from Mafeking in the Union of South Africa, they caught a train to Johannesburg. He had never worked in Johannesburg, the city of his dreams, but had been sent to a farm in Delmas. I asked him whether he would return to the Union.

"Never. When I want work, it will be Bulawayo," he said.

Moyo bent down and pulled his suitcase from under the seat and opened it. I peeped inside. There was an old blanket, two or three battered torches, and, at the bottom of the case, a quantity of sprouting potatoes. He pulled out a Farmer's Weekly Diary of 1957 and a stub of a pencil and began making squiggles on it. He made sounds, incomprehensible sounds, as he made the meaningless squiggles. I thought I head him say verdomde (damned)—Afrikaans which he had most certainly picked up on the potato fields. Granny shook her head pitying the poor boy who would get lost. He took out his ticket and looked at it, making incomprehensible sounds. Moyo couldn't even read the fare he had paid for his ticket home. Moyo had been South. Poor Moyo.

The train swung like a buxom African woman coquettishly flouncing her hips and we swung with it. Moyo adjusted his hat in case it had lost the correct angle. Mweli sat looking at nothings out of his sick eyes. And the old man sat looking at the night through the window. Moses Banda had made a new column of figures: the same figures. He had been a tailor at Iscor near Pretoria for six years. Now he was returning home with three tailor's sewing machines and other things. It was his money which he kept adding over and over again. I had thought he was a miner with hands like that.

The gramophones played in the swinging train. People who had never seen Johannesburg said that the songs reminded them of the city. The woman who had itched for a flirtation clung to her young muscled man, and the young girl of Zulu breed with her thickly powdered pretty face played hard-to-get and wrought havoc with the young men's hearts. And the train swung northward through the night.

The train swung into Francistown, still in Bechuanaland, at five-thirty in the morning. We were approaching Plumtree where our passes would be checked. I grew restless and a flutter of panic drove me to ask to see my companions' passes. Granny did not have one and was defiant about it. She had travelled like that for many years. What was this newfangled thing of passes about, she said. The passes were all different from one another and different from mine. They said mine would do; that it was more official than all.

At Plumtree Rhodesian African policemen in black fezzes and big black boots jumped on the train and asked for our passes. I steadied my hand as I handed mine. The policeman glanced at me and handed it back. I almost sighed with relief. Granny glared at the young policeman.

"Granny, where's your pass?"

"What pass? I've been travelling like this long before you were born! Child, ask your mates for a pass!"

"Get a pass next time, Granny," said the young policeman walking out of the compartment.

I had crossed the border into Southern Rhodesia. Someone whispered in Zulu: "Zishile (it's burnt)," which meant that someone was in trouble. I peeped into the corridor and right next door an African policeman had mounted guard over the door. A white official had been sent for. The man taking his wife and two children to Nyasaland had not taken passes for them. I was terror-stricken. Now there would probably be a re-check on the passes, and questionings. And it wouldn't take much to prove that I was no Nyasa returning home. I should be arrested and handed back to the Union. I couldn't resist peeping into the corridor, and when I next peeped a white official was there. But the man only received a warning —not even a fine.

One of the men returning to Nyasaland began a conversation with the African policeman in the corridor about conditions in the Union.

"There's not a bush, not even grass to hide in," the man was saying. "Here at least you can hide behind a bush. It's like a road, and a policeman sees you miles off." The policeman looked at the bushes in silence.

"But there are Nyangas (medicine men)—where do they get the roots from then?" said the policeman.

"There are quacks galore. . . . As you say, where would they dig the roots from?" said the returning man. "There are quacks without number, that's true."

Then the man from Johannesburg told the policeman about the pass laws. A garden boy had been picked up for a pass right in the garden where he worked and his missis looked for him in vain. A servant who had been sent to the greengrocer's had been picked up for a pass with basket and vegetables and the missis found him after a search at the police station.

"I used to hear it was nice," said the policeman.

"Then go and see for yourself," said the man returning from the Union.

"No," said the Rhodesian policeman. "I'm all right here."

A PARABLE

Bernard B. Dadié

Bernard B. Dadié of the Ivory Coast is a poet who has also written stories and a biographical novel. The parable here given is very much like the traditional spoken stories in form and theme.

Life, having assumed the shape of a handsome young man, went to seek hospitality at the home of a man afflicted with elephantiasis. The latter asked him his name. "My name," said he, "is Life; certain people know me in my going who won't recognize me on my return. I go and I come. When I return here, I shall present myself to you; that will be in seven years. But what, then, is the matter with you?" "Sire," said the man, "I have this ugly illness; it has destroyed my human appearance." "I shall cure you," said Life, "but you will forget me." "Whoever succeeds in curing me," said the man, "I shall never forget!" Life drew out a vegetal powder and put it on the man, whose illness disappeared entirely.

Having taken to his road again, Life arrived close by to a leper, who asked him his name. "My name," said he, "is Life. Certain people know me in my going who will not recognize me on my return. I go and I come. In seven years I shall pass by your house again. I am going to cure your disease, but you will forget me."

"I shall never in my life forget you," said the leper.

Life cured him and took to his road again.

He arrived close by to a blind man who asked him his

name. "My name is Life," he said. "Some people know me in passage, in my going, who will not recognize me in my coming back." He cured him and went on his way again.

Seven years having passed by, he afflicted himself with blindness and went to seek hospitality at the home of the man who, formerly, had been blind. It turned out that the latter was in the fields. His wives said, "Our master will never cease, then, to receive nobodies! For what motive does he welcome this band of blind men? We know absolutely nothing about it."

Life said, "Won't you give me a little water to quench my thirst?" So then the women put some dirty water into an old gourd and gave it to Life.

The host arrived. "Another one of your good-for-nothing men has arrived," the women said. Life moved forward gropingly until he reached the man and said, "I am in passage and I ask to spend the night at your home." The man spread out an old mat for him in a corner of the vestibule and gave him some earth-nuts.

When dawn appeared, Life called his host, restored his own sight in his presence and said, "Hadn't I told you that some people knew Life in his going who wouldn't recognize him on his return? The day I restored your sight you didn't think of today." Then Life went out putting a bit of vegetal powder on his footprints. The man became completely blind.

Life parted. Once he arrived not far from the village of the man who formerly had been leprous, he afflicted himself with leprosy that made swarms of flies pursue him. He went to ask for hospitality at the home of this man, who didn't even give him anything to eat, saying that he was too dirty.

At dawn, Life called him, cured himself, and said, "Hadn't I told you that some people have known Life in his going who don't recognize him on his return? In which circumstances did that take place?" Then Life went out, putting a vegetal powder on his footprints: the man was covered again with a leprosy such that his flesh died of itself.

Arriving near the village of the man who had formerly had elephantiasis, Life afflicted himself with elephantiasis to such a degree that he could only walk by dragging himself. As soon as he arrived at the door of his vestibule, the man ran out to meet him saying, "Oh! Enter! How this handsome lad has been ruined! Come here; you fill me with great pity. I myself had that same horrible disease and a good man took care of me. If I only had the power, I should like to take care of you. You are indeed unhappy! If you consent to stay here at my house, perhaps the same man who cured me will find you and take care of you." Then the man killed a fatted sheep for him, had a plate of rice cooked for him, gave him ten servings of fresh milk, and put him in a fine room.

At dawn, Life changed into the handsome young man he had been before, and said, "You have known Life in its going and you have recognized him on his coming back. You shall remain in your present state, for you are he who remembered the past."

The man gave him seven fine cows and a bull, but he said, "No, I have nothing to do with wealth; if I have acted so, it is in order to let you know that Life is prolific in change."

Translated by Anne Atik

THE MEANING OF AFRICA

ABIOSEH NICOL

Born in Sierra Leone, and educated both in that country and in Nigeria, Abioseh Nicol went on to England for further study where he took a degree in Natural Sciences at Cambridge. He also became interested in writing and has published short stories, articles and poems. He is now the Principal of Fourah Bay College, Freetown, Sierra Leone.

His poem, sober and intellectual in tone, reflects an experience shared by the increasing number of Africans who leave their native soil, spend many years abroad in training, and return with trepidation and love, with hope and dedication to build a new Africa, or as Mr. Nicol more modestly puts it, to till well one "circumscribed plot." Here is not the grandiose voice of a pan-African ideologue, but the quiet contentment of "a small bird singing on a mango tree."

Africa, you were once just a name to me
But now you lie before me with sombre green challenge
To that loud faith for freedom (life more abundant)
Which we once professed shouting
Into the silent listening microphone
Or on an alien platform to a sea
Of white perplexed faces troubled
With secret Imperial guilt; shouting
Of you with a vision euphemistic
As you always appear
To your lonely sons in distant shores. . . .

Then the cold sky and continent would disappear
In a grey mental mist.
And in its stead the hibiscus blooms in shameless scarlet
   and the bougainvillea in mauve passion
   entwines itself around strong branches;
   the palm trees stand like tall proud moral women
   shaking their plaited locks against the
   cool suggestive evening breeze;
   the short twilight passes;
   the white full moon turns its round gladness
   towards the swept open space
   between the trees; there will be
   dancing tonight; and in my brimming heart
   plenty of love and laughter.

Oh, I got tired of the cold Northern sun
Of white anxious ghost-like faces
Of crouching over heatless fires
In my lonely bedroom.
The only thing I never tired of
Was the persistent kindness
Of you too few unafraid
Of my grave dusky strangeness.

So I came back
Sailing down the Guinea Coast,
Loving the sophistication
Of your brave new cities:

Dakar, Accra, Cotonou,
Lagos, Bathurst, and Bissau;
Liberia, Freetown, Libreville,
Freedom is really in the mind.
Go up Country, so they said,
To see the real Africa.
For whosoever you may be,
That is where you come from.
Go for bush; inside the bush,
You will find your hidden heart,
Your mute ancestral spirit.
And so I went, dancing on my way—

Now you lie before me passive
With your unanswering green challenge.
Is this all you are?
This long uneven red road, this occasional succession
Of huddled heaps of four mud walls
And thatched, falling grass roofs
Sometimes ennobled by a thin layer
Of white plaster, and covered with thin
Slanting corrugated zinc.
These patient faces on weather-beaten bodies
Bowing under heavy market loads.
The pedalling cyclist wavers by
On the wrong side of the road,
As if uncertain of this new emancipation.
The squawking chickens, the pregnant she-goats
Lumber awkwardly with fear across the road.
Across the windscreen view of my four-cylinder kit car
An overladen lorry speeds madly towards me
Full of produce, passengers, with driver leaning
Out into the swirling dust to pilot his
Swinging obsessed vehicle along.
Beside him on the raised seat his first-class
Passenger, clutching and timid; but he drives on
At so, so many miles per hour, peering out with
Bloodshot eyes, unshaved face and dedicated look;
His motto painted across "Sunshine Transport, we get you
There, quick, quick. The Lord is my Shepherd . . ."

The red dust settles down on the green leaves.
I know you will not make me want, Lord,
Though I have reddened your green pastures.
It is only because I have wanted so much
That I have always been found wanting.
From South and East, and from my West
The sandy desert holds the North:
We look across a vast Continent
And blindly call it ours.
You are not a country, Africa,
You are a concept,
Fashioned in our minds, each to each,
To hide our separate fears,
To dream our separate dreams.
Only those within you who know
Their circumscribed plot,
And till it well with steady plough
Can from that harvest then look up
To the vast blue inside
Of the enamelled bowl of sky
Which covers you and say
"This is my Africa" meaning
"I am content and happy.
I am fulfilled, within,
Without and roundabout.
I have gained the little longings
Of my hands, my loins, my heart,
And the soul following in my shadow."
I know now that is what you are, Africa.
Happiness, contentment and fulfilment.
And a small bird singing on a mango tree.

EPILOGUE TO APARTHEID

Ezekiel Mphahlele

Out of the stifling, racist police state of South Africa have
escaped some of the best of the new generation of African
writers. One of them, Ezekiel Mphahlele, teacher and writer

from Johannesburg, went to Nigeria, where he became an instructor at the University College in Ibadan, Nigeria. It was only in Nigeria, breathing the oxygen of freedom, that Mphahlele found it possible to finish his autobiography, *Down Second Avenue,* from which we reprint the final chapter. The accents of artistic integrity are to be heard here. Whether this integrity will find subjects and occasions for its employment in the placidity—the "vacuum," as he calls it—of Nigerian life, remains to be seen. Certainly, the liveliness and honesty of this mind, tapping its bottomless "barrel of gall," should not be expected to succumb to any vacuum.

Mr. Mphahlele is now in Paris where he is on the staff of the Congress for the Cultural Freedom.

I CAN NEVER SUMMON enough courage to read a line from any of my stories that were published in 1947, under the title, *Man Must Live.* In ten years my perspective has changed enormously from escapist writing to protest writing and, I hope, to something of a higher order, which is the ironic meeting between protest and acceptance in their widest terms. Maybe from the chaff I have been writing since 1947 a few grains have emerged. One story, "The Suitcase," appeared in *New World Writing,* a New York anthology of prose and poetry, in 1955. The story was recommended to the publishers by Nadine Gordimer, who had already made a name as a novelist and short-story writer. The story was later translated into Dutch for an anthology of Negro stories. It is in essence a true story, told to me by Rebecca about an incident that had occurred in Sophiatown.

No South African journals circulating mainly among whites would touch any of my stories, nor any others written by a non-white, unless he tried to write like a European and adopted a European name. Two or three Coloured writers told me once that they had slipped through the readers' sieve and become immortalized in European pulp. But I have been too busy fighting my own bitterness without trying to prostitute myself in that fashion. Some articles of mine, however, have appeared in the readers' columns in the white press. Then obviously the particular paper was not committed. Very rarely do articles written by non-whites appear in the white press. Every time something has been published that I wrote, I have felt patronized. But then always I wrote because something burned inside me beyond bearing; the desire to correct some stupidly over-enthusiastic cabinet minister or some smug suburban white person who, as grandmother would say, pretends not to know which side of the body the African's heart sits. Moreover, there is only one independent paper run by a Coloured group in Cape Town, *Torch;* independent in the sense that it is not managed by whites. It has no readers' columns, and one has to sympathize with Unity Movement or All-African Convention ideology to write for it. The only one left with a multi-racial editorial board is *New Age.* But it is hardly enough for increasing non-white readership in a country where literacy among non-whites is higher than anywhere else on the Continent. And then *New Age* is always in financial straits.

As soon as I landed in Nigeria in September 1957 and settled into school work, I wrote and finished the second half of this book. Immediately I felt the difference between writing here and in a South African social climate. Somehow it feels like having just climbed down from a vehicle that has been rocking violently for countless miles. I am able to write articles on Nigeria in between times, but I haven't settled down to a short story yet. I have been trying to sniff around and find a distinctive smell to guide me. It has been eluding me. I now realize what a crushing cliché the South African situation can be as literary material.

I admire the white man's achievements, his mind that plans tall buildings, powerful machinery. I used to want to justify myself and my own kind to the white man. I later discovered that it wasn't worth it. It was to myself and to my kind I needed to justify myself. I think now the white man has no right to tell me how to order my life as a social being, or order it for me. He may teach me how to make a shirt or to read and to write, but my forebears and I could teach him a thing or two if only he would listen and allow himself time to feel. Africa is no more for the white man who comes here to teach and to control her human and material forces and not to learn.

Countless times I have dreamt about the deep valleys and craggy mountains of Pietersburg. I have revisited them in my dreams, never in flesh. Every time I have been trapped by the huge mountains, and I have heard endless echoes chasing after me, chasing, while I ran all the time, ran into a dawn of sirens and motor-car hooters and bicycle bells and trolley carts and . . . breakfasts.

I admire that man who, like Bach in his music, can make definite statements of religious faith. Yet I'm impatient of Robert Browning's bloated, blustering certitudes about God. Reminds me: my life up to now has been a series of events through which it seems I was driven by some sort of inevitability. Yes, I've thought, and planned and suffocated and had my share of hate and felt cloyed, no more than my fellow African, but I've always been hurled back into the furnace of reality and I couldn't decide one way or another. And then, it seems, some big wave came and carried me along with it to the inevitable shore, and then I knew I must be doing the right thing. I've felt the heartburn of frustration and didn't feel sorry for my hates. I can't feel sorry even now, removed as I am from it all. The other man shut me off in Second Avenue. And now he has taught me never to expect mercy—but who wants mercy? Never to beg for favours through the kitchen door, but to take by force what I possess while he wasn't looking. He has driven me against the wall so that I never forget I am black. He has taught me to lie to him and feel triumphant. Because he has made me get used to the back door I have bought goods, stolen from his shop by his own Black worker, for less than the cost. And there are millions of me. We know almost everything about him and he knews nothing about us, so we still hold the trump card.

It is the lingering melody of a song that moves me more than the initial experience itself; it is the lingering pain of a past insult that rankles and hurts me more than the insult itself. Too dumb to tell you how immensely this music or that play or this film moves me, I wait for the memory of the event.

All my life people have been at my soul, tugging at it in different directions. I have chafed under unrelenting controls, enthusiastic evangelizing, ruthless police watchfulness. So many other hands have been reaching out for me, and so many voices have been babbling about my ears like the idiotic rattling of wheels of a moving train and I must scream, leave me alone. Downright anarchy, downright individualism, you may say. I enjoy a fair amount of both, at any rate in my thought-life. This Nigerian sun will burn up at least such prejudice and bitterness and hate of thirty-seven years as haven't grown into my system like kikuyu grass. That may amount to very little. But there will always be that smouldering anger against poverty, injustice, and the legalized bullying of the small man by the strong one.

I am sitting in the spacious garden of a Lagos house as I write this epilogue, and it is early January, the heat is much drier than when I came here. Before deciding to write I set on a recording of Vivaldi's *Four Seasons*. As the music floats across to me from the sitting-room, I remember a beautiful winter morning in Nadine Gordimer's big garden in Parktown, Johannesburg. Nadine, Anthony [Sampson], who had come down from London to collect material for a book, and I were listening to Vivaldi in the same fashion. "I find Vivaldi most satisfying," Nadine said. Yes, after Beethoven's roaring furnaces, Mozart's sweet, sad, delicate humour, Schubert's lyrical sweetness, Chopin's melancholy nostalgia, after Tchaikowsky's capricious moods, Bach's overwhelming bigness and after Rimsky-Korsakoff's enchantment, it is a cool and refreshing experience to come back to Vivaldi.

Yes, basking in this Nigerian heat, I feel cool inside me. I stretch myself like the lizards there on the warm concrete wall. I have brought with me prejudices and anger to a country where they are almost altogether alien now. I'm breathing the new air of freedom, and now the barrel of gall has no bottom any more. I shall soon know what to do with this freedom. For the moment, I'm still baffled, and my canoe still feels the momentum that launched it in Second Avenue. But what a glorious sense of release!

There is complacency here. Often, I think, too much of it. The secondary school boys I'm handling and the South African high school boy are worlds apart. In the south the boys and I were caught up in a violent situation. We both carried a pass and we could be stopped any time by the police and searched or arrested the moment we stepped out of the school grounds. We were both hungering for many things and getting little, which in turn sharpened the edge of our longings. I responded to every throb of pain and restlessness in them, and I think they responded to my yearnings. Here, the atmosphere is placid. In a sense there is a vacuum. But oh, what a sense of release. And what a glorious opportunity for Rebecca and me to replenish our moral and mental reserves. The children are very happy, and they will be able to learn something worth while, something that is fit for all mankind, not for slaves.

The Church as an ecumenical force in South Africa has been on the retreat since before Union in 1910. And then the Church, with its emphasis on the value of the individual personality, has continued stubbornly to bring outmoded standards to the situation; a situation where a powerful *herrenvolk* has for three centuries done everything in the interests of the *volk*.

Where persons have been oppressed as a race group, the Church has sought safeguards and concessions for the individual, evading the necessity and responsibility of group action. And while it fixed its gaze on Calvary or kept up an aloofness from political realities, the road has been slipping back under its feet. It never seems to have occurred to the Church that right under its nose has been growing a calculating white barbarism, among those it considered as hereditary custodians of Christianity, custodians who need mission stations in their very midst. I cannot but reaffirm what I said in a B.B.C. talk in 1955 on the African intellectual: that to us, the Church has become a symbol of the dishonesty of the West. I'm still suspending belief and disbelief as far as the necessity or uselessness of organized religion goes. All I know is that I found no use for it in South Africa; that since 1947 when I stopped going to Church, I have become progressively weary of all the trappings of mystical formalism that go together with South African "churchianity." For the moment, I'm content to move on, free of this sort of allegiance, exposing myself to the impacts of as many ways of life as possible. I'm glad that I can at last exercise that right.

THREE POEMS

LÉOPOLD S. SENGHOR

Léopold-Sédar Senghor, the first president of the Republic of Senegal, is a writer about whose work it might be difficult to answer the question: Is it more African than French, or more French than African?

He was born in Senegal in 1906, being brought up in the coastal town of Joal, which had been founded and fortified by the Portuguese. His family are of the Serere people who are mostly farmers, shepherds, and fishermen. Senghor's father was a merchant belonging to the Christian minority in a country where the Moslems were more numerous and the large majority were of the traditional African religions.

After studying locally and at Dakar, young Senghor won a scholarship to the Sorbonne and was well on his way to becoming a distinguished scholar, poet, and statesman. After graduating from the Sorbonne, he was at various times a teacher, a Deputy for Senegal in the French National Assembly, a political director of a Dakar newspaper, a professor of African languages, the author of four books of poetry in French, editor of an anthology of African verse and a resourceful politician on homegrounds in Senegal.

As in the case of such famous French poet-diplomats as St. John Perse and Paul Claudel, Senghor was able to maintain a highly professional standing in both politics and poetry. M. Senghor's verse is thoroughly at home with contemporary French poetry, but at the same time it is unmistakably African in source and ambience.

In an eloquent essay discussing the wellsprings of his poetry, he avows that every creature and every object called up in his poems harks back to his "childhood kingdom" in Senegal, where, he recalls, he was often beaten by his father for his vagabondage among the shepherds and peasants.

In one of his poems he says, "I always confound childhood and Eden much as I mix up Death and Life—a bridge of sweetness links them together." The three poems printed be-

low, while hardly representative of the entire range of
M. Senghor's poetry, do show this deep paradisal feeling and
this heightening of the sense of life by a confrontation with
death. However, to Senghor, as to any unlettered African, the
dead are the inspirers of the living. To Senghor the poet's
inspiration also comes under the sign of the hurricane: the
unruly power of a great destructive wind sweeping away the
past, clearing the air and the mind for new creative effort.

Black Woman

Naked woman, black woman
Clad in your color that is life, in your form that is beauty!
I have grown up in your shade, the sweetness of your hands
    bound my eyes.
And now in the heart of summer and noon, I discover you,
    promised earth, from the tower of your sun-scorched
    neck
And your beauty smites me to the full of my heart like the
    flash of an eagle.

Naked woman, dark woman!
Firm-fleshed ripe fruit, dark raptures of black wine, mouth
    making lyric my mouth
Savanna of sheer horizons, savanna quivering to the East
    wind's fervent caresses
Carved tom-tom, taut tom-tom snarling under the Victor's
    fingers
Your grave, contralto voice is the spiritual of the Beloved.

Naked woman, dark woman!
Oil sweet and smooth on the athlete's flanks,
On the flanks of the princes of Mali
Heaven-leashed gazelle, pearls are stars on the night of your
    skin
Delights of the spirit at play, red gold reflections on your
    shimmering skin.
In the shade of your hair, my anguish lightens with the nearing
    suns of your eyes.

Naked woman, black woman!
I sing your passing beauty, form that I fix in the eternal
Before jealous destiny burns you to ashes to nourish the roots
    of life.

Night in Senegal

Woman, lay your balmy hands on my brow, your hands
    softer than fur.
High up the swaying palms scarcely rustle in the night breeze,
No sound, not even the song of the wet-nurse,
We are rocked in the rhythmic silence.
Let us listen to its song, hear our dark blood beat, hear
The deep pulse of Africa beating through the mist of lost
    villages.

And now the weary moon wanes toward its bed of slack water
And now hushed are the bursts of laughter, and even the
    tellers of tales
Loll their heads, like the child on its mother's back,
And now dancers' feet grow heavy and singers' voices drowsy.

It is the hour of stars and of dreaming Night
Leaning on this hill of clouds, wrapped in her long milky
    loin-cloth.
The roofs of the huts gleam tenderly. What are they confiding
    to the stars?
Indoors the fire dies out in an intimacy of sweet and acrid
    odors.

Woman, light your lamp of butter, around which the fore-
    bears chat like parents, the children in bed.
Let us listen to the voices of the Elissan elders. Like us exiled,
They did not wish to die, their seminal stream losing itself in
    the sands.
Let me listen, in the smoky hut, basking in the glow of
    guardian souls
My head on your breast warm as a *dang*[1] snatched smoking
    from the fire.

[1] *Dang:* a ball- or pancake-shaped bit of food

Let me breathe the odor of our dead, let me gather up and
    repeat their living voice that I may learn
To live, before plunging deeper than any diver into the
    eternal depths of sleep.

The Hurricane

The hurricane uproots everything around me
The hurricane scatters my leaves, my futile words.
Whirlwinds of passion whistle in silence.
But peace on the dry tornado, on winter-time's flight!

You, ardent Wind, pure Wind, fine-season-Wind, burn every
    flower, every vain thought
When the sand falls back on the heart's dunes.
Servant, suspend your statue-gesture, and you, children, your
    games and ivory laughs.
You, may it consume your voice with your body, may it dry
    the perfume of your flesh.
Flame that illumines my night like a pillar, like a palm,
Fire my bleeding lips, Spirit, blow on the strings of my Kôra
That my song may rise, as pure as the gold of Galam.

Translated from the French by Anne Atik

NKRUMAH, KENYATTA, AND THE OLD ORDER

Peter Abrahams

Peter Abrahams, born in a Johannesburg slum of an Ethi-
opian father and a "Cape Coloured" mother, is the best known
of the South African Negro writers. He has written *Mine Boy*
and other novels, as well as an autobiography, *Tell Freedom*.
In the lively article excerpted here, he gives us a piece of can-
did journalism such as few other writers would be in a
position to do, for in writing of his visits with Nkrumah and
Kenyatta he is writing of men who were his friends and in-
timates in the African colony in London before the upsurge of
independent states in Africa. Mr. Abrahams has lived for

many years outside his native continent, first in England and now in the West Indies.

Written in 1959, the article may on some political points be dated; and Mr. Abrahams may have overestimated the damage done to Kenyatta's potentialities by his ambivalent connections with tribal society; but on the whole, it is a valuable portrayal in personal terms of the tensions between nation-building leaders and traditionally oriented masses. These tensions could be of two sorts: in the case of Nkrumah they would seem to be part of a clash between authoritarian centralism and a variety of localisms; in the case of Kenyatta, there seems to be in addition to the political dynamics, an inner struggle of emotional commitments to both African and Western patterns.

IT WAS A HOT, HUMID, oppressive August day in Accra, capital of the Gold Coast that was to become Ghana. The air had the stillness of death. I walked down toward the sea front. Perhaps there would be the hint of a breeze there. As I neared the sea front I was assailed by a potent stench of the sea with strong overtones of rotting fish.

The houses were drab, run-down wooden structures or made of corrugated iron, put together any way you please. The streets were wide and tarred, and each street had an open-drainage system into which young boys and old men piddled when they needed to relieve themselves. I have seen women empty chamber pots into these drains in the early morning. The fierce sun takes care of the germs, but God help you if smells make you sick.

In about eight minutes of walking, some fifteen "taxis" pulled up beside me: "Hi, massa! Taxi, massa! Me go anywhere you go cheap!" They are all private taxis with no meters and driven by strapping young men with flashing teeth. The place is full of taxi drivers willing to go anywhere and do anything cheap.

The street traders here are women. "Mammy traders," they are called. They trade in everything. They sell cigarettes, one at a time; round loaves of bread and hunks of cooked meat on which the big West African flies make sport. They love bargaining and haggling. They are a powerful economic factor in the life of the country. The more prosperous ones own their own trucks, some own fleets of trucks. These "mammy trucks" are the principal carriers of the country. They carry passengers as well as produce and go hurtling across the countryside with little regard for life or limb. Each truck has its own distinctive slogan, such as: Repent For Death is Round the Corner, or Enter Without Hope, or The Last Ride or If It Must It Will. My own favorite, and I traveled in this particular truck, pleaded, Not Today O Lord Not Today.

I passed many mammy traders, many mammy trucks, before I reached the sea front. I crossed a street, jumped over an open drain, and there was the sea. But there was no breeze, and no shade from the terrible sun. In the end I gave in to the idea of "taxi, massa, taxi" and looked about for one. But now there was no taxi in sight. Instead, I saw, suddenly, a long procession of many women and a few men. The procession swung around a corner and came into full view, twenty or thirty yards long. The women wore white flowing robes and white kerchiefs on their heads. The faces were painted into grotesque masks made with thick streaks of black, red, white and yellow paints. The heavy thud of bare feet rose above the hum of the sea.

Then, all at once, the drums burst forth and there was no other sound about me. The marching women began to jig, then dance. As the tail of the procession passed me the drums reached a frenzy. A thin, pure note from a reed rose above the drums. The whole procession became a shivering, shaking mass. The reed note held longer than seemed human. And then, dramatically, there was silence. The thudding feet faded away out of sight and sound. There was silence and a slight racing of my heartbeat and the hum of the sea, and, of course, the overpowering fishy stench.

I thought of Richard Wright, with whom I had had breakfast that morning. This was his first visit to any part of Africa and he seemed to find it bewildering. Countee Cullen, the late American Negro poet, had speculated:

> One three centuries removed
> From the scenes his fathers loved,

  Spicy grove, cinnamon tree,
  What is Africa to me?

Wright was finding the answers and finding them disconcerting. He had been astounded by the casual attitude to sex. There was, he had said, too much sex, too casually given and taken; so that it worked out as no sex, with none of the emotional involvement associated with sex in the western mind. He shook his head with a slight disgust. The open drains into which young boys and old men piddled had led him to conclude that Africans piddled rather more than other people. The sight of young men dancing together, holding hands, disturbed the puritan in him. He expressed to me that morning what he later summed up in his book on the Gold Coast: "I was black and they were black but it did not help me."

What Wright did not understand, what his whole background and training had made difficult for him to understand, was that being black did not of itself qualify one for acceptance in tribal Africa. But how could he, when there are thousands of urban-bred Africans up and down the vast continent who do not themselves understand this? The more perceptive of the urban Africans are only now beginning to comprehend, but slowly.

Being black is a small matter in tribal Africa because the attitude toward color is healthy and normal. Color does not matter. Color is an act of God that neither confers privileges nor imposes handicaps on a man. A man's skin is like the day: the day is either clear or dark. There is nothing more to it until external agencies come in and invest it with special meaning and importance.

What does matter to the tribal African, what is important, is the complex pattern of his position within his own group and his relations with the other members of the group. He is no Pan-African dreaming of a greater African glory when the white man is driven into the sea. The acute race consciousness of the American Negro, or of the black South African at the receiving end of Apartheid, is alien to him. The important things in his life are anything but race and color—until they are forced on him. And "Mother Africa" is much too vast to inspire big continental dreams in him. She is a land of huge mountains, dark jungles and vast deserts. In her rivers and in her jungles and in her grasslands lurk creatures that are the enemies of man: the leopard and the lion, the snake and crocodile. All this makes travel, by the old African methods, extremely difficult and makes for isolation between one group of people and another. The African who is in Britain is likely to be a deal better informed on what is happening all over the continent than would be his fellow African in any of the main centers of both tribal and non-tribal Africa. In terms of communications the man in the tribe lives in the Dark Ages.

Richard Wright was surprised that even educated Africans, racially conscious literate people, had not heard of him and were skeptical of a grown man earning his living by writing. They could not understand what kind of writing brought a man enough money to support a family. Wright really wanted to understand the African, but—"I found the African an oblique, a hard-to-know man."

My sympathies were all with Wright.

The heat and salty rancid fish smell had made me desperately thirsty. Across the way a mammy trader squatted beside her pile of merchandise: cooked meat, sweet potatoes —a whole host of edibles—and some bottles of opaque white liquid that could be either coconut milk or palm juice, as well as the inevitable little pile of cigarettes priced at a penny apiece. I had been warned of the risks involved in eating anything sold by the street traders. But to hell with it, I was thirsty and not exactly a stranger to African germs. I crossed the street, felt the bottles and chose the one that seemed coolest and looked the least opaque.

"How much?"

"One shilling." The carved ebony face looked at me with dead eyes.

I pulled the screwed-up newspaper stopper from the bottle, wiped its mouth and took a swig. I could not decide whether it was coconut milk or palm juice. It had been heavily watered down and sweetened. But it was wet and thirst-quenching. I drank half the bottle, firmly ignoring the little foreign bodies that floated in the liquid. Then I paid her and drank the rest. I put down the empty and began to move away.

"You African?" she asked in her harsh, cold, masculine voice.

I stopped, turned and looked at her face. It was as deadly cold and impersonal as before: not a flicker of feeling in her eyes. Like an African mask, I thought. But unlike Wright, I did not try to penetrate it. I knew the futility of trying. She would show feeling if and when she decided. Not before.

"Yes," I said, and added, "from the south. Far, far south."

She paused for so long that I began to move again.

"You like here?" Nationalism had obviously touched her.

I turned back to her. "No," I said.

"Why you don't like?"

"I don't say I don't like."

"But you don't like?"

I showed her my teeth, African-wise, which is neither smile nor grimace but a blending of the two. "You like Africa?" I asked.

Now it was her turn to show me her teeth. There was a flicker of feeling in her eyes, then they went dead again. She nodded. I had established my claim. Only outsiders—white people or the Richard Wrights—liked or disliked Africa.

I left the mammy trader and carried on up the smelly and hot street. Much and little had passed between us. Out to sea some fishing boats appeared on the sky line. About me were the citizens of Accra. Some wore the cloth of the country— the men looking like pint-sized citizens of ancient Rome painted black and the women looking extraordinarily masculine—and others wore western dress.

My thoughts shifted to my forthcoming meeting with Kwame Nkrumah, Ghana's first Prime Minister. It was well over seven years since I had last seen him, in London. Then he was a poor struggling student; now he was the head of a state and the spokesman for the great Pan-African dream of freedom and independence.

This was the man who later made common cause with the people of French Guinea, when they voted for independence in 1958 and against membership in DeGaulle's Fifth Republic—a move by Nkrumah that can have great significance for the British Commonwealth. Prime Minister Macmillan has indicated that Whitehall is watching Nkrumah's "closer association" moves with Guinea with keen interest. Prediction would be idle, yet it is intriguing to speculate that an ex-colony of Britain might bring an ex-colony of France into the Commonwealth. This could be a dramatic underscoring of the changing nature of colonialism in Africa. And at the center of it is Kwame Nkrumah.

I remembered our past friendship and wondered what changes I would find in him. Anyway, it was now nine A.M. and my date with him was for 9:30. I would soon know.

A few minutes later I flagged a taxi and simply said, "Kwame's office."

A pale-brown West Indian miss was the Prime Minister's secretary. She welcomed me as though I was a V.I.P. The Prime Minister had not come back from a conference yet. This tribal business was taking up a lot of his attention. She told me with indignation how members of the Ashanti tribe had to crawl on their bellies for some twenty yards into the presence of their king, the Asantehene, and how tribalism had to give way or there would be no progress. If she was any indication, then Nkrumah was very worried about the opposition the tribesmen were offering his western-style Convention People's Party.

A number of officials came in. The lady stopped assailing the tribes. Then there was some bustle and the Prime Minister arrived. In something just over five minutes he had seen and dealt with these officials and I was ushered into his office. It was a big pleasant, cool room.

Nkrumah came round his big official desk, took my hand and led me to a settee near the window. The now famous smile lit up his face. As we exchanged greetings, felt each other out with small talk in an attempt to bridge the gap of years, my mind went back to our London days. This poised, relaxed man, with the hint of guarded reserve about him, was a far cry from the friend I had last seen nearly eight years earlier.

For me, the most striking change of all was in his eyes. They reflected an inner tranquillity which was the one thing the Nkrumah in Europe never had.

Even his name had been subtly different then. He had been our friend Francis Nkrumah, an African student recently arrived from the United States, and he had not seen Africa for a decade and more. He had quickly become a part of our African colony in London and had joined our little group, the Pan-African Federation in our protests against colonialism.

He was much less relaxed than most of us. His eyes mirrored a burning inner conflict and tension. He seemed consumed by a restlessness that led him to evolve some of the most fantastic schemes.

The president of our federation was an East African named Johnstone Kenyatta, the most relaxed, sophisticated and "westernized" of the lot of us. Kenyatta enjoyed the personal friendship of some of the most distinguished people in English political and intellectual society. He was subtle, subtle enough to attack one's principles bitterly and retain one's friendship. He fought the British as imperialists but was affectionate toward them as friends.

It was to this balanced and extremely cultured man that Francis Nkrumah proposed that we form a secret society called The Circle, and that each of us spill a few drops of our blood in a bowl and so take a blood oath of secrecy and dedication to the emancipation of Africa.

Johnstone Kenyatta laughed at the idea; he scoffed at it as childish juju. He conceived our struggle in modern, twentieth century terms with no ritualistic blood nonsense. In the end Francis Nkrumah drifted away from us and started his own little West African group in London. We were too tame and slow for him. He was an angry young man in a hurry.

Then he went back to his part of Africa, and Francis Nkrumah became Kwame Nkrumah. He set himself at the head of the largely tribal populace and dabbled in blood ritual. There was some violence, a spell in prison, and finally Nkrumah emerged as the first African Prime Minister in a self-governing British African territory.

Tribal myths grew up around him. He could make himself invisible at will. He could go without food and sleep and drink longer than ordinary mortals. He was, in fact, the reincarnation of some of the most powerful ancestral spirits. He allowed his feet to be bathed in blood.

By the time I visited the Gold Coast the uneasy alliance between Nkrumah and the tribal chiefs had begun to crack. A week or so before my arrival he had threatened that, unless they co-operated with his government in turning the Gold Coast into an efficient twentieth century state, he would make them run so hard that they would leave their sandals behind them. This was a calculated insult to the tribal concept that a chief's bare feet must never touch the earth.

That was the beginning of the secret war. Nkrumah thought he would win it easily. He was wrong. The chiefs have not run, and today their opposition to him is even more clear cut. Some of his own followers, like Joe Appiah, who married the daughter of the late Sir Stafford Cripps, have defected to the tribalists. They are biding their time: waiting and watching.

And they have, negatively, scored their victories too. They have pushed him to a point where his regime is, today, intolerant of opposition. The tribal society brooks no opposition. Nkrumah's government banishes its most active opponents. As a modern socialist leading a western-style government he justifies this as a temporary expedient. But his less sophisticated ministers frankly talk the tribal language of strength, frankly express the tribal impulse to destroy those who are out of step.

There was an air of delicacy about our conversation and we were both aware of this. I asked him how he was getting on with those civil servants who, a little time earlier, had labeled him an "irresponsible agitator." He had nothing but praise for those who had remained. Some resigned, among them the officer in charge of the prison where Nkrumah had been detained, who refused openly to serve under one of his former inmates. One or two other die-hards of the old colonialism also pulled out, but in the main the expatriate civil servants stayed on and rendered loyal service. But he was preoccupied with Africanizing the service, something which has largely come about now.

We touched on local politics. He let off at full blast against the tribalist. I told him I had heard that the Accra Club was still exclusively European. His eyes lit up. "You wait and see," he said.

Then, in relation to nothing either of us had said, he leaned toward me and exclaimed, "This place is rich! God, man, there's so much riches here!"—as though revelation had just been made to him.

But always, throughout our talk, I sensed a new reserve, a new caution that had not been there in the young student I had known in Europe.

As we talked in Nkrumah's cool office that hot August day in Accra, my mind kept slipping back to our mutual friend Jomo or Johnstone Kenyatta, [later to be] imprisoned in his native Kenya for leading the Mau-Mau movement. Significantly, though we mentioned many friends, both Nkrumah and I avoided mentioning Kenyatta. I had decided not to mention him first. I had hoped Nkrumah would. He did not.

A year earlier, I had flown up to Kenya from South Africa and visited Kenyatta. I felt terribly depressed as I got off the plane. Things had grown so much uglier in the Union. The barricades were up in the ugly war of color. When I had left South Africa in the dim-and-distant past, there were isolated islands where black and white could meet in neutral territory. When I went back in 1952, the islands were submerged under the rising tide of color hatreds, and I was glad to quit that dark, unhappy land which yet compelled my love.

It was in this mood that I got off the plane. I had not seen my friend Jomo for years. Now there he was, just outside the airport terminal building, leaning on a heavy cane, bigger than I remembered him in Europe, paunchy, his face looking puffy. And behind him was a huge crowd of Africans.

I began to move toward him when a lean-faced, lean-hipped white colonial-administrator type suddenly appeared beside me and said: "Mr. Abrahams."

I stopped and thought, "Oh, Lord."

Kenyatta also came forward. The two men ignored each other. Lean-face introduced himself and said the Colonial Office had alerted them that I was coming to do some writing for the London Observer and they had drawn up a provi-

sional schedule for me. Had I done anything about accommo-
dation?

Before I could answer, Kenyatta said, "You are staying
with me, of course." The old detachment was back in his
eyes. They seemed to say, "You've got to choose, pal. Let's
see how you choose."

Lean-face said, "We've got something set up for you
tomorrow and—"

"I live in the bush," Kenyatta added.

It dawned on me that I had become, for the moment, the
battlefield of that horrible animal, the racial struggle. I made
up my mind, resenting both sides and yet conscious of the
crowd of Africans in the background. A question of face was
involved.

"I've promised to spend this weekend with Mr. Kenyatta,"
I said.

Lean-face was graceful about it. I promised to call at the
Secretariat first thing on Monday morning. He gave me a
copy of the schedule that had been prepared for me and
wondered, *sotto voce,* whether I knew what I was letting
myself in for. Kenyatta assured me that I would be perfectly
safe, that nobody was going to cut my throat. I was aware
that they were talking to each other through me. I was aware
that they knew I was aware, and that made me bad-tempered.

"Then I'll say good night, Mr. Abrahams," Lean-face said
pointedly.

As soon as he was out of hearing Kenyatta began to curse.

"It's good to see you again, Johnstone," I gripped his hand.

"Jomo," he replied. The hint of ironic speculation was back
in his eyes. A slightly sardonic, slightly bitter smile played on
his lips.

"Welcome to Kenya, Peter," he said. Then, abruptly:
"Come meet the leaders of my people. They've been waiting
long."

We moved forward and the crowd gathered about us. Jomo
made a little speech in Kikuyu, then translated it for my
benefit. A little old man, ancient as the hills, with huge holes
in his ears, then welcomed me on behalf of the land and its
people. Again Jomo translated.

After this we all bundled into the fleet of rattling old cars and set off for the Kikuyu reserve in the heart of the African bush. Kenyatta became silent and strangely remote during the journey.

We stopped at the old chief's compound, where other members of the tribe waited to welcome me. By this time the reception committee had grown to a few hundred. About me, pervading the air, was the smell of burning flesh; a young cow was being roasted in my honor. Before I entered the house a drink was handed to me. Another was handed to the old chief and a third to Kenyatta. The old man muttered a brief incantation and spilled half his drink on the earth as a libation. Jomo and I followed suit. Then the three of us downed our drinks and entered the house.

A general feasting and drinking then commenced, both inside and outside the house. I was getting a full ceremonial tribal welcome. The important dignitaries of the tribe slipped into the room in twos and threes, spoke to me through Kenyatta for a few moments, and then went away, making room for others.

"Africa doesn't seem to change," Kenyatta murmured between dignitaries. There was a terrible undercurrent of bitterness behind the softly murmured words. I was startled by it and looked at his face. For a fleeting moment he looked like a trapped, caged animal.

He saw me looking at him and quickly composed his face into a slightly sardonic humorous mask. "Don't look too closely," he said.

And still the dignitaries filed in, had a drink, spoke their welcome and went out.

The ceremonial welcome reached its high point about midnight. Huge chunks of the roasted cow were brought in to us, and we gnawed at the almost raw meat between swigs of liquor. Outside, there was muted drumming. Voices were growing louder and louder.

Suddenly, in the midst of a long-winded speech by an immensely dignified Masai chief from a neighboring and friendly tribe, Kenyatta jumped up, grabbed his heavy cane and half staggered to the door.

"Come, Peter," he called.

Everybody was startled. I hesitated. He raised his cane and beckoned to me with it. I knew that this would be a dreadful breach of tribal etiquette.

"Come, man!" he snapped.

I got up, aware of the sudden silence that had descended on the huge gathering. By some strange magic everybody seemed to know that something had gone wrong.

"Jomo," I said.

"I can't stand any more," he snapped. "Come!"

I followed him to the door. I knew the discourtesy we were inflicting on the tribe. I also knew that my friend was at the breaking point. We walked through the crowd of people, got into Kenyatta's car and drove off into the night. The African moon was big and yellow, bathing the land in a soft light that almost achieved the clarity of daylight.

He took me to his home. It was a big, sprawling, empty place on the brow of a hill. Inside, it had nothing to make for comfort. There were hard wooden chairs, a few tables and only the bed in the bedroom. There were no books, none of the normal amenities of western civilization. When we arrived two women emerged from somewhere in the back and hovered about in the shadows. They brought in liquor, but I never got a clear glimpse of either of them. My friend's anguish of spirit was such that I did not want to ask questions. We sat on the veranda and drank steadily and in silence until we were both miserably, depressingly drunk.

And then Kenyatta began to speak in a low, bitter voice of his frustration and of the isolated position in which he found himself. He had no friends. There was no one in the tribe who could give him the intellectual companionship that had become so important to him in his years in Europe. The things that were important to him—consequential conversation, the drink that represented a social activity rather than the intention to get drunk, the concept of individualism, the inviolability of privacy—all these were alien to the tribesmen in whose midst he lived. So Kenyatta, the western man, was driven in on himself and was forced to assert himself in tribal terms. Only thus would the tribesmen follow him and so give him his position of power and importance as a leader.

To live without roots is to live in hell, and no man chooses voluntarily to live in hell. The people who could answer his needs as a western man had erected a barrier of color against him in spite of the fact that the taproots of their culture had become the taproots of his culture too. By denying him access to those things which complete the life of western man, they had forced him back into the tribalism from which he had so painfully freed himself over the years.

None of this was stated explicitly by either Kenyatta or myself. But it was there in his brooding bitter commentary on both the tribes and the white settlers of the land. For me Kenyatta became that night a man who in his own life personified the terrible tragedy of Africa and the terrible secret war that rages in it. He was the victim both of tribalism and of westernism gone sick. His heart and mind and body were the battlefield of the ugly violence known as the Mau-Mau revolt long before it broke out in that beautiful land. The tragedy is that he was so rarely gifted that he could have made such a magnificent contribution in other circumstances.

BARBING DAY IN THE TOWN OF SHORT GHOSTS

Amos Tutuola

Amos Tutuola, a Nigerian worker with little schooling, has written in his own intriguing English four remarkable books of fantasy, which as far as he is concerned are not fantasy at all. He has been there, he says, in that bush of ghosts. In a way, this is the simple truth.

His four books—*Palm-Wine Drinkard, My Life in the Bush of Ghosts* (excerpted here), *Simbi and the Satyr of the Dark Jungle*, and *The Brave African Huntress*—are far from being the fabrications of one man's imagination. They are merely Amos Tutuola's private paths through the dense forests of traditional West African narrative. He undoubtedly adds something to the old themes by his extraordinarily graphic style, which is helped and not hindered by his limited education. We can only speculate about the forms that this traditional material will take in the work of more sophisticated literary artists in the future; but Tutuola's success is a sign that very old themes and motifs of African oral literature will not be completely cast aside.

Before coming to the town of short ghosts, the lost but resourceful hero of Tutuola's story has had many fearsome and bizarre encounters and escapes. The ghosts are of an unimaginable profusion: there are the "smelling-ghosts" who wear live scorpions and snakes as jewelry; there are golden, silvery, and coppery ghosts; there is a television-handed ghostess, burglar-ghosts, homeless ghosts, marrying ghosts and many more. The town of short ghosts is ruled by the "flashed-eyed mother" who sits permanently in the rain and sun, day and night, vast as a hill, filling the town; and on her body grow innumerable baby heads all talking and clamoring to be fed. So powerful are this queen's eyes that with their flashes she can set fire to wood, or fiercely flog offenders even at a great distance. Although she is a paragon of filth, covered all over with excreta and spittle ("the dirt was her beauty"), nevertheless her charges do have a rare and awesome "barbing day."

As all the heads which were on the body of "flash-eyed mother" and also all short ghosts' heads were full of much thick and dirty hair like weeds, so they were only barbing once in a century when the "Secret Society of Ghosts" festival is near.

So that a special full day is reserved for barbing their heads and their barber is one of the "fire creatures" who was qualified for barbing heads with the clippers and knife of fire. But when it was announced by the "flash-eyed mother" that the barbing day would be tomorrow I thought our heads would be barbed with the ordinary clippers, scissors and knives as in my home town, so I was jumping up with gladness because I was never barbed once since about fourteen years that I entered the Bush of Ghosts. So when the day was reached all of us were bound to be in one spot. After a few minutes there I saw a creature who was fire and held the clippers of fire which were blazing with the flame of fire. First, he started to barb for those heads as everything must first start from them. But I was very surprised to see that all of these heads were shouting with joy as these clippers of fire were touching their heads instead of crying. Again it was this day I noticed carefully that uncountable beetles, bees, wasps and many other kinds of biting insects were living inside the hair of these heads as their homes and also their mother's head was full up with numerous small birds which built their nests inside the hair of her head as on the trees. Having barbed all the heads and their mother then he started barbing for the short ghosts. But after he barbed half of them all the heads reported to their mother that they were feeling hungry, then she ordered those half who had been already barbed to go and kill an animal from the bush, so at this stage I had a chance and mixed with those who had been already barbed as if I had barbed my own too. So it was this way I saved myself from barbing my head with the clippers of fire.

One day, when I was seriously sick, I was detailed to be at home by the short ghosts to be serving the mother with anything that she wanted to do. I was greatly surprised to say that it was that day I knew that she was selling the flash fire of her eyes to other kinds of ghosts who were coming from the various towns to buy it, and a flash was worth a heavy amount of ghosts' money.

THE AFRICAN WORLD-VIEW

K. A. Busia

Kofi Abrefa Busia of Ghana is of Ashanti origin. He is a sociologist with a B.A. in philosophy and economics, and a Ph.D. in anthropology from Oxford. He is the author of a well-known work, *The Position of the Chief in the Modern Political System of the Ashanti.*

In 1959, he had to flee Ghana because of his opposition to the Nkrumah regime. He then became professor of African sociology at the University of Leyden, Holland. Later he came to the United States as a spokesman for those oppositionists who have been imprisoned by the Nkrumah government. He is continuing research on Africa for the Phelps-Stokes Fund and the New World Foundation, both of New York.

We give here an extract from an address to a Conference

on the Christian Faith and African Culture held in the Gold
Coast (now Ghana) in 1955. Dr. Busia examines the reasons
for the lack of any great success in christianizing the Africans.
Aware that many African church members are at the same
time adherents of older African views and practices, Dr. Busia
suggests that this is due to the African's deeply held views of
nature and man. These views are not necessarily in contradic-
tion to the essence of Christian belief and should command
respect even from those who do not share them. Dr. Busia
implies that where such respect is withheld, efforts toward religious conversion can be a form of psychic violence, a
spiritual domination no less repugnant than economic exploitation or political oppression.

MY SUBJECT IS the African world-view, but I should say at
once that though there are religious ideas and social values
that are widespread in Africa, there are also diversities. For
there are many and not one African community. There are
numerous communities on the vast continent of Africa which
have lived in self-contained isolation, under varying conditions of life and experience.

Certain beliefs, nevertheless, such as animism, the concept
of ghosts and spirits, polytheism and magic, are common
patterns which afford valuable guides for understanding particular communities in Africa.

When we think of a people's world-view, we consider their
concept of the supernatural, of nature, of man, and society,
and of the way in which these concepts form a system that
gives meaning to men's lives and actions.

All peoples have beliefs regarding the supernatural. But
what is considered as falling within the natural, what can be
explained in terms of a people's experience and empirical
knowledge, differs from one community to another. Europeans
in Africa, for example, will find that many things are ascribed
to supernatural causes, which they will ascribe to natural
causes, on the basis of their scientific knowledge. This does
not mean, as some Europeans have, I think, erroneously
concluded, that the African has no concept of causality, but
only that the sphere of the supernatural for the European is

narrower. This is so, because of the European's wider knowledge of natural phenomena.

Africans believe in a Supreme Being, the Creator of the world and all the things in it. The ideas as to the attributes of the Creator vary, but all believe that He is charged with power, both beneficent and dangerous. This belief in a Supreme Being who is omnipotent is held along with belief in lesser deities who are also charged with power, both beneficent and dangerous. These supernatural entities or gods are not always held to have bodies like men, but their values, attitudes, and thoughts, i.e. their personalities are like those of men.

They take notice of men's actions; they desire human attention and are pleased when honour is paid to them, as well as displeased by neglect. They can further man's welfare, in conformity with the society's desires and goals; they can make crops grow, increase the fertility of soil, beast and man, sanction established morality, and punish those who depart from the established rule of the society. Such punishment occurs in this world, and not in another. The punishment may bring misfortune, disease, or even death. The gods are not invariably good; they have moods, and are sometimes destructive and whimsical. The relationship between the deities and men, and between one deity and another is conceived in human social terms; the gods speak through their priests, they give promises, they make demands, they issue threats, they show anger as well as pleasure, they listen to prayers, they accept or reject sacrifices, they institute rites in which the worshippers join.

I may digress to point out that the problem of evil so often discussed in Western philosophy and Christian theology does not arise in the African concept of deity. It is when a God who is not only all powerful and omniscient but also perfect and loving is postulated that the problem of the existence of evil becomes an intellectual and philosophical hurdle. The Supreme Being of the African is the Creator, the source of life, but between Him and man lie many powers and principalities good and bad, gods, spirits, magical forces, witches, to account for the strange happenings in the world.

Nature, too, can have power, and even spirits. It must be

noted that in farming, fishing, stock raising, and other economic activities the African shows a knowledge of natural
causes. The difference with Europe lies in the fact that the
control that Europe has gained over nature is greater and
therefore Europeans can give naturalistic or scientific explanations to a greater range of happenings than Africans. But
there are theories of reality in Africa just as in Europe. When
the African offers an egg to a tree, or food to a dead ancestor,
he is not expressing ignorance of material substances, or
natural causes, but he is expressing in conduct a theory of
reality, namely that behind the visible substance of things lie
essences, or powers which constitute their true nature. Those
who have read Western philosophy are familiar with such
formulations, but because the African does not formulate his
problems in terms familiar to the Europeans, or may not
even be able to express his awareness in words, his conduct
is often grossly misinterpreted. In Western metaphysics, the
known world is divided into two, mind and matter, and a
human being into soul and body. Some have said that matter
alone is real and mind is an illusion; while some now hold
that both mind and matter are structures composed of more
primitive stuff which is neither mental nor material. The
African has not offered learned and divergent disputations
to the world in writing, but in his expression in conduct of
awe, and reverence for nature, no less than in his use of
natural resources, he demonstrates his own epistemology. I am
not aware of an agreed Christian view of nature, but I submit
that there is an African one which is that nature has power
which may be revered as well as used for man's benefit.

With regard to man himself, there is a widespread belief in
Africa that he is a compound of material and immaterial substances; man is a biological and spiritual being. Physical death
is not the end of men. The soul concepts of African peoples
are many and elaborate. Among the Ashanti, for example, as
I have shown elsewhere, "Man as a biological being inherits
his blood from his mother; this gives him his status and membership within the lineage, clan, and the tribe, and his obligations as a citizen. . . . As a spiritual being, a man receives a
two-fold gift of the spirit: that which determines his character
and individuality he receives through his father; but his soul,

the undying part of him, he receives direct from the Supreme Being."

Among the Dahomey, as Herskovits tells us, "all persons have at least three souls, and adult males have four. One is inherited from the ancestor, and is the 'guardian spirit' of the individual. The second is the personal soul, while the third is the small bit of the Creator that 'lives in every person's body.' " The first in Euroamerican thought is to be conceived as the biological aspect of man; the second, his personality, and the third his intellect and intuition. The fourth soul of adult males is associated with the concept of destiny. This soul occupies itself not only with the affairs of this world, but also with the collective destiny of his household, since "the Dahomean reasons that when a man reaches maturity, his own life cannot know fulfilment apart from the lives of those who share that life with him."

P. Mercier (*African Worlds,* p. 227) has stated that he thinks Herskovits was not accurate, but Mercier himself says "The human soul (*se*) has many forms, although its essential unity is insisted on: there is the *joto,* the soul handed on from the ancestor of whom each living man is the representative, and who is his guardian; the *se,* which strictly speaking is a portion of *Mawu,* the great *Se* of the world; the *selido,* which is life, feeling, personality, the individual's peculiar qualities with which *kpoli,* the destiny revealed by *Fa,* is identified; finally, there is the *ye,* this is the term most commonly used, and denotes the shadow, the indestructible portion of the individual, which, at the time of burial, becomes invisible and leaves the body.

Those two examples must suffice. The African view of man in society in general lays more emphasis on his membership of a group than on his individuality. The membership of the group continues beyond death into the life beyond. The dead, the living, and the yet unborn form an unbroken family, and this concept is given emphasis in institutions and ritual.

A people's interpretation of the universe is shown in conduct: in day to day activities, in human relations, and in rites; in avoidances as well as observances. The sociological field of religion and cosmology includes the emotions and beliefs prevalent in a social group regarding the supernatural, the overt behaviour, the material objects, and the symbols and rites associated with such beliefs.

I have given merely some signposts. I am aware of their inadequacy, but I could not fill in the details for every African community; I have neither the time nor the knowledge. I have said enough, I hope, to show what I consider to be the crucial problem. I have said that I do not think the diversity in cultures and moral values constitute an argument that there can be no rational ideals capable of universal recognition and acceptance. But I would submit that the people's interpretation of the universe must be appreciated if Christianity, or any faith based on the universality of moral values, is to become meaningful within their culture. I submit further that until Christianity has come to grips with this problem, not only in Africa, but in other non-European countries, Christianity will remain an alien and superficial addition to more hospitable creeds. Hospitable, because none of the creeds preaches the dogma that it alone is true and all others are false. This is the dogmatic claim of the Christian religion, and that dogma imposes on those who share it or propagate it the duty of understanding and correcting the errors of other creeds. Lastly, Christianity is a way of life; but the world is the richer for its diversity of cultures. Every people may claim that its culture is God-given; a part of its life.

Can the African be Christian only by giving up his culture, or is there a way by which Christianity can ennoble it? Something, I believe, must die, but only in order that it may bear fruit. To us is entrusted the husbandry.

THE DIGNITY OF MAN
The 1961 Nobel Peace Prize Acceptance Speech

ALBERT LUTHULI

Albert John Luthuli was born in 1899 and grew up at a local mission where his father was serving as an interpreter and evangelist. He was educated in the mission schools of Natal, and was graduated from the Congregationalist Adams College in 1921, where he remained as a teacher of Zulu language and music. In 1935, he abandoned the comforts of his academic career to become the elected chief of the Amakholwa people in the Groutville mission reserve. Several of his ancestors had also been tribal chiefs.

Encouraged by his success as chief, he entered politics as a member of the Native Representative Council, but he was dissatisfied with the essential powerlessness of this advisory body. Chief Luthuli joined the African National Congress, a multiracial organization, and soon became its president.

In 1952, he helped launch a campaign of passive resistance against the racialist policies of the South African government. The government reacted by jailing thousands of Africans, stripping Luthuli of his chieftainship and declaring the African National Congress illegal. Mr. Luthuli refused to resign from the presidency of the ANC and was subjected by the government to speaking bans, imprisonment, and in 1959 banishment to his rural home district for five years. In 1960, he was fined $280 for publicly burning his identity card.

During his confinement, he lives on his ten-acre farm in a five-room cottage that is filled with books on religion, politics and philosophy. After supervising the work on his farm by day, he spends his evenings on his writing. On Sundays he attends the local Congregational Church. He has been on the executive council of the Christian Council of South Africa, of which he was vice-president for four years. In 1962, he published his autobiographical book, *Let My People Go*.

Luthuli's position is that of a religious Christian and an African nationalist. His policy of non-violent militancy, which is eloquently restated in the address reproduced here, has won him a great following among Africans. In its award, with the cash prize of $43,615, the Norwegian Nobel Committee wanted to pay tribute to Luthuli's long, non-violent struggle for his people's rights. Perhaps it was also trying to strengthen the hand of a man of moderation against the white and black extremists in a situation which could lead to a holocaust. This historic first Nobel prize to be awarded an African received a fitting response in Luthuli's stout attack on "the most terrible dream in the world"—the totalitarian racialism of South African "apartheid." His ringing affirmations on behalf of the dignity of man, and the fullest democratic rights for all, are a challenge not only to the South African government, and to the whole non-African world, but to the dozens of newly independent African states as well.

THE NOBEL PEACE AWARD that has brought me here has for me a threefold significance. On the one hand it is a tribute to my humble contribution to efforts by democrats on both sides of the color line to find a peaceful solution to the race problem. This contribution is not in any way unique.

To remain neutral in a situation where the laws of the land virtually criticized God for having created men of color was the sort of thing I could not, as a Christian, tolerate.

On the other hand the award is a democratic declaration of solidarity with those who fight to widen the area of liberty in my part of the world. As such, it is the sort of gesture which gives me and millions who think as I do tremendous encouragement.

There are still people in the world today who regard South Africa's race problem as a simple clash between black and white.

Our government has carefully projected this image of the problem before the eyes of the world. This has had two effects.

It has confused the real issues at stake in the race crisis. It has given some form of force to the Government's contention that the race problem is a domestic matter for South Africa.

This, in turn, has tended to narrow down the area over which our case could be better understood in the world.

From yet another angle, it is a welcome recognition of the role played by the African people during the last fifty years to establish, peacefully, a society in which merit and not race would fix the position of the individual in the life of the nation.

This award could not be for me alone, nor for just South Africa, but for Africa as a whole.

Africa presently is most deeply torn with strife and most bitterly stricken with racial conflict.

Ours is a continent in revolution against oppression. And peace and revolution make uneasy bed fellows.

There can be no peace until the forces of oppression are overthrown. Our continent has been carved up by the great powers. In these times there has been no peace. There could be no brotherhood between men.

But now, the revolutionary stirrings of our continent are setting the past aside. Our people everywhere from north to south of the continent are reclaiming their land, their right to participate in government, their dignity as men, their nationhood.

Thus, in the turmoil of revolution, the basis for peace and brotherhood in Africa is being restored by the resurrection of national sovereignty and independence, of equality and the dignity of man.

It should not be difficult for you here in Europe to appreciate this. Your age of revolution, stretching across all the years from the eighteenth century to our own, encompassed some of the bloodiest civil wars in all history.

By comparison, the African revolution has swept across three-quarters of the continent in less than a decade, its final completion is within sight of our own generation.

Again, by comparison with Europe, our African revolution to our credit is proving to be orderly, quick and comparatively bloodless.

Our goal is a united Africa in which the standards of life and liberty are constantly expanding, in which the ancient legacy of illiteracy and disease is swept aside, in which the dignity of man is rescued from beneath the heels of colonialism which have trampled it.

This goal, pursued by millions of our people with revolutionary zeal, by means of books, representations, demonstrations and in some places armed force provoked by the adamancy of white rule, carries the only real promise of peace in Africa. Whatever means have been used the efforts have gone to end alien rule and race oppression.

There is a paradox in the fact that Africa qualifies for such an award in its age of turmoil and revolution. How great is the paradox and how much greater the honor that an award in support of peace and the brotherhood of man should come to one who is a citizen of a country where the brotherhood of man is an illegal doctrine.

Outlawed, banned, censured, proscribed and prohibited; where to work, talk or campaign for the realization in fact and deed of the brotherhood of man is hazardous, punished with banishment or confinement without trial or imprisonment; where effective democratic channels to peaceful settlement of the race problem have never existed these 300 years, and where white minority power rests on the most heavily armed and equipped military machine in Africa.

This is South Africa.

Even here, where white rule seems determined not to change its mind for the better, the spirit of Africa's militant struggle for liberty, equality and independence asserts itself, I, together with thousands of my countrymen, have in the course of struggle for these ideals been harassed and imprisoned, but we are not deterred in our quest for a new age in which we shall live in peace and in brotherhood.

It is not necessary for me to speak at length about South Africa. It is a museum piece in our time, a hangover from the dark past of mankind, a relic of an age which everywhere else is dead or dying.

Here the cult of race superiority and of white supremacy is worshiped like a god. The ghost of slavery lingers on to this day in the form of forced labor that goes on in what are called farm prisons.

It is fair to say that even in present day conditions, Christian missions have been in the vanguard in initiating social services provided for us. Our progress in this field has been in spite of, and not mainly because of, the Government. In this the Church in South Africa—though belatedly—seems to be awakening to a broader mission of the Church, in its ministry among us.

I, as a Christian, have always felt that there is one thing above all about "apartheid" or "separate development" that is unforgivable.

It seems utterly indifferent to the suffering of individual persons, who lose their land, their homes, their jobs, in the pursuit of what is surely the most terrible dream in the world.

This terrible dream is not held on to by a crack-pot group on the fringe of society. It is the deliberate policy of a Government, supported actively by a large part of the white population, and tolerated passively by an overwhelmingly white majority, but now fortunately rejected by an encouraging white minority who have thrown in their lot with nonwhites who are overwhelmingly opposed to so-called separate development.

Thus it is that the golden age of Africa's independence is also the dark age of South Africa's decline and retrogression.

Education is being reduced to an instrument of subtle indoctrination. Slanted and biased reporting in the organs of public information, a creeping censorship, book-banning and black-listing, all these spread their shadows over the land.

But beneath the surface there is a spirit of defiance.

The people of South Africa have never been a docile lot, least of all the African people. We have a long tradition of struggle for our national rights, reaching back to the very beginning of white settlement and conquest 300 years ago.

We, in our situation, have chosen the path of nonviolence of our own volition. Along this path we have organized many heroic campaigns.

The bitterness of the struggle mounts as liberty comes step by step closer to the freedom fighters' grasp. All too often, the protests and demonstrations of our people have been beaten back by force, but they have never been silenced.

Through all this cruel treatment in the name of law and order, our people, with few exceptions, have remained nonviolent.

Nothing which we have suffered at the hands of the Government has turned us from our chosen path of disciplined resistance. It is for this, I believe, that this award is given.

The true patriots of South Africa, for whom I speak, will be satisfied with nothing less than the fullest democratic rights.

In government we will not be satisfied with anything less than direct individual adult suffrage and the right to stand for and be elected to all organs of government.

In economic matters we will be satisfied with nothing less than equality of opportunity in every sphere, and the enjoyment by all of those heritages which form the resources of the country which up to now have been appropriated on a racial "whites only" basis.

In culture we will be satisfied with nothing less than the

opening of all doors of learning in non-segregatory institutions on the sole criterion of ability.

In the social sphere we will be satisfied with nothing less than the abolition of all racial bars.

We do not demand these things for people of African descent alone. We demand them for all South Africans, white and black.

Let me invite Africa to cast her eyes beyond the past and, to some extent, the present with their woes and tribulations, trials and failures, and some successes, and see herself an emerging continent, bursting to freedom through the shell of centuries of serfdom.

This is Africa's age—the dawn of her fulfillment, yes, the moment when she must grapple with destiny to reach the summits of sublimity saying, ours was a fight for noble values and worthy ends, and not for lands and the enslavement of man.

Still licking the scars of past wrongs perpetrated on her, could she not be magnanimous and practice no revenge? Her hand of friendship scornfully rejected, her pleas for justice and fair play spurned, should she not nonetheless seek to turn enmity into amity?

Though robbed of her lands, her independence and opportunities to become—this, oddly enough, often in the name of civilization and even Christianity—should she not see her destiny as being that of making a distinctive contribution to human progress and human relationships with a peculiar new Africa flavor enriched by the diversity of cultures she enjoys, thus building on the summits of present human achievement an edifice that would be one of the finest tributes to the genius of man?

In a strife-torn world, tottering on the brink of complete destruction by man-made nuclear weapons, a free and independent Africa is in the making, in answer to the injunction and challenge of history:

"Arise and shine, for thy light is come."

Acting in concert with other nations, she is man's last hope for a mediator between the East and West, and is qualified to demand of the great powers to "turn the swords into ploughshares" because two-thirds of mankind is hungry and illiterate.

Africa's qualification for this noble task is incontestable, for her own fight has never been and is not now a fight for conquest of land, for accumulation of wealth or domination of peoples, but for the recognition and preservation of the rights of man and the establishment of a truly free world.

PART TWO
AFRO-AMERICAN RESPONSES

Chapter 4

Affirmations:
The New-World Negro and His Heritage

THE FEAST

RENÉ MARAN

René Maran wrote a number of books about Africa, of which the most famous is *Batouala* (see also the general introduction).

In the following chapter from that novel, we see the Banda tribe come together at the summons of their chief, Batouala, for a wild revel while the commandant of the Government station is away. The time is the First World War. The region is the French Congo. The dance festival is held to honor the *ga'nzas*—those who are about to be initiated into manhood or womanhood. It is an occasion not only for emptying the jars of hemp-wine and meal-beer, but also for draining the vials of bitterness and rage. Tormented by the taxes, the injustices, and the hypocrisies of the white rulers, the people give vent to their grievances and despair. They take what comfort they can from reports that far away in Europe the whites are slaughtering each other.

Here is a glimpse of the raw and festering results of colonial administration at nearly its worst. It explodes any myth of African docility under exploitation. These folk see through the white man's deceits with stark clarity. They do not seek refuge in illusions about either their masters or themselves.

THE FULL MOON traversed the region of the stars. The festival of the *ga'nzas* was about to begin.

What a stroke of good fortune! A week before, the commandant had left Grimari on a tour of inspection in the neighborhood of Bamayassi. The billygoat away, the nanny-

161

goats will play. Swarms of natives overran the grounds of the Government station—the only place that offered room enough for the full sweep of the various figures and the dance of the warriors.

A large empty space, as broad as it was long, reached from the commandant's house down to the Bembe. And only one man had been left in charge, only one native gendarme, one *tourougou,* Boula, for whom the natives didn't give a tinker's curse—Boula in sole charge of the administration building and annexes, the training camp and the guardhouse.

Who really did care about a *kouloungoulou*—the nickname they had given Boula because, they said, he crawled like a milleped.

The *ga'nzas* not having arrived yet, the *yangba* was not in full swing, but the indications were that it was going to be wonderful.

A dozen *li'nghas* scattered about seemed to be waiting expectant. These were not ugly little tom-toms, dirty from use, weatherbeaten, wormeaten. On the contrary, each of them visibly swelled with pride over its double convexity, the great round of an enormous tree trunk patiently hollowed out. They had been given a pale coat, made of mixed white clay and manioc meal, with a broad band of red running lengthwise and breadthwise.

On the ground were spread baskets of millet, manioc cakes, whole clusters of bananas, dishfuls of caterpillars, eggs, fish, bitter tomatoes, wild asparagus. There were quantities of meats, either sun-dried or grilled over a fire—antelope meat, elephant meat, quarters of wart hog and buffalo. There were the tubers that the whites despised—*dazos,* for example, every bit as good as their white potatoes. There were *bangaos* or sweet potatoes, both the red-skinned and the yellow-skinned sorts. There were *baba's-sos* or yams. There were great jars brimming over with the drink made of fermented millet or maize. And there were a few bottles of Pernod.

The Pernod had been bought from the *boundjoudoulis* (white tradesmen) and was reserved for the chiefs, head-men, and elders.

From the numerous fires arose volumes of smoke, black, heavy, and very pungent from the damp wood.

The roads from Kama, Pangakoura, Pouyamba, and Yakidji swarmed with the latecomers hastening toward these fires visible from afar—men, women, children, boys, boyesses, slaves, dogs.

They had come, and still were coming, from their kagas, their thickets, their muddy *patas-patas,* or their plantations, armed with arrows and javelins, and carrying burning pieces of wood to light their way in the wooded strips through which they had to pass before they reached the small lakes.

The women, as soon as they arrived, set right to work with their *koufrou* to pound the maize and millet and manioc into meal, and while pestles banged in wooden mortars they sang the song of the *kouloungoulou.*

> The kouloungoulou, as is known, lives in dung.
> That's all he eats, too, they say. Think of it!
>> Kouloungoulou, kouloungoulou,
>> Kouloungoulou, ho! Ia-hey!

> His wealth consists of but one thing.
> He got it from the boundjou (white man).
> And excellent husband that he is
> He passed it to his yassi.
> She passed it to their daughter.
>> Kouloungoulou, kouloungoulou,
>> Kouloungoulou, ho! Ia-hey!

> How is it that we saw a kouloungoulou,
> Wearing a tourougou's chechia,
> Passing through our lovely fields?
> Yassis, yassis, take care, beware
> Of the filthy kouloungoulou.
> He's no friend for you.
>> Kouloungoulou, kouloungoulou,
>> Kouloungoulou, ho! Ia-hey!

There were bursts of laughter. The merriment became general. They laughed for the sake of laughing. They talked without knowing just what they were going to say: the *kéné* was already working. They drank maize-beer on top of millet-beer, and drank and drank without cease.

A wonderful gathering. All the M'bis and all the N'gapus were there with their elders.

Batouala and his old parents formed the center of a group of chiefs and their head-men.

He held forth.

The death of several whites had been reported at Bangui. . . . It was said that the Governor was soon going to Bandorro . . . that over in France in M'Poutou (Europe) the Frandjes were fighting the Zalemans.

While talking he stuffed the garabos within reach with hemp[1] and tobacco, lit them, took several puffs, which is the custom, and passed them round.

"You know, Batouala, I have just come back from Krebedge," said Pangakoura, the great Mandjian chief. "One learns a good deal traveling, doesn't one? For example, that the whites don't like each other. Here's proof, absolute proof —I had a complaint to make against a Portuguese and I went to the commandant, the one we call Kotaya on account of his huge paunch. I told him my story, trimming it up a little, of course.

" 'Pangakoura,' he said, 'you certainly are an idiot, the most idiotic idiot I've ever come across. What! you poor old dunderhead, don't you know a Poutriquess doesn't count? Listen. At the beginning of things—you follow me, do you?— at the beginning of things the N'Gakoura of the whites took the best he had on hand and created the whites. Then he gathered together the leavings and created the dirty niggers like you. Much later, he wanted to make the Portuguese and looked about for something to create them from. There was nothing left but the offal of the blacks. Out of that he kneaded the first Portuguese.' "

Volleys of laughter.

"Don't you think that the drop in the price of rubber is an unexpected piece of luck for us?" asked Batouala. "Even if the commandant had been away, we should not, but for this chance, have been able to come here to the Government grounds to warm our livers. There would have been one of those wretched *boundjoudoulis* on the spot to make us pay

[1] Contains a strong narcotic—Translator's note.

a *pata,* yes, five francs, for what the whites wouldn't have to pay more than a *meya,* ten sous."

"Your words are like clear water," said Yakidji. "We must give thanks to N'Gakoura. All the traders, on account of this happy crisis, have had to go back to Krebedge or Bangui. May they rot to death, their mouths open, their feet in filth."

"And that isn't all. Oh, that isn't all, Batouala," said Yabada. "On account of the grand palavers between the white Zalemans and the white Frandjes, the *yongorogombes* are going to be shipped to M'Poutou. Yes, they're all going off to war at M'Poutou, all the long muskets,[2] all the black soldier-trash. Probably our present masters will join them. I myself think they will."

"Yabao!" quavered Batouala's old father, "as sure as my hairs are white, I think you're taking *kagas* for rivers and your wishes for the reality. Soon it will be three seasons of rains since the Frandjes and the Zalemans have been palavering. Have the Frandjes given any sign of wanting to leave? Not a bit. There's danger over there. Why should they go there to get killed? Each man looks out for his own skin, Yabada."

Louder laughter.

"You're always right, elder. I admit it. But will you allow me to hope that the Zalemans will lick the Frandjes?"

"Ah, you boundoua Yabada! Zalemans—Frandjes: whites all the same. Why change one for the other? We are under the Frandjes, we know their good qualities and their bad qualities. They play with us like a *niaou* with a mouse. In the end the *niaou* always eats the mouse with which it has played. Since sooner or later we're going to be killed and eaten, what use is there to wish for different *niaous* than those we have? It's like escaping buffaloes to fall into the clutches of a lurking panther."

The discussion became general.

"He's right. Why change? The new ones might be worse."

"They don't like us. And we pay them back in their own coin."

[2] "Long muskets" is the nickname for black troops not native to Ubangi-Shari, but brought by the French from the coast and other districts—Translator's note.

"We ought to murder them."

"We ought."

"We will some day, later on."

"When the Banziris, Goubous, Yakomas, Sabangas, Dacpas, all, in short, who talk the Banda or the Mandjia or the Sango language, stop their old quarrels."

"That will be when the Bembe flows backward."

"And Macoude catches the moon in his nets."

Laughter again, so long and loud that one scarcely heard a great noise that sounded in the distance.

"Either you are all sons of a dog," cried Batouala under the influence of pipe and drink. "Or else you are all drunker than I am. Are you men, yes or no? Have the *bazi'nguers* of Snoussi castrated you? I don't know. At any rate I for my part can't help cursing the whites. I remember the time when the M'bis lived peacefully along the Niou-Bangui, between Bessou-Kemo and Kemo-Ouadda. As soon as the first whites appeared, most of us picked up our fetishes, our pots, poultry, mats, dogs, women, goats, children, ducks, and withdrew to the country near Krebedge.

"I was very little then."

"There were struggles; there were huts to build and fields to sow. All useless. The whites settled at Krebedge.

"Another move. We liked Griko. We halted at Griko. The same difficulties getting established there; but we thought we'd be able to draw a peaceful breath. Wrong! The whites— the whites again!—descended on Griko.

"We started off once more. To Grimari. There was a fine location for us in Grimari between the Bembe and the Pombo. We settled there. Alas! before we had completed our building and planting the whites were upon us again. By that time we were worn out and discouraged. Besides, we had lost so many men taking land away from others by force that we were afraid our tribe might be destroyed. So we stayed where we were, and—looked pleasant. . . ."

The great noise in the distance drew nearer.

"No use. Our submissiveness didn't bring us the good will of the whites. Not content with trying to suppress our customs, they wanted to impose theirs on us. We had no right to play *patara* for money. We had no right to get drunk. Our singing and dancing interfered with their sleep. But—pay them a tithe, and they'd deign to put up with our singing and dancing. Pay, pay, pay, always pay! The Government treasuries are insatiable.

"Yet after all, we'd give into them, the mean bullies, if only they applied the same logic to themselves that they do to us. They don't. Listen. Two moons ago that beast Ouorro, drunk as a white man, beat up one of his *yassis*. She was bruised and swollen from head to foot. Blame him if you feel like it. But who of you—eh?—has never beaten his *yassi?*

"The jade actually went to the commandant to complain. It so happened that he had several white guests stopping with him. As a rule, he is that rare thing among the whites—sober. On this occasion he was full to toppling over. He ordered a *tourougou* to place Ouorro under arrest. The *tourougou* carried out his orders rather gently, and the commandant went into a fury and threw an empty bottle at his head. The *tourougou* fell down, the blood streamed from his forehead. He made a face from the pain, and all the whites laughed as though it were a huge joke. That's the way they treat us.

"Yabada, see for yourself. Dare to risk two francs at *patara* under the eyes of the commandant. What'll you get for the awful crime? A lashing with a knotted whip, and with that you'll come off easy. Only the whites may play games of chance."

Batouala's eyes were bloodshot, he shouted and stammered.

"The whites are good for nothing. They call us liars, and treat us accordingly. Our lies don't deceive anyone. If we embellish the truth sometimes, it's because the truth isn't good enough; manioc without salt is tasteless. But the whites! They lie for nothing. They lie with method. They lie by rote, as naturally as they breathe. That's what gives them the advantage over us.

"They say the Negroes under one chief hate the Negroes under another chief. La, la! How about the *boundjoudoulis,* the long muskets, the *Mon Pères* (priests), and the commandants? Do they agree? And if they don't why should we? A man's a man, no matter what his color, here as well as in M'Poutou. . . ."

The huge sound in the distance had become more distinct,

like the droning of thousands of blue or green *voumas* (flies)
about a carcass.

Batouala rose to his feet, and shouted and gesticulated.

"I will never allow anyone to deny the meanness of the
whites. What I blame them most for is their lying and their
cheating. The things they didn't promise us! 'Later on,' they
said, 'you'll see, it's only for your own good that we force you
to work. We'll take only a very, very small part of the money
we make you earn. We'll use what we take to build villages
for you, roads, bridges, machines that run on iron rails by
means of fire.'

"Where are they—the roads, the bridges, the wonderful
machines? Where I ask? Nowhere! Not a sign of them.
Nothing, nothing! And so far from taking only a tiny part
of what we earn, they rob us of our last sou. Aren't we to be
pitied? I ask you, aren't we to be pitied?

"Thirty moons ago we got three francs a kilo for our
rubber. Overnight the price went down. Without offering the
shadow of an explanation, they paid us only fifteen sous for
the same quantity of *banga*. And the Governor chose that
very moment to raise our tax from five to seven and ten
francs.

"Now there isn't anybody who doesn't know that from the
first day of the dry season to the last day of the rainy season
we work just to swell the taxes—if not also to fill the pockets
of our commandants.

"We're nothing but flesh to feed the taxes. We're nothing
but beasts of burden. Beasts? Not even that. Dogs? They
feed their dogs, and tend their horses. We? We're less than
their animals, we're the lowest of the low. They're killing us
by slow degrees. . . ."

A drunken crowd pressed up behind the group of which
Batouala was the centre.

They reviled the whites. Batouala was right, a thousand
times right. Of old, before the coming of the whites, they had
lived happily. They had worked a little, for themselves, they
had eaten and drunk and slept. From time to time they had
had bloody palavers and had plucked the livers from the
dead to eat their courage, and incorporate it in themselves.

Such had been the happy days of old, before the coming of the whites.

Now they were mere slaves. There was nothing to be hoped for from a heartless race. For the *boundjous* (whites) were heartless. They deserted their children by Negro women, and these children, knowing they had sprung from the whites, scorned to associate with the blacks. They were full of hate and envy, these *boundjouvoukos,* these half-whites-half-blacks. They were lazy, mischievous, rotten with vices.

As for the white women, no use talking about them. For a long time they were considered precious objects, and were feared and respected like fetishes. Now they had come down a few pegs. Now it was known that they were just as easy as the black women, and more venal, and had vices the black women were innocent of. . . . But what was the use of talking about it?

And the white women wished to be respected!

Batouala's father held out his hand. The uproar subsided as if by magic. Not so the sound of music and singing that filled the air.

"My children, everything you say is so. Only, you should see there's nothing to be done. Resign yourselves. When the *bamara* (lion) roars, the antelope fears to bell. You are not the stronger. Keep quiet.

"Besides, to be quite frank, we are not here to curse the *boundjous.*

"I am old. While you were discussing, my tongue got dry. Let us shout less and drink more. Next to the bed and the easychair, Pernod is the most important invention of the *boundjous.* My eyesight is not so good, but I thought I noticed several bottles of absinthe. Do you mean to brood on them, Batouala?"

The tension relaxed. They went into fits of laughter. Batouala himself had tears of laughter in his eyes as he hastened to satisfy the waggish old man's desire.

TO AFRICA

Aimé Césaire

In 1939, as he was about to complete his university studies

in Paris and return to his native island in the French Antilles, Aimé Césaire published one of the most remarkable poems of modern times, *Memorandum on My Martinique* (*Cahier d'un Retour au Pays Natal*). Its language was hammered out at white heat in the forge of a volcanic indignation; its apocalyptic voice declared that "for centuries Europe has stuffed us with lies and bloated us with pestilence . . . but the work of man has only begun . . . no race has a monopoly of beauty, intelligence, strength."

Born in Martinique in 1913, M. Césaire received his secondary schooling there, and then went on to Paris, where he spent much time discussing Africa with Léopold S. Senghor, his fellow student at the École Normale Supérieure.

An embattled partisan of his race, Césaire has been, like his friend Senghor, a politician as well as a poet. In 1945 he was elected mayor of Fort-de-France, capital of Martinique. He was also elected a deputy to the French National Assembly, a position he still holds. He has published several volumes of poetry and a tragedy, *And the Dogs Were Silent*.

To Aimé Césaire, who speaks of his "Bambara ancestors," Africa is more than the land of his forbears: it is the country of his selfhood, the redemptive negation of every wrong which the blacks have suffered at the hands of the whites. He is usually credited with the coining of the much discussed term "negritude." (See also selections by Samuel Allen and T. L. Hodgkin.)

In the poem given here, we can see the intensely personal manner in which Césaire identifies himself with the soil of Africa and its people. "I am your son," he avows, but this is much more than a conventional or sentimental gesture. The proof of this is in the style and texture of the verse which is itself a truly tropical soil burgeoning and bursting with sensual life. Whatever the difficulties of his surrealistic imagery, we cannot miss the basic themes: the catastrophe of Africa's enslavement—that "famous plague" which disordered nature; the tenacity of the dream of freedom in the midst of suffering ("whose harrow in my chest makes the rampart of a city"); the beautiful visions of a redeemed land whose miracles are being prepared by each stroke of the peasant's *daba* or hoe. Africa is Césaire's muse as surely as Beatrice was Dante's.

To Africa

(for Wilfredo Lam)

Peasant strike the soil with your *daba*
there's a haste in the soil unravelled by the event's syllable
I remember the famous plague
there hadn't been an announcing star
but only the earth in a wave without shingle kneading from
    space a loaf of grass and reclusion

Strike peasant strike
the first day the birds died
the second day the fish ran aground
the third day the animals emerged from the forest
and girdled the towns in a great belt hot and very strong

Strike the soil with your *daba*
in the soil there's the chart of transmutations and the guiles of
    death
the fourth day the vegetation wilted
and everything from agave to acacia turned to acid
in tufts in resounding vegetal organs
where the prickly wind played flutes and trenchant odors

Strike peasant strike
in the skies windows are born that are my spurting eyes
and whose harrow in my chest makes the rampart of a
    city which refuses to give way to the muleteers of despair
Famine and of yourself swell
mass where a nod risks the anger of the future
strike Anger
at the foot of our fairy-castle is a ballroom for
    the meeting of blood and landscape where the dwarfs
    aiming their mirrors listen in the bends of stone or of salt
    to swell the sex of the gaze

Peasant may there emerge from the mountain's head she
   who wounds the wind
may there cool in her throat a draught of bells
may my wave devour itself in her wave and bring
   us back to the sand drowned in the flesh of torn
   guavas in a purifying hand in beautiful sea-weed
   in flying grain in bubble in recollection in
   precarious tree
let your gesture be a wave that howls and withdraws
   towards the hollow of beloved rocks as in perfecting
   a rebellious island to be born
in the soil there is tomorrow in scruple and the word
   to charge as well as the silence

Peasant the wind where keels glide halts round my face
   the distant hand of a dream
your field in its plunder bursts into life with sea monsters
which I can't ward off
and my gesture is pure as a forehead of forgetfulness
Strike peasant I am your son
at the hour of the setting sun the twilight under my eyelids
   plashes yellow green and tepid unassuaged iguanas
but the beautiful ostrich messenger suddenly born
   of the woman's stirred forms waves to me
   friendship's signs from the future

Translated by Anne Atik

African Dance

PEARL PRIMUS

That great musical realm, American jazz, is known the world
over as of Negro, and ultimately of African, origin. The same
is true of many of the dances of the Americas.

It is not surprising therefore to find the American dancer
Pearl Primus going to Africa, as she has done repeatedly
since 1948, to study African culture and dance. She has been

in Liberia in an official capacity to direct the African Center of Performing Arts at Monrovia.

Miss Primus was born in Trinidad and came to the United States as a young child. She earned her A.B. at Hunter College, her M.A. at New York University, and has been doing work toward a doctorate in anthropology at Columbia University. She is well known as a dancer, choreographer, and scholar of the dance.

For the creative dancer, there can be no situation more inspiring than a society in which the dance accompanies and expresses every significant occasion of life. This inspiration Miss Primus found in African dance. In the following selection, she vividly describes the many dances of Africa which stirred her deeply. Her enthusiasm is the fusion point of her love of the dance and her identification with her African heritage.

AFRICAN DANCE IS basic, vital! For me it is the source, the well from which I draw inspiration for my work. African dance is complete. It ranges from the subtlest and most lyric of movements to the most dynamic, from the most sophisticated presentations to the simplest. It can defy space in fantastic leaps into the air or burrow into the earth. It does not limit itself to any one part of the body but employs the use of even the most minute muscle. It varies from the slowest and stateliest of court dances to those which move so rapidly the eye cannot hope to register all that is happening.

It is hard for me to think of Africa without hearing again the great drums, witnessing once more in memory the elaborate ceremonies and experiencing, as if still there, the inexplicable ecstasy of dancing with the greatest of dancers. Again and again I stand in awe above the plunging rapids of the mighty river Congo or kneel before the Oni of Ife to receive my name, *Omowale,* child returned home. These are but part of the memories which ignore the travelling hands of the clock. I must pause in the writing to quiet that part of me which cries out "Dance!"

It is possible for purposes of this discussion to divide Africa, as the anthropologist does, into the nine culture areas. It is even possible to classify it according to the three big areas thought of by students of art. However, I choose to use the purely original and arbitrary division of city and jungle. In Africa the people do not like the word jungle. They feel, and rightly so, that movies have so distorted and falsified accounts of life in the interior that most foreigners on hearing the word jungle immediately picture frightful areas of tractless land with wild animals constantly raiding villages and with men wilder than the animals destroying each other. The word bush is used.

I use the word jungle to mean other than city. I am well aware that of this vast continent only a relatively small portion—in fact, one fourth—is covered with true jungle. Another fourth is made up of lakes and deserts, and grassland in varying degrees occupies nearly one-half of Africa. I like the word, for it suggests the music of the interior—whether that music be of voices, birds, instruments, rivers or silence. It is with respect that I speak the word jungle. It is with unmistakable pride that I write of the rich heritage of a great people.

To expect to do more than scratch the surface of an introduction to dance in Africa in these few pages would be attempting the ridiculous. Even if I were to consider the dances of only one tribe, I would not be able to fit all the material into one article, for dance in Africa is not a separate art, but a part of the whole complex of living. What I shall try to do is to capture its essence by discussing briefly certain essential elements.

Dance was and still is of vital importance in the life of the African people. I do not usually say much about the dance in the cities of Africa for many of these cities are very much like parts of America and Europe. Many of the people dress in European clothing and hold heated discussions on world affairs. They travel to and from all parts of the world for study, business or vacation purposes. When they dance, if they do, it is the fox trot, the rhumba, the waltz and even the lindy hop. The native dance is often called pagan and in many cities it is completely forbidden by the officials. The hi-life, which is a dance now common along the entire West Coast, is the African version of Calypso. While it is most exciting and enjoyable, one must leave it and travel up country into those areas where every important phase of life is still accompanied by dance.

Here people use their bodies as instruments through which every conceivable motion or event is projected. The result is a strange but hypnotic marriage between life and dance. The two are inseparable. When a child is born, when a man is buried, there is the dance. People dance the sowing of the seed and the harvest, puberty rites, hunting, warfare. They dance for rain, sun, strong and numerous children, marriage and play. Love, hatred, fear, joy, sorrow, disgust, amazement, all these and all other emotions are expressed through rhythmic movement.

As if their bodies, developed through centuries of dance, sunshine and struggle, are not enough to portray their feelings, they create powerful rhythms and songs to accompany their movements. Priests, warriors, hunters, doctors were primarily dancers. I once knew a herbalist, as the native medicine man is called. When he moved, he was like fire hurling itself with terrifying control into space. He would wrap himself around the trunk of a tree, and, using his long arms and neck, he would become a serpent. Then, filled with the healing power of the deity he invoked, he would unwind himself and encircle the sick (The snake is a symbol for many things, among them the healing power). So he would dance until the spirit crept from him.

Dance is only a part of the whole or the complex. The ceremony is the complex. For the ceremony, the master artists carve and paint fantastic masks. The designers create strange and wonderful costumes. Geniuses draw music from everywhere.

I group the ceremonies of fertility, birth, initiation, engagement, marriage and death under the term life cycle, for each normal individual within a tribal setup passes through each phase. These ceremonies are mostly religious in nature.

There are many types of fertility dances, for no two tribes have identical folkways. But each fertility dance has the same purpose. Each one is a prayer before the sowing that the seed may take strong root and grow well. In certain instances it is believed that the dance will chase away all evil, thus allowing the seed to germinate. Aside from the hypnotic beauty of these dances, there is a very interesting concept involved. The prayer is offered not only for fertility of vegetable and animal life but also for fertility of thought. If a chief has to make a great decision for his tribe, the dancers are called forth to dance, so that his mind will become fertile with strong thoughts.

Among people living along its banks, the river is a symbol of fertility. It overflows onto the land, watering and fertilizing the soil. It rises sometimes from an unseen source and journeys with its burden of life to the larger waters. So it is at a certain time during the year before the seed is sown, the women come forth dressed in the green of growing things. Like an endless river they move, their bodies fitting one behind the other—curve of abdomen into curve of back and each hand, each foot, each hand moving alike. These women, themselves the bearers of seeds, become the river flowing in the intricate and winding patterns set by tradition.

The ceremonies for birth vary among the tribes and fall into several broad categories. (1) There are those thanking God for the numerous births and the good harvest of the past season. These are communal and are usually danced once a year at the planting season. (2) There are those called by individual families to celebrate a birth or to pray for divine assistance during a difficult or prolonged passage of the unborn child into the world. (3) There are those danced by pregnant women for "good birth" and for fertility and continued blessings for their people. (4) There are those danced at the Naming Ceremony, for only when he receives his name will the infant become a part of his tribe. This classification does not include dances by secret societies or individual medicine men or doctors. Nor does it include any of those ceremonies which occur on singular occasions. For instance, among the people of Makamba, the *Ikinyabugiga* is performed only when twins are born. While celebrating the birth, the ceremony achieves another purpose. He who excels in the dance may choose a wife without having to pay a bride price.

The next of the great religious ceremonies is called the initiation or, more correctly, the period of the Initiation, known to us as puberty rites. This is perhaps the most important and fascinating of all the phases through which man must pass. The term is used to include both sexes. Bared of its trappings, the Initiation means simply this: Man cannot live with fear. Man must meet fear, conquer or be conquered by it. The very existence of a group depends upon the individuals within that group. A weak person is a threat to his society. Therefore, from babyhood, the individual is prepared physically and psychologically to endure the most severe tests. Then at a specific time, which varies with the tribe, he is placed on his own to face fear. Fear may be in the form of masked dancers depicting the ancestors returning to chastise. Fear may be in the form of silence and loneliness. Fear may be excited by physical pain, hunger, thirst. Fear may be excited by the thunder of seen or unseen forms. Whichever way it comes, it must be conquered.

Those who fear the period of the Initiation remain forever children. They cannot marry. They must run in the fields and endure the scorn of their society. Those who conquer, emerge as men and women ready to take up the occupation of life— to marry and to augment their tribe. Circumcision usually accompanies the Initiation, and in certain areas clitorectomy is still practiced.

The newly initiated dance with the pride and power of the conquest. These dances are so energetic and compelling that they seem spontaneous, as if created on the spot. The truth is this: during the period of childhood and the actual preparation in the bush schools, the individual learns these dances. There is not only strict emphasis upon the technique, sequence, timing and execution of the dance but also drill to achieve perfection. When the initiated has conquered fear, a new dimension is added to his personality. He has lived through this period. He has experienced the terror and the exultation. At the root of his being, he has experienced deep ecstasy. He is a human volcano. The technique, the sequence he has learned become a vehicle in which his soul can leap to the heavens. Where before he merely jumped because he should, he now defies the laws of gravity. He soars through space because he must. Where he was taught the technique of a turn he now becomes a top, spinning himself into the earth. A child left the village but a man returns!

Among most of the tribes, the ceremonies of engagement and marriage are still accompanied by the dance. Among groups living at the southern tip of Urundi, the maidens dance their acceptance of a proposal. Imitating the crown bird, they dance in a circle. Then with tiny running steps, they fly down the green sloping mountain sides and seem to disappear in the rich vegetation. But in most areas it is the marriage which is the occasion for feasting and dance—the marriage, before or after it is consummated. Sometimes the ceremony is exceedingly simple. After a brief reminder by her women folk about the role of a good wife, the bride takes her belongings and follows her husband to his house. Sometimes the entire village gathers, singing and throwing teasing remarks at the couple, and the dancing will go on long after the bride has left the compound or entered her new home.

The last phase—the final passage—or, as the Bushongo people say, "the return"—death! The spirits of the ancestors are all around, never wandering too far to return either to help or punish the living. In certain tribes, when a person dies, it is the duty of the living to rejoice and to celebrate with great dancing so that the spirit of the deceased will not feel slighted. Sometimes by dance and song the spirit is encouraged to journey to a place of rest before returning. It has been recorded that dancing was continuous for two and a half months after the death of a chief of the Lamba people of Northern Rhodesia.

This belief in the ancestors as having spiritual existence in the invisible world around them has caused much trouble between European and African groups. Whole villages are sometimes ordered to move to make way for roads, stores, offices of dwellings for the European. Land is not just a matter of so much earth, a house, a path, a market! It is part of a way of life. It is an intangible shared by the living and the dead. It is loved, respected, handed down from generation to generation. To leave the land is to desert the ancestors, the sacred shrines and the essence of all that was and is. Dance is a part of living and no part exists without the influence of other parts to make the whole. The culture of displaced tribes soon becomes dissipated. The struggle to live in a new environment is acute. The dances, even when performed, soon lose their meaning and their form.

The life cycle is completed by the return to the invisible. A common belief that there is no mourning or weeping permitted when a death occurs is based upon the exuberance of the dancers, the chants, the excited drumming, the gaiety and the feasting. But sometimes the weeping is inside the house. True it is controlled, because tradition often decides who may or must weep. Often professional mourners are hired to wail from the moment death occurs until the interment. These people, superb performers, seemingly schooled in the use of effective timing, are in direct contrast to the display of happiness about them. For the African there is no thing or person or situation which is not in itself a duality. No good without bad, no happiness without sorrow, no strength without weakness, no pride without shame, no life without death. This is often projected into visible and audible forms as here—wailing mourners, rending their garments and rolling in the dust contrast with the dancers in gorgeous costumes performing among the festive villagers.

But for the people who live with the magic language of the dance, these occasions for dance are not enough. There are dances to accompany the hunt. Even now among tribes where hunting is becoming an occupation of the past, men still dance the glories of the big hunt. They still costume themselves in spectacular skins and vines and to the throbbing of drums and the sharp notes of bells, they stalk imaginary animals.

Among other dances which speak of the past, are those done by the warriors. Today most of these dancers are old, but they need only the whisper of encouragement to bring forth the powerful war dances of their youth. Old men! But once the cry is sounded, once the chant begins, wrinkles disappear, thin bodies become powerful, the squinting eye opens, piercing the present. The war dance begins! The mantle of age is flung aside for a while. I have stood in the village of Mushenge experiencing emotions for which I can find no words, as the old men of the once powerful Bakuba tribe danced the ancient Bushache. Their faces were lit with inner exultation as they lifted their knees high in the sureness of the attack. Then turning their backs abruptly on the unseen enemy, the muscles of their torsos like trembling snakes of defiance, they would describe vigorous circles with their wands of fur and sprays of manioc leaves. The very air was waiting. Then, suddenly, a cry like mountains ripping in half burst from the throats of the drummers. The earth jumped! the dancers attacked! the imaginary enemy crumbled to the ground!

There are dances which are the exclusive property of certain occupations. For example, the bronze workers of Benin, Nigeria, can tell exactly what type of work a man does, how long he has been doing it and what level of achievement he has attained—all by the dance. There are dances which accompany story telling. Legends and tribal histories are told in words and with dance. Secret societies have special dances. Medicine men or herbalists are trained to excel in certain dances. There are dances to ward off sickness and those to cure it. There are dances to celebrate the harvest, to welcome visitors, and to mark the coronation or stepping into office of a new chief.

Among the most exciting dances are those like the Attilogu of the Ibo people of Nigeria. Every muscle shouts the joy of being alive. Most lovely are those which portray the beauty and grace of the chief of the tribe. The royal dancers of the king of the giant Watusi dance his elegance, his strength, his invincibility. They say he is as graceful as a bird, as swift as lightning. When he speaks, they cannot move and when he is absent, they must not be seen for they are his voice. I see them now, their hats waving, their bells sounding over the hills, their faces brilliant with ecstasy, their skins gleaming under the golden sun.

There are countless others, but we can sum up by saying that any occasion within the life of the tribe is one for the dance. The dance is strong magic. The dance is a spirit. It turns the body to liquid steel. It makes it vibrate like a guitar. The body can fly without wings. It can sing without voice. The dance is strong magic. The dance is life!

THE GOOD GRAY BARD IN TIMBUKTU

M. B. TOLSON

The prologue to the present volume consists of the first section of Melvin B. Tolson's *Libretto for the Republic of Liberia*. Our epilogue is taken from the last section of the same work where the future of Africa is symbolized by an exhilarating suite of passages about a futuristic transportation network. The second section of the *Libretto* which we give here evokes the legendary past of Africa: medieval black empires, concourses of learned men, and the final victory of the "locusts"—the rapacious Europeans

Melvin B. Tolson was born in Moberly, Missouri and was educated at Fisk, Lincoln, and Columbia Universities. He is Professor of Creative Literature and Director of the Dust Bowl Theater at Langston University in Oklahoma. Tolson's interest in the theater shows up in the powerful forensic effects of his verse. As these excerpts witness, he has made his own the poetic discoveries of Hart Crane and other modern masters, so that the visual and auditory impact of his language is extraordinary. Tolson is also the author of a work-in-progress, an epic poem on the Negro in America, entitled "Harlem Gallery."

The Good Gray Bard in Timbuktu chanted:
"Brow tron lo—eta ne a ne won oh gike!" [1]
Before Liberia was, Songhai was: before
America set the raw foundling on Africa's
Doorstep, before the Genoese diced west,
Burnt warriors and watermen of Songhai
Tore into bizarreries the uniforms of Portugal
And sewed an imperial quilt of tribes.

[1] I am informed that variations of this eironeia or mockery may be found in scores of African languages. It means here: The world is too large—that's why we do not hear everything. *cf.* Pliny, *Historia Naturalis,* II: "There is always something new from Africa." Also Swift:
So geographers, in Afric maps
With savage pictures fill their gaps. . . .

In Milan and Mecca, in Balkh and Bombay,
Sea lawyers in the eyeservice of sea kings
Mixed liquors with hyperboles to cure deafness.
Europe bartered Africa crucifixes for red ivory,
Gewgaws for black pearls, pierres d'aigris for green gold:
Soon the rivers and roads became clog almanacs!
The Good Gray Bard in Timbuktu chanted:
"Wanawake wanazaa ovyo! Kazi yenu wazungu!" [2]

Black Askia's fetish was his people's health:
The world his world, he gave the Bengal light
Of Books the Inn of Court in Songhai. Beba mzigo! [3]
The law of empathy set the market price,
Scaled the word and deed: the gravel-blind saw
Deserts give up the ghost to green pastures!

Solomon in all his glory had no Oxford,
Alfred the Great no University of Sankore:
Footloose professors, chimney sweeps of the skull,
From Europe and Asia; youths, souls in one skin,
Under white scholars like El-Akit, under
Black humanists like Bagayogo. Karibu wee! [4]

The Good Gray Bard in Timbuktu chanted:
"Europe is an empty python in hiding grass!"

Lia! Lia! The river Wagadu, the river Bagana,
Became dusty metaphors where white ants ate canoes,
And the locust Portuguese raped the maiden crops,
And the sirocco Spaniard razed the city-states,
And the leopard Saracen bolted his scimitar into
The jugular vein of Timbuktu. Dieu seul est grand!

And now the hyenas whine among the barren bones
Of the seventeen sun sultans of Songhai,
And hooded cobras, hoodless mambas, hiss

---

[2] "The women keep having children right and left. It's the work of you white men."
[3] "Lift the loads." This repetend is tacked on *ex tempore* to ballads growing out of a diversity of physical and spiritual experiences.
[4] Among primitives hospitality is a thing poetic and apostolic. *Jogoo linawika: Karibu wee.* "The rooster crows, 'Welcome!'" *Mbuzi wanalia: Karibu wee.* "The goats bleat, 'Welcome.'"

In the gold caverns of Falémé and Bambuk,
And puff adders, hook scorpions, whisper
In the weedy corridors of Sankoré. Lia! Lia! [5]
The Good Gray Bard chants no longer in Timbuktu:
"The maggots fat on yeas and nays of nut empires!"

POLITICAL ELITES AND AFRICA'S FUTURE

St. Clair Drake

An American Negro sociologist, St. Clair Drake, here offers
a compass for the use of African political leaders in navi-
gating the heavy seas of social change. The compass has only
one fixed point: "the expansion of productive effort." All
other points are to be relative to this. He calls this perspective "pragmatic pluralism."

Dr. Drake realizes that in following such a perspective the
black elite may exert severe pressures—often as coercive as
any hitherto used by white colonialists—against the "backward" ways of their own people. As a countervailing force
against the overly pragmatic, Dr. Drake hopes the new re-
gimes would permit the free functioning of poets, artists,
thinkers, and religionists. However, the question remains
whether rulers of their own volition choose to put up with
such "encumbrances."

Dr. Drake is professor of sociology at Roosevelt College,
Chicago and has also served as head of the Sociology Department at the University College of Ghana. He is senior author
of *Black Metropolis,* an important study of Negro life in
Chicago.

AGAINST THE background of the basic socio-cultural reality,
the African political elites have to decide what phases of their
cultures they will defend, which they will ignore, and which
they will denounce. They must decide which specific cultural
manifestations they will encourage and which they will suppress. They must also decide such issues as how much force
to use and when and where, as well as the tantalizing prob-

---

[5] The word means weep and seems to follow the patterns of
otototoi in the Aeschylean chorus.

lems of timing, posed in the question: How long can we wait? In the past, the onus for forcing the pace of social change, for disrupting old patterns, has rested upon the outsider— the European or Asiatic invader. Increasingly in the future, the hostilities, the resentments, and sometimes the violent attacks of traditionalists and conservatives will be directed at the new African elites. The experiences of Nehru and Sukarno in Asia and of the rulers of the new Ghana and Sudan indicate that these issues will not be easily resolved.

Pragmatic pluralism, like cultural relativism, concedes that all of the varied schemes for living on the African continent have had their usefulness, but squarely faces the fact that they are now in a state of constant change and that they are all suffering from social disorganization incident to accelerated contacts with the products of Western thought and technology and with Islam and Christianity.

Pragmatic pluralism implies the acceptance of responsibility on the part of intellectual and political elites within so-called backward and underdeveloped areas for trying to guide the process of re-integration. The approach to the problem is pragmatic in the sense that no fixed and final goals are set up, and no doctrinaire methods of dealing with change are accepted. The approach is pluralistic in that it does not evaluate any one society and its cultural products as being more desirable than another, and it accepts the desirability, as well as the inevitability, of cultural diversity within the emerging new nations.

Pragmatic pluralism does not view social disintegration as an unmitigated evil, but rather as a dialectical process in which social reorganization proceeds concurrently with social disorganization. Old cultural forms are constantly undergoing modification because of the impact of outside ideas and because of changes induced from within the social system. It recognizes the fact that one response to rapid change is a tendency for some people to cling more tenaciously to the old and to utilize old forms in the pursuit of new goals amid the insecurities of urbanization and industrialization. An attempt is made to conserve what is suitable in the old social structures and customs and to deliberately ban customary behavior only when it clearly militates against the goals of the emerging adjustment pattern.

Pragmatic pluralism accepts only one value as the key value toward which all other values should be ordinated, and that value is the desirability of increasing the productive capacity of the group and its per capita income and of raising the material standard of living of the people. This is a democratically derived value, for there is no doubt about the fact that the world masses, however much they may disagree on everything else, not only desire an improvement in their political well-being but also repudiate any political leadership that does not cater to this revolution of rising expectations. Dramatic evidence is sometimes available of the desire for a better standard of living, such as that revealed in a report by a U.N. Trusteeship Council Visiting Mission in Africa:

> However contrarily the Haya people may have acted in the past, the Mission heard and saw evidence that suggests that they have greatly improved themselves in very recent times . . . They have gone far in the democratization of their local government. . . . Their development plan fund provided more money in 1953 than was spent on the Government and the Native authority development schemes in the whole of neighboring Sukumaland. . . . Their cooperative coffee-marketing system, only five years old, is rapidly approaching the same stage of development as the much older organization of the Chagga on Mount Kilimanjaro.

All customs are judged first in reference to whether they do or do not hamper this expansion of productive effort. Appeals are made to the people in terms of this broadest common denominator of value.

Pragmatic pluralism involves an eclectic approach toward specific borrowing from other societies. It leads to a refusal to condemn either capitalist or socialist systems wholesale or to adopt either in toto. Doctrinaire economic and social schemes are considered unrealistic.

Pragmatic pluralism accepts economic priority as a planning and engineering device, fully realizing that new non-economic values are the real ends of human endeavor. However, it would be presumptuous to try to set such goals. They grow. It is recognized that the media of mass communications and the agencies of rapid transportation, as well as political and commercial factors, have bound all the societies of the earth together into one world, whether they like the fact or not. Any local society now is just one facet of a world society. The great debate goes on continuously as to what kind of basic values all will eventually adhere to. Pragmatic pluralism tries to involve everyone in the debate. In the United Nations, the debate goes on in the Economic and Social Council where people from the ends of the earth frame the Charter of Human Rights, sign pronouncements against forced labor and try to outlaw discrimination against women and to curb the drug traffic. And in a remote Afghanistan village where the people have secured their livelihood for many generations by growing poppies for making opium, it is patiently explained that this is now considered antisocial. And the people vote to change their mode of subsistence, asking only for teachers and equipment in order to learn a new way! Instances could be multiplied to illustrate the process of new values in the making. At any given moment, it is perhaps possible to make a rough assessment of the cultural traits and social usages which the world elites who have shared in the common stock of "civilized" ideas would rate as "desirable" and "undesirable." Today in most of Africa, judgments on African culture traits would probably run somewhat as follows:

JUDGMENTS OF EDUCATED ELITES	TRAITS SURVIVING FROM TRADITIONAL AFRICAN CULTURES	TRAITS CHARACTERISTIC OF THE NEW TRANSITIONAL AFRICAN SOCIETIES
Highly Disapproved	1. gustatory cannibalism 2. ritual cannibalism 3. Pharaonic operation 4. human sacrifice 5. sorcery witchcraft 6. mutilations at initiation ceremonies 7. inefficient technology 8. tooth filing and evulsion	1. increasing sexual promiscuity 2. juvenile delinquency 3. gangsterism and hoodlumism 4. neglect of hygiene and sanitation 5. drunkenness 6. illiteracy 7. political apathy

JUDGMENTS OF EDUCATED ELITES	TRAITS SURVIVING FROM TRADITIONAL AFRICAN CULTURES	TRAITS CHARACTERISTIC OF THE NEW TRANSITIONAL AFRICAN SOCIETIES
	9. pawning and slavery 10. consulting oracles for serious decisions 11. secret societies which murder 12. complete public nudity on the part of adults 13. intertribal warfare 14. cruel punishments	
Moderately Disapproved	1. curing disease by magic 2. ornamental scarification 3. eating of foods which the West defines as "disgusting" 4. seminudity in public on the part of adults 5. polygyny 6. animal sacrifice 7. trial by ordeal 8. kin avoidance and other taboos	1. lack of thrift by masses 2. "frivolity" of youth 3. tendencies toward political dictatorship by new elites 4. half acculturated behavior in public
Approved If It Does Not Hamper "Progress"	1. excessive discussion of problems by elders 2. lavish hospitality 3. retention of native clothes 4. ancestor cult 5. matrilineality 6. marriage gifts 7. celebration of funerals 8. extended family ties 9. communal land tenure	1. paid employment for urban women 2. voluntary associations 3. Christianity 4. Islam 5. new professional and trade associations

Most of the traits which are listed as highly disapproved have already been eliminated during the past hundred years, except in some internally marginal areas. Witchcraft is a significant exception, being on the increase in many areas because of new insecurities. Nowhere do any elite groups feel that it is necessary to make massive onslaughts and crusades against these remnants of the past. Sometimes an attack on some one aspect of the traditional arises as a part of the ongoing new political process, as in Ghana in 1954, when Ashantis belonging to the Convention Peoples Party attacked the very validity of the belief in the Golden Stool, the soul of the nation, because the Ashanti ruler had thrown the weight of the stool against the CPP. On the other hand, in the case of Mau-Mau, traditional forms of oath-taking and social organization were revived to aid in a political struggle. In some instances the attack on the disapproved traits is vigorous and direct, as in the case of Liberia's laws against the Leopard Society and similar "subversive organizations" or as in the case of Tunisia's law against polygyny with supporting sanctions quoted from the Koran! Sometimes they are very indirect, as when recently the Eastern Region of Nigeria appointed a commission to study the rise in the "bride price." The Commission took the opportunity to point out in the preface that although all of the groups who had testified in hearings defended polygyny, the members of the committee wanted to go on record as opposing it and hoped it would eventually die out. Pragmatic pluralism avoids making an issue of customary behavior unless it indisputably hampers productive efficiency, outrages the emerging "world conscience" or holds the group up to extreme ridicule by outsiders.

This evaluative scheme, which seems to be emerging among the elites of "backward areas" and which I have called "pragmatic pluralism," could find vigorous reinforcement from the approaches developed by the anthropologists, although many of the leaders no doubt see anthropology as the "handmaid of imperialism." As Africans take on the role of ruling elites, they need detached and careful studies of the customs of their own people, if they are to make intelligent decisions. They need the kinds of analyses that point out the costs that will have to be paid in human terms if various forms of alternative action are pursued. They will particularly need to know the probable unintended consequences of various social actions. Imperialist governments sometimes found the use of government anthropologists to be a wise investment in helping them to implement specific programs. Why should not the new governments also find anthropologists helpful? Anthropology gave us the original framework of cultural relativism, which taught the detachment necessary to view societies objectively. In recent years new fields such as applied anthropology and action anthropology have come into being to use the findings of the discipline for carrying out action within some specified framework of value.

Any type of pragmatic philosophy runs the risk of turning into opportunism or cynicism. The only guarantee that a society with its political elites operating pragmatically will serve the common good is the presence within the society of a considerable minority of social scientists who remain cultural relativists; of poets and artists who refuse to abandon the point of view of romantic primitivists; and of relentless social critics—religious and intellectual—who measure all action by the criteria of absolutes. This becomes the really creative type of pluralism within a society, as opposed to that arising from ethnic differences. The lot of this evaluative minority will not always be an easy one, just as it has not been an easy one in Western societies. Practical men always have a measure of distrust for those who, as James Branch Cabell phrased it, have "heard the music from behind the moon"; or those who say, "Our Kingdom is not of this world"; or those who refuse to consider any custom or social usage sacred. But if Africa is to develop truly "civilized" societies, however small—and we must never forget fifth-century Athens—it must eventually produce from within its own bosom such evaluators. It must produce its own Socrates, Voltaire, Martin Luther, and Karl Marx. Their contributions will be not African, but universal.

THE BLACK POET'S SEARCH FOR IDENTITY

SAMUEL W. ALLEN

In this extract from his essay, "Tendencies in African Poetry," Samuel Allen, a poet himself, examines the growth of a positive racial consciousness, and an African orientation, among the Negro poets, a consciousness that defiantly shakes off "the censorious presence of European thought and judgment." He is mainly concerned here with the French-writing Negroes of the Caribbean area.

Mr. Allen, a graduate of Fisk University and Harvard, is a lawyer, a poet, and a student of the humanities. His first volume of poems was published in Germany in a bilingual edition under the pen name, Paul Vesey. During an extended stay in Europe after World War II, Mr. Allen contributed to the important magazine, *Présence Africaine,* published in Paris. In 1961, he joined the United States Information Agency in Washington.

AFRICA, "A STAR IN ILL REPOSE," has begun to rouse from a troubled sleep. The political fact of Africa's epoch of liberation is presently accompanied and has been preceded by the effort of African writers to cast off the cultural imprint of colonial Europe, in whose schemata too often the African feels his "road follows the tortuous curves of abasement and his future, lost wretch, shall be his shameful present." [1] Although the African literary enterprise is as yet modest in its claims, the poet is clarifying the spiritual significance of the unfolding of a different world. Jean-Paul Sartre in "Orphée Noir," [2] his remarkable preface to Léopold Senghor's anthology of Negro poetry, has pointed out that the poet as *vates* or prophet, in the original Greek sense of the word, has announced the suppressed aspirations of the Negro and is the forerunner in the double process of destruction and creation implicit in the formation of a new imaginative world free of the proscriptions of a colonial West.

The task is one of fashioning a truer sense of identity, a renewal of that organic vision of the world without which political and economic enfranchisement will be a mere setting forth of another people on the modern road to their mechanistic, streamlined salvation, barren of any inner meaning. Our attention in this development is drawn not only to Negro poets of the African continent but also to the large

[1] David Diop, "Un Blanc m'a dit," *Anthologie de la nouvelle poésie nègre et malgache,* ed. Léopold Senghor (Paris: Presses Universitaires de France, 1948), p. 175.

[2] Jean-Paul Sartre, "Orphée Noir," trans. S. W. Allen, *Présence Africaine* (1st series, "l'Art Nègre," Nos. 10-11). It is a tribute to the catholicity of the French intellectual tradition that in "Orphée Noir" for the first time in either hemisphere a philosophic talent of the magnitude of Sartre has devoted his critical concern to the unique cultural situation of the Negro African in Western society.

body of those poets of the Caribbean area, particularly those writing in French, for most of whom Africa is felt to be the fertile source of their inspiration, both the origin of their enslavement and the spiritual goal in their quest for liberation. In this group would fall Césaire, Roumain, Dépestre, Damas, Laleau, and Niger, who for the most part are more intense in their reaction to the estrangement of the African in the West than the poets of the continent itself are.

These poets, like poets the world over, deal with the great themes of human life: love, death, religious experience, friendship, etc. There is, however, common to all of them a passionate concern for the alien role of the Negro in the West, a preoccupation which, as Richard Wright has noted in regard to the poetry of the American Negro, has evoked varying reactions on the part of the white world, from a fraternal admonition to treat more "universal" themes to expressions of a rather bored annoyance with the "eternal obsession with race." In this regard it is significant to note that there is in modern African poetry a strong self-assurance, a new feeling of confidence in the expression of racial and cultural pride. This poetry shows indifference to the attitudes of those who are strangers to the Negro poets' world attitudes which involve, moreover, a failure to perceive that the proscriptions of the Negro in the West have been for him, except for certain varying superficial aspects, as absolute and inevitable a part of human life as the usual subjects of poetic concern are for the poet writing in a dominant tradition. It is apparent that the modern African, however, writes more and more for the African, or for himself, and less for a European public which would by its critical direction influence and blunt the instruments of reconnaissance which his poems are.

In the works of these poets there is a recognition of the painful reality of the destruction of an ancestral way of life, which inevitably holds in retrospect much of the idyllic character that a pastoral Greece has held for a post-Renaissance Europe. Senghor opens his anthology with the striking poem of Leon Damas, of French Guiana, "They came that night," in which the frenzy of the African dance is suddenly frozen and transformed before the reader's eyes into a museum relic:

They came that night when the
tom
    tom
        rolled from
                rhythm to
                    rhythm
                        the frenzy
the eyes
the frenzy the hands the frenzy
the feet of statues
SINCE THEN
how many of us
are dead
since they came that night when the
tom
    tom
        rolled from
                rhythm to
                    rhythm
                        the frenzy
the eyes
the frenzy the hands the frenzy
The feet of statues.[3]

And David Diop, from Senegal, evokes the same disaster:

My women pressed their lips
To the hard thin lips of the cold eyed conquerors
And my children yielded their peaceful nudity
To uniforms of blood and steel.
Your voice, too, is dead.
Slavery's chains have bruised my heart,
Tom toms of my nights, tom toms of my fathers.[4]

Back beyond the desperate moment when the enslaver loomed in the village pathway, there appears in the poet's

[3] Senghor, *Anthologie,* p. 6. Unless otherwise indicated, the translations are by Samuel Allen.
[4] Olumbe Bassir, *An Anthology of West African Verse* (Ibadan, Nigeria: Ibadan University Press, 1957), p. 54. The excellent translations of this and other French poems in the Bassir anthology are by Margaret Peatman.

vision the nostalgic image of an Africa of human warmth and
pastoral beauty, of tribal dances and story telling by the old
men at night around the fire. Jacques Roumain, the Haitian
revolutionary, whose poetry is both intensely militant and at
the same time expressive of the most exquisite pathos in its
search for the spiritual peace of a lost heritage, gives effective testimony to this void:

> That is the long way to Guinea
> Death leads you there
> There are the branches, trees, the forest.
> Listen to the rustling of the wind
>   in its skein of eternal night . . .
> That is the long way to Guinea
>   no brilliant reception is prepared for you
>   in the black country of black people:
> Under a smoky sky pierced by the shrieks of birds
> Where around the eyes of swampy rivers
> The trees open their eyelashes upon a fading light,
> There waiting for you is a quiet village
>   at the water's edge,
> The hut of your fathers and the family stone
>   on which your brow rests at last.[5]

In this poetry Africa appears as a lost paradise, an idyll of
a vaguely remembered youth, where the self was undivided
and unharassed by the subsequent pervasive surveillance of
a civilization alien to the poet's origins and his inspiration. It
is important to realize that it is not an Africa geographically
fixed and determined that is most significant here, although
the physical reality of a "homeland" holds a transcending
value for most peoples. Independently of this aspect, however, Africa emerges from this poetry as a symbol of man
in his pristine integrity, at one with himself and his world, a
part of all he surveys.

African poetry today is concerning itself with the task of
restoring not the identical vision of the African world before
its invasion and enslavement, but a vision in which the Afri-

[5] Jacques Roumain, "Guinea," *Black Orpheus*, No. 2 (Jan. 1958,
Ibadan, Nigeria), p. 27.

can can claim an integral part and which is not eternally clouded by the censorious presence of European thought and judgment. This central concern is evident in the work of African poets of both English and French expression. In English, however, there has not thus far been a development assuming the stature of a literary movement, as in the French language.

It was in the late thirties that Etienne Léro, a Martiniquan poet and student in Paris, turned from his purely literary studies to philosophy, as a result of his constant reflection upon the problems of the West Indian writer and the obstacles to his creative effort. In association with Jules Monnerot and René Menil, he founded the literary journal, *Légitime Défense,* of which Senghor writes:

> More than a review, *Légitime Défense* was a cultural movement. Beginning with a Marxian analysis of the society of the West Indies, it discovered in the Caribbean the descendants of the Negro-African slaves held for three centuries in the stultifying condition of the proletariat. Léro affirmed that only surrealism could deliver them from their taboos and express them in their integrity[6]

Léro died shortly thereafter, and though he had adopted surrealism as a method, it did not prove in his hand the liberating influence he had conceived it to be. His work as theoretician, however, provided the weapon for others to use later in eliminating the cramping tutelage of Europe.

The French language itself is not the perfect instrument for the expression of the African poet in his integrity. French is the language of a people distinguished for their analytical genius, for the precision of their logic—a language excelling in its mastery of the abstract, but not in its description of the concrete. The African poet finds that his impulse is essentially passionate and concrete, having little to do with the logical exposition of abstract ideas. The Haitian poet, Laleau, is specific in his complaint:

> This beleaguered heart
> Alien to my language and my dress
> On which bite like a brace

[6] Senghor, *op. cit.,* p. 49.

The borrowed sentiments and customs of Europe;
Mine is the agony
The unutterable despair
In breaking with the cold words of France
The pulsing heart of the Senegal.[7]

The French symbolist Mallarme said of his language, "It is the neutral language *par excellence,* since its genius requires an attenuation of all colors too vibrant or variegated." [8] Senghor has observed that the Negro African inspiration is characterized by the quality of its passion. It is evident that a language evolved over the centuries by a people neutral in affective disposition would find a more deeply passionate ethos excessive and resistant to its representational grasp.

Accordingly, the "black apostles," as they have been described, find themselves obliged to "edit their gospel" of liberation in the language of the oppressor, the language they were forced to begin to learn amid the death cries of their murdered ancestors, the language that has since become the vehicle for the rationale of their proclaimed racial inferiority and the daily instrument of their abasement:

> The white man killed my father
> My father was proud
> The white man seduced my mother
> My mother was beautiful
> The white man burnt my brother
>   beneath the noon day sun
> My brother was strong.
> His hands red with black blood
> The white man turned to me
> And in the Conqueror's voice said
> "Hey, boy! a chair, a napkin, a drink!" [9]

A thousand and one derogatory connotations roused by the language recall the image of the "ignorant black savage,"

[7] Senghor, *op. cit.,* p. 108.
[8] Sartre, *loc. cit.,* p. 226.
[9] David Diop, "Le Temps du Martyr," *An Anthology of West African Verse,* p. 53.

of the superstition of a "darkest Africa," from which the "native" is rescued to share, insofar as he is able, in the "blessings of civilization." *Légitime Défense* held that it would be only by the radical surrealistic use of the language that these age-old associations could be shattered and the way prepared for the expression of the African psyche in its integrity, uncensored by the shadow of colonial Europe. It was necessary to break up these habitual associations by throwing together the most unlikely words to produce rational and acceptable meaning in juxtaposition. Out of the defiance of rational thought, in the drunken flood of words and image, would emerge the deep suppressed direction of the poet's being:

> With little steps of rain of caterpillars
> With little steps of draughts of milk
> With little steps of roller-bearings
> With little steps of earthquakes
> The sweet potatoes march in the earth with great strides
>   of gaps of stars.[10]

It is an automatic creation similar to that of the surrealist painter Max Ernst, who employs this method in casting up his terrifying cosmic visions to encompass and express the "crisis of consciousness" of our times.

It was Léro's compatriot, Aimé Césaire, who became the most eloquent spokesman in this use of the surrealist technique to achieve the unfettered expression sought by Léro. Sartre describes the manner in which the moribund surrealist movement in France—having proved an unsuitable literary medium for the poets of the social revolution, because it was antagonistic by nature to the precision necessary in the day-to-day struggle of the worker toward his economic emancipation—was seized upon by Aimé Césaire and made the principal weapon in his assault upon the cultural and racist taboos of the West. He quotes from Césaire's "Sun Serpent":

> The seas liced with islands crackling under
> rosy-fingered flame throwers and my body untouched
> by the thunderbolt.

[10] Sartre, *loc. cit.,* p. 228.

Here is the apotheosis of the lice of black grief jumping through the hair of the water, sunlit islands, crackling under the finger of a celestial delousing rosy-fingered dawn, the dawn of Greek and Mediterranean culture, snatched from the sacred Homeric poems by a black thief. The dawn whose fingernails, delicate as those of an enslaved princess, are suddenly forced by a Toussaint L'Ouverture to explode the triumphant parasites of the Negro sea; the dawn which suddenly rebels and transforms herself, pours forth fire like the savage weapon of the whites—the flame-thrower, weapon of scientists, weapon of executioners—blasts with her white fire the great black Titan who rises intact, eternal to spring the attack of Europe and of the heavens. In Césaire the great surrealist tradition is achieved, takes its definitive sense, and destroys itself. Surrealism, European poetic movement, is stolen from the Europeans by a black who turns it against them and assigns it a rigorously prescribed function.[11]

This preoccupation with the situation of the Negro in a culturally alien world common to the vast majority of Negro African poets has given birth in the French language to the central concept of "négritude." The term is not amenable to easy definition. It appears to serve in somewhat varying roles for those who employ it. It represents in one sense the Negro African poet's endeavor to recover for his race a normal self-pride, a lost confidence in himself, a world in which he again has a sense of identity and a significant role. It is, in Sartre's figure from classic mythology, his Eurydice recovered by Orpheus from Pluto, his lost beloved, his ultimate identity, his vision of the world and not that of a culture holding him in derision and contempt. It is not a goal to be accomplished, but rather, more basically, an affective disposition, in Heidegger's existentialist term, the Negro's "being-in-the-world." Senghor points out that the négritude of a poem is less the theme than the style, the crucial nature of which we shall consider later. It includes the characteristic impulses, traits, and habits which may be considered more markedly

[11] *Ibid.,* p. 234.

Negro African than white or European. It is thus something which the poet possesses in the wells of his being and simultaneously something which he is seeking to recover, to make manifest. Négritude is a subjective disposition which is affirmed and which objectivizes itself in the poem. Writes Césaire:

> My négritude is not a rock, its deafness
>   hurled against the clamor of the day
> My négritude is not a film of dead water
>   on the dead eye of the earth
> My négritude is neither a tower nor
>   a cathedral
> It plunges into the red flesh of the earth
> It plunges into the burning flesh of the sky
> It pierces the opaque prostration by its
>   upright patience.[12]

In these lines, Césaire emphasizes the dynamic quality of this concept: négritude is an act, an active becoming, a vital force dynamically, but patiently and stubbornly, active in the earth and the sky and the elements. Amid the insufferable tensions of his estrangement, négritude is that area the poet has carved out for himself in the poem where he may live and dwell and have his true and absolute being:

> The words surpass themselves. It is indeed toward a sky and a land whose height and depth cannot be troubled. It is made of the old geography. Yet there now emerges at a certain level an area curiously breathable. At the gaseous level of the solid and liquid organism, white and black, night and day.[13]

It is worth while here to remark that a common reaction among Americans—tutored in a society strongly egalitarian and integrationist in avowed direction and ideal, however delinquent in deed—to such racial concepts is one of surprise that the Negro African, who above all has been the victim of

[12] *Ibid.*, p. 236.
[13] *Ibid.*, p. 232.

racial persecution, should affirm racial qualities. To hear the presiding genius of the movement quote, with evident approval, Gobineau, the hobgoblin of every student of Klineberg, Herskovits and Charles S. Johnson, appears to be the parallel in reverse of the devil's tricks with scripture. The American, and more particularly the American Negro, is inclined to feel that to affirm the rights and the dignity of the Negro as a man among men is one, and a valid, thing but that to acclaim a specific quality or a complex of traits or attitudes as peculiarly Negro—an aspect of what the French African poets have termed *la négritude*—is distinctly another matter and smacks of the racism American social scientists have patiently been attempting to erase since the original impact at the turn of the century of Grant and Stoddard and their disciples.

Further examination of the concept, however, and a consideration of the historical circumstances giving rise to its development tend to make clear its justification, and more, its necessity. The reaction to centuries of humiliation and contempt is not one of calm objectivity. The pendulum can only gradually achieve dead center. It is elementary that each age, each people, has its own historical necessity. Although it is true, for example, that there is no equivalent contemporary literary assertion of racial identity among white poets, it is also true that there is apparently no real and present danger of an "I am an Englishman" day. In this connection, Sartre has used Hegelian concepts, which serve well here, to describe the movement.[14] Negritude in African poetry is an antiracist racism; it is the moment of negativity as reaction to the thesis of white supremacy. It is the antithesis in a dialectical progression which leads to an ultimate synthesis of a common humanity without racism. This is undoubtedly too neat a formula for the actual operation of the influences involved; yet it does provide a ready and roughly accurate framework for the comprehension of the conflicting tendencies at play here.

[14] *Ibid.,* p. 245.

PART THREE

THROUGH THE EYES
OF OTHERS

Chapter 5

The Old Order:
Personality in the Matrix of Tradition

THE SOOTHSAYER

R. S. RATTRAY

The Leopard Priestess, a novel fashioned out of an old African story, was written by a man who spent a lifetime among West Africans and became a great authority on their language, art, laws, and customs. Having published several scientific treatises, Robert Sutherland Rattray decided to portray Africans in a work of fiction that would embody his intimate knowledge of them.

As background for the selected chapter, "The Soothsayer," the following basic elements of the story should be known.

Amalagane and Opoku's love was forbidden not only because they were both of the leopard totem, but also because the girl was the Priestess of the Pentia shrine, consecrated to the preparation of arrow poison for the tribe's hunters, and as such had to remain sacrosanct for the term of her office. Moreover, the lovers had compounded the transgression by embracing on the bare earth, thus defiling a deity.

The reader needs to know also that in olden times, it was the custom of this tribe for the old and decrepit "to meet their ancestors" by jumping into a pool inhabited by crocodiles. In our story, Amalagane's grandmother, at the "jumping of the ancients" had hesitated and seemed about to speak. Amalagane had, with her foot, pushed her grandmother into the pool, not only because the old woman's hesitation would bring disgrace upon the clan, but perhaps also because she feared that her grandmother meant to voice her suspicions about the unlawful love between Amalagane and Opoku. Rumors of untoward happenings were already stirring up uneasiness among the people, and a visit to the soothsayer became inevitable when a lioness attacked the villagers.

While many elements of Rattray's tale are now archaic, the visit to the diviner is very much a living custom over most of Africa.

EXCITEMENT IN THE VILLAGE had subsided somewhat, but had given place to an uneasy feeling as to what the future still held in store. The strangers who had attended the dance had all returned to their homes, and the village of the leopard clan had again settled down to its normal routine of cultivating, hunting, pottery, basket-making, and other activities in a life in which even the little children have little time for play. The lioness had escaped, having leaped through the cordon of men, flames, and smoke; and the lion clansfolk were convinced that she was none other than Amalagane's grandmother come back; nor did the others need much convincing that such was really the case. Was it not clearly proven by the fact that the beast had seized Amalagane's right foot, that offending member which had been used, on the day of the "jumping" to kick her grandmother to the crocodiles? Indeed, but for the heavy anklets which she had worn, Amalagane must surely have lost her leg. As it happened, she had suffered little serious injury, and, save for a few lacerations and many bruises, was none the worse for the adventure. Several others had received injuries from burns, more serious than either she or Opoku had suffered from the lioness.

The next thing to be done was, clearly, to consult the soothsayers.

The Master of the Earth and the Elders were in constant deliberation. So far, however, the affair had still to be regarded as falling within the household, and as such, those in higher authority had not, as yet, any right directly to interfere.

Amalagane and Opoku were both members of certain family groups. They had been attacked and mauled by a wild beast. For this there must certainly be some very notable cause. Such things could not possibly be classed as among the ordinary natural happenings to be expected in normal, well-conducted lives, either of lions or of human beings. There must obviously be supernatural forces at work. The Master of the Earth had hinted as much to the head of the leopard clan settlement, who had in turn passed it on to the seniors of Amalagane's and Opoku's kindred groups, and these had finally instructed the heads of their compounds that the affair was viewed as being possibly serious. In consequence, the result of any family-conducted inquiry was to be duly reported through proper channels for the further consideration of those in higher authority.

All this was strictly in accordance with African law and procedure. These decree that a man's business is his own affair only just so long as it in no way jeopardizes other members of his family group; that a family's affairs are no other family's concern, so long as the consequences of anything they do may reasonably be expected to be confined within that family circle; that a kindred group's affairs are its own business, so long as other kindred groups are not involved; that a clan's business only concerns that clan, provided any trouble it raises can be localized. Beyond this it becomes of tribal, of national moment. This climax is attained when a member of a small family group, however insignificant he or she may be, commits a sin, that is, violates a red taboo. For such a lapse, until duly expiated, the punishment will fall not only on the original guilty party, but upon the whole loosely knit community, which thus becomes for a time closely united in face of a common danger. In such a case the Master of the Earth is called upon as the final adjudicator.

Even he, however, does not dare attempt to carry into execution his own judgments. He leaves that to the spirits and to the gods. Such, stated in a few sentences, was the old African Law and Constitution.

The first step to be taken by the heads of the families concerned was to consult a soothsayer. The manner in which this is done must be described for a European, to whom it is as strange as would be to Africans the method by which Europeans get a swift answer from persons far away beyond the sea.

The soothsayer's stock-in-trade consists of a skin bag. This contains among other things, a rattle, a wand—forked at one end and shod with iron at the other—a slab of wood in which have been cut two shallow sockets into which are sunk two iron disks.

In addition to these, there are a great variety of nondescript objects, comprising among others the following: a fragment of a pumpkin shell, a piece of string, a hair ball out of the stomach of an old cow, a corn cob, feet of hens and cocks, a shea butter nut. To each of these things, and dozens more like them, is assigned a particular meaning, well known to everyone. The oracle man squats down, turns out the contents of his bag, and calls up the spirits, which then enter his body. The consulter thereupon lightly touches the wand which the soothsayer himself holds. It hovers over and darts among varied objects, picking out one and another from the heap. The consulter, who has already formulated his question in his own mind, need not speak; he need not even inform the soothsayer what is his business. All that is necessary is that he touch the wand; it will give him the answer he seeks by sorting out the lots, which may then be interpreted as one would read picture writing. This supernatural power which guides the wand, and in each case decides its ultimate objective, may be derived from many and varied sources. Often it is that of an ancestor of the soothsayer's, but it may also be some nature or even animal spirit.

It would not be just to dismiss all this as chicanery. It is the African's way of seeking an unbiased answer for his doubts and questionings, and thus, to ease his mind. It enables him also to place the onus of certain unpleasant but wholesome truths on the shoulders of the spirits and to fix in the same quarter the opprobrium of carrying out unpopular but salutary measures.

It is equally good psychology and policy, because in nine cases out of ten the soothsayer's wand will bend to the trend of public opinion.

Bakologo was the most noted soothsayer in the leopard clan. Once upon a time, after sacrificing a fowl in the customary manner at the shrine of his ancestor, he had been seized with convulsions and had fallen down as if dead. On his recovery he had narrated how he had gone to the spirit world and there conversed with the dead, who had told him that they were prepared to place their powers at the disposal of the living if they wished to invoke them. What, therefore, had been hitherto his ordinary ancestral shrine, concerned only with the affairs of the descendants of that ancestor, became a public soothsaying shrine for all who cared to consult it. It was, then, to this soothsayer that the housefathers of Opoku and Amalagane resorted, two evenings after the dance.

They found the old man sitting in front of his shrine against which he was idly leaning. After the customary greetings and some desultory talk, the soothsayer held out his bag to one of the Elders, who placed a hand on either side and said:

"I hold your sides, but not your mouth. Behold! I hold your waist, leaving your mouth free to speak; even if it be cruel, do not have pity; drag me among the stones, seek not out the smooth places; the facts, the facts, not 'it is like this and that'; tell me the real thing."

Bakologo tipped the contents of his bag on the ground before him. He then sought out two flat stones from the heap, licked one side of each, then cast them down and noted which sides fell upwards. The spirit thus declared its readiness to be consulted.

"Take the wand," he commanded.

Opoku's house-father took hold of the stick, near the iron-shod end, between the thumb and forefinger of his right hand, while the soothsayer held it near the forked end in his right —holding the rattle aloft in his left hand.

Bakologo then spoke, addressing the spirit:

"My father, after the day breaks, I cannot know what they have come for; you will tell them. My father, I call upon you that you too may call upon your fathers that they may come and sit with us. I know these people sitting here, but I do not know the reason that they call me; you know what it is."

He commenced to sing in a droning, humming tone, as he swayed backwards and forwards:

"*Nweyomm; nweyomm:* Strike hard, strike hard. Supposition is not soothsaying. *You* will know who is angry; *you* will tell them who is offended. Father, I am still rattling. Hit straight, hit hard."

The Elder addressed the Soothsayer who was now staring with unseeing eyes.

"Do they then consent that I may consult, that I may see or may not see?"

"Yes, yes, call my father, call my mother," droned the oracle.

"Then I hold you," answered the Elder.

The wand hovered over the *yala,* as the contents of the bag are called, and began to sort them out, touching now this one, now that, searching among the pile for another, retouching the first. Amalagane's father leaned forward eagerly as the wand picked out the various objects, and broke from time to time into sharp exclamations, "See! a foot! now a calabash; have they made a mistake? No, no! See! again! a foot! What! the Pentia shrine? Defiled? Can it be? Earth-Goddess, blood upon her! What more? Nothing!"

Their hands fell off the wand, which rolled among the objects strewn about the ground. The soothsayer stretched himself as if awakening from sleep, looked foolishly at the two men, then recognized them, and smiled at seeing two old friends. He then began replacing the *yala* in his bag. The séance was ended.

SPRING SOWING

JACK H. DRIBERG

A very important thing to the African is his relationship to the earth that sustains him. His labor, his prayers, his sacrifices and taboos, his communion with his ancestors, his songs and his dancing—all are woven into a pattern of piety to keep the earth fertile and friendly.

The following selection brings us into the very midst of New Year's rites of a Sudanese clan who are beginning the year's tilling of the soil. We see the Keeper of the Lands "making right" the earth. We watch with the elders of the clan at their vigil under the living calendar of sun and stars, finally heralding with trumpets the propitious beginning of the planting season. We listen to the comradely joking and singing of relatives and friends at work in the garden of Lokuryamoi, who had married into the clan and was now one of them.

"Spring Sowing" is fiction, but it comes from the pen of a man who had long experience in East Africa. Mr. Driberg was a devoted student of African ethnology over many years, producing a number of useful books. He was also a lecturer in anthropology at Cambridge University. (See also note on page 50.)

EARLY NEXT MORNING Lokuryamoi went to the forest, where he found Lomingamoi and many of his clansmen. Of them all Lomingamoi alone carried an axe; for there was to be no real work that day, but only the sanctification of the forest for the new year's cultivation.

Since his father's death Lomingamoi had become Keeper of the Clan Lands, an office which his family had held from the beginning of the Idoto clan. He too wore a cap of bark-cloth like his fellows.

He was responsible for all the cultivation within the bounds of the clan lands, and no alien from another clan, such as Lokuryamoi, could cultivate in them without his permission. None might weed his crops until Lomingamoi had chosen a day and had first pulled up a handful of weeds, and when the earliest ears of corn appeared it was his duty to sacrifice a goat for the clan, that the ears might fatten and that no mischance might overtake the harvest.

Now, however, it was only the forest which concerned him. He had to make it safe for all his comrades, and he received from each a knife or hoe as his reward.

Slipping off his baboon-skin cape he hung it on a laurel bush, spat on his hands, and swung his axe to loosen the joints of his shoulders. Lomingamoi vigorously felled a tree while the others watched, and for another year his people might cut timber and hew the brushwood without danger from the spirit of the woods.

Resting a foot on the fallen trunk, Lomingamoi stretched his arms out towards the forest and prayed:

"O Earth, wherever it be my people dig, be kindly to them. Be fertile when they give the little seeds to your keeping. Let your generous warmth nourish them and your abundant moisture germinate them. Let them swell and sprout, drawing life from you, and burgeon under your fostering care; and soon we shall redden your bosom with the blood of goats slain in your honor, and offer to you the first-fruits of your munificence, first-fruits of millet and oil of sesame, of gourds and cucumbers and deep-meshed melons.

"O trees of forest and glade, fall easily under the axe. Be gentle to my people. Let no harm come to them. Break no limb in your anger; crush no one in your displeasure. Be obedient to the woodman's wishes and fall as he would have you fall, not perversely or stubbornly, but as his axe directs. Submit yourselves freely to my people, as this tree has submitted itself to me. The axe rings, it bites into the tough wood. The tree totters and falls. The lightning flashes, its fire tears at the heart of the wood. The tree totters and falls. Before the lightning the tree falls headlong, precipitate, knowing neither direction nor guidance. But the woodman guides the tree where he wills and lays it to rest gently and with deliberation. Fall, O trees of forest and glade, even as this tree has fallen, hurting no one, obedient, observant of my will.

"O rivers and streams, where the woodman has laid bare the earth, where he has hewn away the little bushes and torn out the encumbering grass, there let your waters overflow. Bring down the leafy mould from the forest and the fertilizing silt from the mountains. When the rains swell your banks, spread out your waters and lay your rich treasures on our gardens.

"Conspire together, O earth and rivers: conspire together, O earth and rivers and forests. Be gentle and give us plenty from your teeming plenty. For it is I, Lomingamoi of the clan of Idoto, who speak, Keeper of the Clan Lands, Warden of the Forest, Master of the Clan."

*   *   *

It was still dark when the elders gathered below the rock of Buthi. Flickering torches had lighted them along the winding mountain tracks, and others could be seen on their way, little dots of flame waving up and down with the motion of the walkers, vanishing and reappearing as they passed behind trees or rocks or were lost in a fold of the hillside.

It was a fine night, so clear that the stars seemed almost

within hand's touch, and Buthi stood like a monstrous finger reaching out at them.

The early rains had washed away the dust of the two dry months, and there was a freshness in the air which made the elders glad of the huge fires, round which they huddled waiting for the dawn. The damp wood sizzled and spluttered resin-blue flames, and the smoke folded filmy gray veils over the ground. The earth was alive once more and the odour of growing things mingled with the smell of burning wood.

Buthi rock stood on a lower ride of the mountains, and behind it to the East, separated by the Idoto valley, the main range chiselled a sharp line against the starry sky. Buthi ridge curled round the valley like the tail of a sleeping leopard.

Already the pale light of the false dawn was throwing the distant range into a blacker silhouette. The night air felt cooler to the elders, and they huddled more closely round their fires. But as the Eastern stars gradually dimmed and were effaced in the grayness of early morning, the elders stood up and stretched themselves. When the first tinges of red flecked the sky and the arrows of golden-red shot upwards from behind the mountains, they gathered silently round a low flat-topped stone. Facing the sunrise they waited and watched. Unregarded the fires sank low. With the falling of the night wind the smoke hung heavily, and already the mist had begun to creep up from the valleys and to throw damp tendrils toward the watchers.

Swiftly the East grew lighter. A scurry of clouds obscured for a moment the breaking day, but they passed almost before the elders had glanced apprehensively at each other. The higher clouds were the first to catch the morning and fired to flaming scarlet. The rim of the sun appeared above the mountains, and as its first ray shot over it was caught by the tip of Buthi rock, which blackened and seemed to tower gigantically above the watchers. It caught the first ray of the sun, and its shadow was flung exactly in the center of the flat-topped stone.

A shout of welcome broke from the elders. For ten days they had watched thus every morning, and for ten days they had seen the shadow creep ever nearer to the point where it should fall. The Seven Maidens were in the right quarter, and it wanted but this to fulfil their reckoning. This was at last the New Year for which they had been eagerly waiting. Now they could plant their crops again; the rains would soon be on them; the lean months were past. Moon by moon they had measured the months. Madidili led to Ukhudo, and Ukhudo to Lodunge. But always the reckoning went a little awry, and each year they awaited the return of the Seven Maidens and watched for the morning shadow of Buthi, that they might know when Lodunge and the New Year had truly come.

The trumpeters stood in a row behind the elders. Six faced the rising sun and six the West. They raised the long, straight trumpets to their lips and blared forth the New Year. From village to village resounded answering notes. Trumpets silent for a year caught up and passed on the message. All the mountains proclaimed the sunrise of the New Year.

Lokuryamoi heard the trumpets in his own village, and stepping on to a ledge of rock sounded the call also. He returned the trumpet to the shelf on which it would rest till the next New Year, and called in his wife:

"It is the New Year, Amongin. Did you not hear? Up and get busy. We shall dig our garden today. There will be forty of us, or perhaps more, as your brother promised to help me and said he would bring three or four of his friends as well. My cousin, Lojyo, is also bringing some men from Lotuke."

Yawning, Amongin stretched her shapely arms and threw some wood on the fire. Her husband pulled a hoe out of the corner and examined it. The edge was worn away till only a thin band of metal remained, so narrow as to make it useless for digging. It was good enough still to scrape the weeds round his village, but that was all: soon he would grind it down for a razor. He threw it back and dragged out his wooden hoe. The edge of this also was blunted, but that could be remedied with fire and a little scraping, and otherwise it was as good as new. Its ten feet of handle gave perfect poise and balance.

"However, metal hoes are better while they last," he remarked. "We shall have to grow more grain this year,

Amongin. We might buy three hoes, perhaps, as I ought to give your mother one. It is a pity that the Locheka will only take sheep for their hoes, as it means that I shall have to take some grain down to sell to the Dodoth. Their sheep always fetch the best hoes. Do you think that your father will lend me his donkey when I go?"

"Hullo, sluggards! We have been calling you, Lokurya, from the stream where we bathed. Come out!"

"There is my brother," laughed Amongin. "Coming, Aura," she called through the door as she tied her apron.

But her husband was out first. He found Auranomoi outside with five of his friends, all dancing with impatience to start work. So hurriedly sharpening his hoe he went back for a goat, while his wife chattered with her brother.

"We need some hoes," he heard her saying, and caught the woods "Dodoth" and "grain."

He led the way to his garden on the river bank, where for the past month he had been busy clearing the trees and making the ground ready for digging as soon as the New Year was come. They found the others awaiting them there.

"How is my uncle, Lojyo?"

"Well enough, Lokurya, but he is rather worried about the baboons this year. There are more of them than ever at Lotuke, and they are becoming a nuisance. You will have a busy time with your other garden there, when the grain starts to ripen. . . . Have you heard? Lokumanoi's wife has given birth to a son, his first since Lokuta was killed."

"No!"

"Is that so?"

"How glad he must be!"

Everyone was pleased, as Lokumamoi's popularity since his great victory was undiminished. His wife's pregnancy had been a matter of interest to the whole tribe, and everyone had hoped for a son to take Lokuta's place.

"Greetings, Loera. I am glad to have come," said Lokurya-moi. "I wanted someone of your clan to sacrifice this goat, and I would sooner have you than anyone else."

"Willingly, Lokurya," he replied politely, taking the goat from Lokuryamoi. He sacrificed it and sprinkled the blood over the ground which had been cleared.

"Earth of my clan," he prayed, "accept this offering, I entreat you. Drink the blood which I pour on you. This goat, which is the goat of Lokuryamoi, is the price of your bounty. Deal kindly with Lokuryamoi, for he is our friend; and stranger though he be, grant him a harvest as rich as our own. Let Nagitak, the grain blight, shrink from touching his garden, and let the beasts of the forest and the birds of the air know that Lokuryamoi is as one of us."

The meat was cut up and spitted, and a small boy who had accompanied Lojyo's party watched over the fire while it cooked and then hung it on a tree. Lokuryamoi showed them what had to be done and promised as much beer as they wanted when the work was finished. For a time they laboured to the tune of an old gardening chorus:

The Seven Maidens await their lovers.
 Dig, brothers, dig.
The great lovers come from the East, the Seven Sons of the
  Bright One.
 Dig, brothers, dig.
The red lovers come from the East, and they bring a gift of
  tears.
 Dig, brothers, dig.
They bring a gift of tears for the Seven Maidens.
 Dig, brothers, dig.

The broken tussocks of young green grass lay tossed upside down, and the damp red soil clogged heavily to the feet of the workers; for the dew still clung in shining drops to every blade of grass.

As the sun grew hotter there were longer pauses, and one would lean on his hoe and shout a question to another far down the line. A joke caused general laughter, and they started singing again and digging rhythmically, their hoe handles rising and falling together in time to the music.

Aryemungimoi started to tell a story, but was shouted down: for who could dig to a story?

Lokonoi, the fool, happening to pass, stopped to gape at them. He mimicked their gestures, with grunts as of great exertion.

"Dig, you cripples, dig," he shouted, imitating Lokuryamoi's voice. "Did I invite you to sit and gossip in my garden all day?"

He spied the meat and snatched at a piece, but Auranomoi's dog snapped at his leg. "Good dog." "At him, Buffalo," laughed the workers, while Lokonoi ran as fast as he could till he was out of sight.

THE GOLDEN AGE OF CHIEF NJEMANZE

Sylvia Leith-Ross

Here we have the portrait of a beguiling African patriarch, romanticized in the memory of a fond granddaughter. His people are the Owerri of the tribe of Ibo in Nigeria, a very independent tribe whose women made history with the famous Aba riots of 1929, which they carried out with the verve of practiced revolutionaries. The plenty dispensed by Chief Njemanze would naturally be remembered for a long time in a country where poverty and hunger were much more usual.

ONE CHARACTER stands out, that of the old Chief Njemanze, dead in 1920. The tales of him, told me by his grandchild, an attractive girl of seventeen, captured the imagination. They seem worth recording as evidence of a golden age, local and short-lived though it was, and of a man who even amongst the ultra-democratic Ibo had succeeded in imposing himself. It is true his title of Chief given to him by the white man had no real meaning, but he had obviously been a leader, holding incontestable authority. "No one made peace or war without consulting him. His permission was asked before anything could be done."

I often visited the quarter to which he had belonged, that of Ama Awom. It was a huge rabbit warren of little huts and courtyards divided by mud or palm-branch walls. It was still fairly full of people coming and going, women preparing food or cooking it over small wood fires, men talking in the *obi* near the gate, children playing, young girls coming in with firewood or water from the nearby stream; but one felt the absence of the master spirit, one saw evidences of slackness and decay, the light of glory no longer shone upon its walls. It was only while I listened to Salome as she sat, wide eyed, looking back into her own babyhood, mixing her own slight memories with all that she had heard of her grandfather's life, that I was able to reconstruct this golden age which had flourished for a few years and then died down, all the more remarkable because so few people or facts ever stand out clearly from the apparently colourless maze of the Ibo past.

Chief Njemanze was a rich man for, beside his fifty wives, he had about two hundred servants. "He loved children too much," and had built for them, inside his compound, rest-houses (slight shelters of mud and palm) to which all might come. "In the middle was the 'big' rest-house, which must have had a hundred poles, some carved, some covered from top to bottom with the skulls of all the cows and the sheep and the goats he had eaten. From the roof hung the corn-cobs which the servants had brought in from the farms, in big baskets, on their heads. Some of the corn cobs would be given to the children. Then wood would be brought and as many as twenty fires would be lit before which the children roasted their cobs with play and laughing." Or they would race to see who could climb fastest up the poles, clasping the carved monkeys and the parrots; and when the boys came back from school, they would have games of touch-wood between the poles.

Salome sat still, seeing again the golden cobs hanging from the smoke-darkened roof, hearing again the laughter of the chasing children. Then she went on: "In his *oba*, he had at least twenty rows of stored yams. Any poor person could go and help himself. Often there would be two or three rows of men and women in the compound, each with a basket of yams. Njemanze, my grandfather, would come out, walk up and down the lines and say: "That is right, my people. I see what you have taken. It is all right."

Again she came back to his love of children: "If he heard a woman beating her child, he would tell her never to do such a thing again. He would take the child to his own hut and give it something to eat or a little present, whispering to it not to tell its mother. On big market day, he would give a shilling to all his children to buy fairings with. He would also buy pieces of cloth and give a yard to all the girls about to be married; he would also provide food for all his people on the feast of Oru Owerri."

Every morning, Salome, who was his son's first-born, went to salute him. She could just remember him. He was tall and stout, and very fine. He wore coral beads round his neck and a necklet of black medicine which he had inherited from his father and which showed he had taken his father's place. He would say to her: "Come here, my child!" The remembered softness in the intonation as imitated by Salome all these years after was remarkable. He would give her a yam which she would carry back to her mother, strutting, the big yam clasped to her stomach.

"While he was eating, there was silence in all the compound, no one would dare so much as to pick up a twig. Two or three of his wives would sit by him while he ate. Children would bring their bowls and he would give them little bits off his own plate. . . . There was always peace in his time. . . ."

Doubtless Salome exaggerated but probably the picture of plenty was true, the wives bending over the cooking-pots, the servants coming in from the farms laden with baskets, the poor people going off rejoicing, the big rest-house hung with the glowing corncobs, skulls, and medicines, and the children running, shouting, between the high carved poles. And clearest of all, one sees Njemanze, rich, strong, and generous, flinging round his shillings or striding between the huts, a child upon his shoulders, undermining maternal discipline.

Now all that is left of the old rest-house are the stumps of a few poles and some of the poles themselves, cunningly carved, lying rotting on the ground. "No one bothers to take care of the old things." Njemanze's own meeting-house still stands but is hardly used. It is nearly square with steeply pitched roof and remarkably well built bamboo frame to which is lashed the palm-leaf thatch. The walls have wooden pegs driven into them on which are stuck old bottles and drinking-horns. In one corner stood a large wooden box which might have been meant for a coffin. There were two old drums and, hanging from the roof, various baskets and odd-shaped round bundles which might have been human skulls, but "no one knows now what they mean." Yet, though all other glory has departed, one marvel remains. Njemanze was a pagan but his children became Christians. When their father died, he was buried according to custom in the courtyard outside his own hut, but over his grave rises a life-size marble angel, finger pointing heavenward, a look of mild surprise upon its face. The marble coping, spattered with the blood of sacrificial fowls, bears the name of a monument mason in Kensal Green.

For a long time, the angel was such a thing of wonder that people came, a hundred at a time, from far and near to gaze upon it. So new and splendid did it seem that expert modellers, engaged upon a nearby *mbari* house, came to look at it and forthwith rushed back to copy it, in clay and coloured chalks, for the adornment of the shrine of Ologba. The angel's whiteness was a "mystery." At night, people hardly dared pass by it, fearing it might be the spirit of Njemanze himself, and when they wanted to relieve themselves, they would go ten at a time to the latrine, running past it very quickly. It is still known as "the monument" and strangers are taken to see it and to read the inscription, in English, to "the greatest chief Owerri ever had."

THE BLIND SINGER

BWEMBYA

We find this little story among the reminiscences of Bwembya, the headman of a small village in Northeastern Rhodesia. A man of small wealth but great dignity, Bwembya is proud of being a grandson of the Chitimukulu (the title of the paramount chief of the Bemba tribe). Like many an old man, Bwembya likes to dwell on things of the past, the grand and the sad. In his vignette of the blinded singer, one feels a classic pathos such as one would find in Homer or the Bible.

The story was recorded by the English anthropologist, Audrey I. Richards.

YOU WANT ME to tell you some more about the court of Mwamba? Well, I will tell you something, for I, Bwembya, remember all things of the past. You ask about the drums and the dancing? No, no one would dance inside the chief's enclosure. They were too much afraid. But the young men and the girls danced outside in the village when the moon was full, and we boys of the royal court would slip through the palisade and dance with the rest. But inside the enclosure only the chief's praise-songs could be sung. Old men, usually blind, sang songs in praise of the chief. They sang all day long. Whenever it came into their hearts to sing, they would leave their huts, with some little boy to lead them across the village. They sang all the way with their young men behind them beating the drums. This was the way they honored the chief. Dreams would come to them in the night, and in the morning they would wake and say, "I have dreamed good things. I have dreamed a praise-song to Mwamba," and they would walk round and round the village singing, so that the chief's heart would be lightened, and he would give them great rewards.

I have heard them say that sometimes such a chief would be filled with pride at these songs and he would say, "This singer shall never leave me to go to another court." Then he would begin constantly to find fault with the man, until one day he would put out his eyes for some little fault, not a grave charge at all. But I did not see such a thing done myself. It is only a story they tell. Of course the blind singer you saw at the Chitimukulu's court last month had his eyes put out because he stole one of the chief's wives. That was a long time ago. They call him *Chishale shale* ("a thing which is left behind"), because he is so old and his fellows are dead. But for weeks after he had been blinded such a singer would sit in silence, because his heart was heavy and bitterness had caught him at the throat. He would sit inside his hut in the dark all day long, and every day the chief would send him presents—pots of beer the people had brought him as tribute, or meat, or honey or the like. This he did to appease the blinded man. Then after a time his heart would grow still again, for his eyes had healed so that they no longer pained him. And then, all of a sudden, he would begin to dream new songs. Yes, and he would sing again in praise of that very chief! For you know what such men are. They sing because it is in their hearts to sing and they cannot keep silent long. Besides, such a man would be afraid to fly to another village, for what can a blind man do without his people, alone in a new country?

THE SKIES OF CHILDHOOD

OTTO F. RAUM

The magic and poetry of childhood have a special affinity for all the turns of the weather. In the following brief selection from his book, *Chaga Childhood,* Otto F. Raum distills the essence of East African childhood. The games, the charms, the incantations are pure poetry, but are never far from one over-riding mundane concern: hunger.

Dr. Raum, whose father was a missionary among the Chagas for forty years, was himself born and brought up among the people he writes of. *Chaga Childhood* is a thorough and pene-trating study of all the ways in which a tribal society educates and prepares its young for the life they are to lead. This educa-tion, while well adapted to serve all practical needs, does not interfere with the natural poetry of the human being as he faces his weathers and his seasons.

INDOORS, CHILDREN pass their time in dancing, singing, playing hide-and-seek, and pinching one another in the dark. When the rain subsides, they rush out into the yard, throw each other down into the mud and slide down slopes. Hail is greeted with great joy. They take the hailstones into their mouths and enjoy their pleasant taste. Children collect them in receptacles and use them as cough medicine. Boys occupy themselves with catching rats by flooding their burrows. Inci-dentally, they help thereby to protect the sprouting crops, whose roots suffer then more than at any other time from the ravages of vermin. During the first heavy showers, the winged termites come out of their dwellings and the children run about collecting them. Part of the catch is eaten raw, but they taste better roasted. Another species of white ant lives in the plains, where it builds picturesque ant-heaps. The children organize expeditions there, shade the exits with leaves and blow air into the passages to induce them to come out.

As the rainy season wears on through several months of cold and wet weather, the children begin to long for the return of the sun. God, they are told, is sick. Thus they sing on the pasture: "Sun, shine! I will give you good broth, old man! Sun, shine! We shall roast a yam for you under yon tree! Sun, shine, and I shall slaughter the red cow for you!" Another song is rather boorish in tone: "Sun, shine! so that I can brew beer to give to my father. It is sure to make him drunk! He will beat my mother, she will run away, and leave her house and food to me. I shall lick the pot then and grow very, very big!" The appearance of a rainbow leads to a competition. One shouts: "It's mine!" and another, "It's mine!" When the quarrel has continued for some time, they agree that each claimant should own one of the coloured bands. When the sun sets, boys climb into trees to see him sink behind the distant horizon. They say: "He is sure to bring us something lovely tomorrow!"

The sight of the moon provokes the children to a quarrel as to whose yard she is in. The halo of the moon is considered an omen of death. Yet the children, quite undaunted, spit at her and ask her to grant certain requests: "Moon, I have seen you! May my father's cow give birth to a heifer that I shall have the milk! May my mother's brother's cow give birth to a steer, that I may obtain a sister's son's share of meat!" When there is a full moon, the children run about in the yard playing hide-and-seek and other games.

When the stars come out on a dark night a boy may point at a particularly bright one and say: "I love that child. It will have to be my wife!" When a shooting star is seen, they are told that it shows the direction in which their future wives live. Children try to count the stars and compare the star-studded sky to a marketplace: "Look, that's where they sell sugar cane, and there are bananas!" A cluster of stars may be interpreted as a slaughtering scene. As they are told that many stars mean a fertile year, they become concerned if there are only a few to be seen: "I shan't get food this year, but may be mother will find something to cook!" Thus Chaga children prove the truth of the saying: "Man, though dependent on his body, has the sun and the stars as the playthings of his mind."

Chapter 6
Between the Old and the New:
Ways of Life in Transition

THE QUARREL

AUDREY I. RICHARDS

The role of a young husband among the Bemba in Northern Rhodesia is traditionally a circumscribed one. He lives in his wife's village under a sort of probationary regime, and is only gradually allowed to take on the functions of a head of the household.

Our present informant, the distinguished anthropologist Audrey I. Richards, tells us that:

"After a period varying from five to fifteen years he is ceremoniously admitted to his wife's family to make him enter in (*ukumuingishya*), and after this feast and dance the keeping of the in-law taboos is at an end. This rite takes place when the marriage appears absolutely stable and two or more children have been born, and the ceremony is no mere picturesque survival at the present day. . . . I heard of a case in which a man performed the *ukumuingishya* ceremony for his youngest son-in-law after a period of two years, because he was a steady, likeable fellow, but postponed the rite for ten in the case of his eldest daughter's husband who was less dependable. It is only when husbands are scarce, under modern conditions of absentee labour, that fathers are afraid to exert their jurisdiction over sons-in-law in the traditional way."

Here we have a portrait of a ne'er-do-well who finds his playground, as it were, in the transitional zone between older tribal control and modern economics. However, he does not have things completely his own way, as the following anecdote of a domestic quarrel indicates. Amusingly, his mother-in-law has the last word, but it is directed against her daughter, who also has lost the old sense of propriety in this unsettled world of today.

THE LAST SON-IN-LAW, ShiMutale, was an interesting character, as he represented a special type of graceless good-for-nothing found in the Bemba country today [written in the 1930s], a young man who gets all he can from his wife's people under the old system of kinship obligations, but gives little or nothing in return. ShiMutale was always elegantly dressed in a spotless white shirt, frequently washed and ironed in public. He was constantly parting and arranging his long hair in a small mirror according to the latest fashion, and spent most of his time lounging in the *nsaka,* playing with his baby son or twanging a Bemba lyre. His most active amusement was bicycling madly around the village swearing at the children in English, of which language he knew no other phrases. I watched him from my tent door during this month, and I must admit that I had not believed it possible that an active young man of twenty-five could have done nothing so consistently for so many days on end without feeling the time drag. ShiMutale had at one time worked for Europeans and sometimes announced his intention of doing so again, but in the meantime he stayed where he was. He had paid no *mpanga* for his bride, claiming the cross-cousin relationship as an excuse for not doing so, and worked six days out of twenty as compared with his father-in-law's twelve.

This case is described in detail because it illustrates the way in which a certain number of young Bemba contrive to shirk their marriage obligations under modern conditions, and thus place a heavy strain on the economic resources of the matrilocal group. They do so usually on the plea that they are resting after their work at the mines, or are about to take other jobs "soon," and they are able to flout their duties with impunity, since the shortage of men in the district makes parents willing to put up with sons-in-law whom they would never have tolerated under the old regime. A quarrel which broke out between ShiMutale and his wife during this month illustrates this fact, and also shows clearly how the period of matrilocal marriage acts to a certain extent as a time of trial for the young husband, even under the changed conditions of the present day.

On this occasion ShiMutale asked his wife, who seemed devoted to him in spite of his laziness and violence, to boil some sweet potatoes for him early in the morning so that he could entertain his friends. The potatoes were his own possession, since he had dug the beds on which they grew, although he had made no millet garden. NaMutale refused, because this would have made her too late to join her mother and sisters at work in the gardens. ShiMutale swore at her and pushed her roughly and she, after the manner of all Bemba women when insulted within earshot of their relatives, shot out a piercing yell. In a moment every one was at their doorway staring, and NaMukonda flung herself across the village in full torrent of abusive defense. This is a regular stage in every matrimonial quarrel among the Bemba—the arrival of the girl's mother, and, if possible, the man's too. People look at each other significantly and say, "Look there! The mother has come." They mean that the battle is set.

On this occasion the villagers gathered together, and even the quiet Malalo followed in the wake of his more violent wife to support their insulted, but scarcely injured, child. The next stage in this typical quarrel came quickly. The angry women forced their way into the hut and threw out the cooking and carrying baskets, and removed the pots—all the women's possessions in fact. This is also the prescribed conduct in a serious matrimonial squabble. The onlookers, like a chorus, commented: "See, they have thrown out the pots." Malalo finally led his sobbing daughter away, and the "beaten" girl retired to her mother's hut with NaMukonda and her other daughter following, shouting obscene abuse.

The woman's family refused to cook for the husband, and though there was no chance of ShiMutale starving, more especially as he had a number of his own relatives in the village, yet the strike of the cooks had a special significance. It was a repudiation of the legal obligations of the marriage contract, just as the removal of NaMutale's cooking pots in the first instance was a sign that a serious quarrel had begun. ShiMutale strolled about the village all day long, twanging the Bemba one-stringed lyre with elaborate unconcern. His young friends idling in the men's shelter amused themselves by shouting to him slyly from time to time, "Getting hungry, sir?" To which he replied on each occasion with would-be jauntiness, "No sir! I am extremely full." He must have known, however, that he was not in a strong position as a son-in-law who had paid no *mpanga* and was known as a wastrel. Taunts to this effect had been freely shouted by NaMukonda in the heat of the quarrel, and the refusal of the in-laws to cook might have meant anything from a public protest to the beginning of a definite break, and in the latter case, ShiMutale as a father who had paid nothing at his marriage and had done no years of service, would have no legal rights to his small son.

The quarrel in this case ended quickly. MaMutale forgot her injuries and slipped back to her husband's hut after dark. NaMukonda, apparently rather worn after the morning's screaming, sat brooding on the veranda of her hut alone. Her comments on the affair were instructive. She had not liked the marriage, but the man was a cross-cousin. "There are no husbands for the girls nowadays"—the Bemba mothers' inevitable refrain. If things went on like this the marriage would break up and the child would belong to "us." But then NaMutale was in the wrong in this quarrel! "Really, the young people of today!" she said. "The girls give their husbands no respect. A woman should always submit to her husband but now they just disobey. Then their husbands beat them and then," ruefully, in memory of the morning's agitation, "it twists their mothers' hearts. And then what do you think? In the evening they say, 'I like him again.' They don't want to sleep alone on a bed all night, and so they go back to their husbands all the same."

"Really!" she repeated with a shrug, and eyes raised heavenwards in protest, "The young people of today!"

A NEW EARTH

Elspeth Huxley

Elspeth Huxley spent her childhood in Kenya, where her

parents were settlers for over thirty years. She has since spent many years not only in East but in West Africa and is considered one of the best informed and most sympathetic writers on African life. Her books are characterized by a special gift for seeing broad problems in terms of the individual human beings involved and their daily existence. We see this gift in the two extracts given here from her book, *A New Earth*.

In the first selection, we learn of the struggles of a farmers' co-operative club in Kenya and also of a young African woman's aspiration toward a degree of independence via her vegetable garden. In the second selection, independence is staunchly asserted in action by an old woman leading other women to build a huge dam to serve their people, when the young men would not do it.

Changes on the Land in Kenya

As you go north the land becomes rather less crowded, there are patches of combretum bush and scattered erythrina trees with their flaring scarlet blooms. Fear of the Nandi, who occupy the hills above, once kept it empty; now it is filling up, but belongs to a tribe called the Kabras who do not welcome infiltration by Maragoli. They have taken kindly to farmers' clubs, and I met the members of one. We sat, as usual, under a tree, men on one side, women on the other, at the home of Mark the president, an oldish Quaker whose living-room was adorned with holy pictures. For most of his life Mark had worked as a cook for Europeans. Then he inherited a farm and retired to put into practice as many as he could afford of the methods he had seen. He had a Sahiwal bull and regularly sprayed his seventeen cattle; he owned a plough, a chicken-house, a Rhode Island cockerel; the chug of a hired tractor breaking his land accompanied our talk.

"I will tell you the club's history," Mark said. "We began four years ago, with six members who wanted to help each other; we paid ten shillings each and bought seeds. Our maize was yielding very little then. Our first step was to fence our land and put up cattle sheds by working together as people used to, without payment. Then we ploughed, and put on manure from the sheds. We planted in rows instead of everywhere. In one year we saw a big change, and I got twenty-four bags of maize to the acre.

"Then we bought wire netting for poultry runs and planted orange trees, pineapples, and vegetables. The instructor helped us with everything, and the Veterinary Department helped us with sprays and better bulls. Then the Medical Department decided to buy our milk; one of our members takes it on a bicycle to the main road and it goes to Kakamega on the bus. The money goes into a bank account and is shared out between us, and now we have fourteen members.

"We do not let anyone join, only those who have enclosed their farms and decided to follow these new methods. It is hard work, but we see now that it pays. We are asking the Government for a loan to make a reservoir and pipe water to our farms. This will be a big thing. Now our main need is for another cash crop besides maize.

"In the past," this dignified old man added, "Europeans have come and taken photographs of us as if we were gorillas; now I hope that they can see that we are people like everyone else."

Then the women spoke. All wore clean, neat cotton dresses and head-scarves, and sat gravely listening until their turn came. One, a schoolteacher, spoke excellent English, but it was the older woman, Mrs. Mark, who did the talking, while the younger translated.

"We have planted vegetables," she said, "onions and tomatoes and carrots, but we cannot find a market; it is the same with eggs; we cannot sell them. What can be done? How can we benefit from our work if we cannot sell the produce?"

The same story was told by a young woman who turned up, on her own initiative, at a co-operative sugar factory I saw later in the day: a schoolteacher with a husband and two small children at home, she entered the office where the manager—whose name really was Mr. Manager—was giving us tea and said she wished to speak.

"Some of us, the younger women," she said, "are growing European vegetables; if we sell them we keep the money, and this is the only way we have of ceasing to depend upon our husbands for everything. But how can we sell these vegetables?

At the market, people do not buy them. How do you manage in Britain? Can you tell us what to do?"

Alas, I could not help her, for the answer to this cry for markets, a desperate cry I heard everywhere, can lie only in great social changes far beyond her power, or any individual's, to invoke. It must lie in the rise of industries which will support urban populations and draw people off the land. Some 87 per cent of the Americans live in cities and buy from the farmers who remain, and over 90 per cent of British citizens are urban. Yet in both these rich countries, despite all the resources of science and high levels of efficiency, despite the immense market on their doorstep, farmers must be subsidized to survive.

What hope of expanding markets can be offered to peasants in a country where 95 per cent of the people live on the land and are self-supporting, leaving only a tiny market in the towns? "You must wait," was all I could truthfully have said to this young woman, "until industries thrive and perhaps half the population has left the land." Meanwhile, as her vegetables so hopefully planted grow to waste, so do the needs of emancipation, germinating under a soil of age-long female subjugation, find scant encouragement. Onions had become for her the symbol of freedom. I could only wish her well.

"All the Kamba Are My Children"

MOST AFRICAN women are more reserved than men; their hard life and habit of obedience combine to make them cautious and they do not display their personalities until they have ceased to be strangers. One of the liveliest exceptions to this rule, if rule it be, is an old woman—she must be about eighty—called Kisembe, whom I met on the shores of an enormous dam. It was the right place to meet her, for this was her dam: she built it. By sheer force of personality she recruited about five hundred women and girls who scooped out every grain of earth with a pick and shovel, carried it on their heads to form the barrier and, in three months, completed a cavity which now holds 25 million gallons of water.

Kisembe arrived at the head of a file of gaily dressed girls

who intoned a marching song. Wrinkled like a June apple,
she wore a red tarboosh, a boldly striped scarf attached to it
by a safety-pin, and a yellow shuka. Her history is a strange
one. When, in 1898, a great famine ravaged the country,
followed by smallpox, she lost first her only child, then her
husband, and finally the brother-in-law who had inherited her.
No African woman is ever without a family but she, it
seemed, repudiated hers, and lived alone in the old style of
Kitui house, a cigar-shaped hut like the Masai's, made of
plaited grass.

"I have no children," she had said, "so all the Kamba are
my children"; and she became a leader among women, someone set apart, a little queer, but respected. And in old age
came this dam, which will be her memorial. I asked why it
was built by women, not by men.

"The men had gone away," she said, "to Mombasa and
Nairobi, to seek work; and the women who were left here in
Migwani had to walk as much as eight miles to fetch water,
and back again. And then the D.C. called on people to make
dams. "That was bwana Kelly, he went about and planted
sticks and said: the dam should be here.

"But the young men who had not gone away would not
do it. Why? There was the Migwani Youth League; they were
defying the Government. They were disobeying the chiefs.
Even our chief here, Kasina, who is wise and strong. So I
called upon the women to build the dam, and they came, and
we built it. And now everyone is glad."

Kaliluni lay beneath us, a big lake, with watering-places
for cattle: perhaps a reproach to the young men, certainly a
boon to the women. Kisembe beamed at it proudly: surely
one of the great women of the country, who can remember
the days of the *murati*, the Arabs who came and took people
to the coast, never to return. She has very little patience with
with young politicians and they, probably, only the kind of
respect for her one gives to a legend or an image from a past
one wishes to forget.

THE "FREE WOMEN" OF CONGO CITY
Basil Davidson

Industrialism and city life have been growing rapidly in certain parts of Africa like the Katanga province of the Congo. The result has been an often spectacular tearing down of older ways and values and a throwing up of wild new folkways. In Katanga, Africans drive electric locomotives, captain river vessels, do skilled work in steel mills and operate costly machine tools. More than one quarter of all Congo people now live in cities, some of them in their own homes built by themselves or by African contractors.

The new African city is in many respects a wide-open frontier type of town where drink, sex, and money are the centers of attention. In the chapter here reprinted from Basil Davidson's *The African Awakening,* we have much interesting testimony from African sources on the startling adaptation of older attitudes in radically new situations. Prostitutes, for instance, carry over from the close mutuality of village life the practice of protective associations. Mothers living in the hinterland avidly accept the earnings of their loose-living citified daughters. Huge drinking parties reminiscent of village festivals are also the occasion of a new pattern: money-making.

Mr. Davidson, who has also written books on China and Germany, has more recently been concentrating on Africa. *The African Awakening,* published in 1955, was the fruit of some four years of study and travel in various parts of Africa. In 1962 he published an historical study of the slave trade, *Black Mother.*

PRIDE AND CENTRE of Congo city life is the bar. It is the apex of this urban civilization that capitalist contact has brought into being, the peak of ambition for everyone with money in his pocket, and the envy of everyone without.

Inquiries conducted in 1953 found that "officially there are 300 bars in the old Native City of Leopoldville and 400 altogether in the African quarters. We estimate there is one bar for every 500 inhabitants: in Belgium, there is one café for

every 484 inhabitants." And this, of course, without counting
the practically uncountable—the private reunions for the
drinking of liquors other than legally permitted African or
European beer. Even the indefatigable Monsieur Mons, who
administers a good deal of African Leopoldville, admits that
he is unable to keep up with all the combinations and permu-
tations of alcohol consumption in the sprawling African sub-
urbs under his care.

Full-flowering product of civilization according to European precedent and example, these Congo bars are nonetheless as far from Belgium's mournful little *bistros,* from her
shadowy holes at the foot of six-storeyed cliffs of sooty
granite, as the *Folies Bergères* from a Salvation Army meeting. Nor is there anything in common between these Congo
bars and those cosy *salons de rendezvous* which pass by the
name of bar in the more moneyed and less moral neighbour-
hoods of Paris: except, no doubt, in the making of rendezvous.
Finally there is no remote connection other than the purely
alcoholic between a Congo bar and a British pub. I doubt if
there ever would have been. When my father was a little boy
in Scotland he used to assist his village friends in carting
home their fathers of a Saturday night as soon as the publican
threw them out, dead to the world: late in the evening but
early enough, my grandfather fondly hoped, for them not to
have defiled the Sabbath. They would turn up in kirk next
morning, scrubbed and shamed, and enjoy a powerful and
ennobling sense of guilt while my grandfather preached
against their sins of luxury and drink. My grandfather was
strong on the subject, I have always understood; even if he
had not been, no doubt the sense of shame would have been
satisfyingly general.

There is nothing sodden, sad or shamed, so far as I can see,
in the whirling swirling life of these Congo bars; and Monsieur Mons, who knows practically everything about this sort
of thing, assures me I am right. Everyone spends to the limit,
his own money or someone else's if he can only get hold of
it: so that the night or so after pay day, which is generally
once a fortnight, will attain a full tide of animation that ebbs
thereafter to a mere trickle in the dog days when everything
is spent.

On the main road through the old township *Congo Bar* is as brilliant as its proprietor's lighting system can possibly make it. *La Joie Kinoise* does as well or better. Both are glowing—and most of the other two hundred and ninety-eight are glowing—in deep saffron light winking with particles of dust. All is as public and companionable as a widely open-fronted shed, mounted on pillars and furnished with a multitude of little tables and chairs, can make it. There is gaiety and light and noise, dancing and jiving, the making and taking of sentimental vows. There is the drinking of innumerable bottles of Simba, thoughtfully provided by a European brewery established in the city.

The girls of the town are much in evidence. At *La Delicatesse,* as I remember, they are banded together in an association of their own, a sort of prostitutes' co-operative, which is chaired by a European trader in cotton clothes. Everyone is satisfied: the trader has mannequins wherewith to publicize his products, the girls are assured of new robes every few weeks, and customers can rest assured they are paying absolutely top prices. Somewhere on the wall of one of these bars, I cannot remember which, there is even a picture of a group of girls, inscribed with their names and offered with the compliments of Monsieur So-and-So, who sells cotton garments and is making lots of money. Some of these bars have European financial backing.

Normal dissolution of city life? Not really. Nothing here is normal in the European sense: nothing is to be explained in familiar terms. M. Grevisse has estimated that a quarter of all the women in the African townships of Elisabethville are *femmes libres,* "free women," and M. Mons thinks that the proportion may be about the same for the African quarters of Leopoldville.

What are these *femmes libres?* They are not really prostitutes, although their way of life is to sell their sexual services to the highest bidder for a period of weeks or even, now and then, of months at a time. In a sense, they represent a kind of concubinage which testifies to the inevitable breakdown of African marriage customs, once numerous populations shift into the towns. But they also represent something else. Even though obscurely, they represent a deliberate act of feminine emancipation. These *femmes libres,* more or less brilliantly dressed and made-up, with bold eyes and lacquered finger-nails, audacious, determined, frivolous, fickle, seizing life with both hands, dominate the city life of Congo Africans: on that everyone seems agreed. They flock to the bars, laugh the inno-cents out of their fears, initiate the village boys new to the city, corrupt the stolidly married husbands, organize in their own defence, fleece the lascivious European, and generally carry on in gross defiance of Morality and Family Order.

But why so many?

"It's because of the money," one of them has explained. "Only a husband has money. A wife has usually no more than what her husband gives her."

Not a very clear response; but she goes on: "In the old days we women had possessions. We had our place, our work . . ." Women in tribal life, that is, had and still have inalienable rights, both of work and of property; and these compel masculine respect and ensure a measure of independ-ence. But in towns only men work for wages, for the women of the Congo have yet to undergo the industrial revo-lution and take employment; so that the *femmes libres* repre-sent a transition between the urbanization of large numbers of African women and the utterly different situation which may be expected as soon as many of these women earn wages on their own account.

However that may be, all African males who have un-burdened themselves on the subject are at one in condemning their wickedness. "In these days," writes M. Henry Bongolo, "African women are disgustingly emancipated from the severe restrictions which tribal custom rightly applied to them; and this emancipation of our women is a festering sore not easily cured, because it is gangrened with prostitution. At industrial centres, where only men are employed, men are generally more numerous than women. With money thrown at them from all sides, these women soon acquire a clear notion of their 'market value,' thanks to the prostitution by which most of them earn their living. So they become contemptuous of marriage. . . ."

"Another thing about Catherine," M. Bonaventure Makonga has written of an imaginary case which he regards as typical, "is that she has been to school. . . . Of course she has mis-understood and misinterpreted those destructive words, 'equal-ity and emancipation.' . . . Now she believes she is the equal of a man, and as free to do what she likes as he is. At the least quarrel . . . she abandons her marriage. She goes home, ends by joining the ranks of the prostitutes—often to the vivid satisfaction of her parents."

Whereas in tribal life, M. Makonga points out, it is cus-tomary to say to a flighty young thing:

> *Wanengena teka,*
> *Le buya badiaboo.*
>
> You are beautiful; but learn to work,
> For you cannot eat your beauty.

The *femmes libres* know better: they do eat their beauty. Fifty years ago, in the days before industry liberated Euro-pean women, Mrs. Warren put the matter squarely. "The only way for a woman to provide for herself decently is for her to be good to some man that can afford to be good to her."

Disarray in marriage, in the social relations between men and women, is one obvious sign of tribal disintegration in these new African cities. In the African quarters of Brazza-ville, on the French side of Stanley Pool, Professor Balandier lately found that no less than 60 per cent of legal cases over a reasonably long period were concerned with "adultery, divorce, disputes over children, complaints over failures to carry out sexual duties in marriage, and even incest."

When young, Professor Balandier notes, the African girl in town "prefers to go with bachelors who pay her rather than get married, for then she has nothing to do but prepare meals, take part in sexual intercourse, and *faire toilette*—she gains by a complete upsetting of society. This sort of situation costs a man perhaps 2000 colonial francs a month (about $11) and the usual present of a piece of cotton cloth. Sometimes it may lead to marriage and a family; but that seems to be rare until the woman begins to feel herself growing old.

"These expensive women are accessible only to men who

are economically strong—the rest go with prostitutes. Prostitution is often with the complicity of parents who speculate on their daughters as they would on rare goods. Such is the burden of a song one may hear in the streets of Poto-Poto (African quarter of Brazzaville):

> Listen, my friends:
>> God has given us mothers. . . .
> Mothers who are killing us
>> For money and for more money. . . .

At Brazzaville, as in the Belgian Congo, "prostitution is institutional. 'Associations' conduct it, more than a dozen of them: Dollar, Diamond, Brilliant Star, Lolita, Violette, etc.: and these"—as in the Congo—"curiously mingle mutual aid (aid to each other and to their parents) with amusement and with prostitution."

M. Bernard Mambeke has made a collection of their songs. One of them runs:

> Come along, why be afraid?
>> I'm married no longer.
> For I married too soon, you see.
>> Thinking there were no other men.
> But if only I'd known!

"Free enterprise" could scarcely go further. "Everything," laments M. Bongolo, "is dominated by money. . . . In this way, so far as marriage goes, the value of the bride-price (traditional in all tribal Africa, being a dowry paid by the man to his bride's tribal group) rises higher and higher in Leopoldville where it is no longer rare to find parents asking six, eight, or ten thousand francs (between \$125 and \$200) in hard cash, without counting certain payments in kind which the would-be bridegroom also has to make. . . .

"Take, for example, this or that pretty girl who, being in regular relations with a European, or a Gold Coaster, or a Senegalese, carries back to her parents five or six hundred francs a month. . . . Far from shameful, prostitution becomes rather the ideal of many parents of young girls. In these conditions, to ask the hand of such girls in marriage is like asking for the daughter of a Maharajah. . . ."

"Let us consider," writes M. Boniface Mwepu in a mood of reasonable indignation, "the various devices which these women use in order to seduce their victims." Note that we are dealing not with a handful of sluts, but with a big proportion of the feminine population of any of these new cities—women who are by no means weakened in their grip on life.

"For instance, instead of dressing properly, they dress in the fashion called *Jibula*. This fashion allows the woman to show her thigh, and very often her groin, when she is walking. The object," complains M. Mwepu, "is to disturb the man and more easily seduce him.

"Or these women wind round their buttocks, under their robes, a *jikita*. This is made of the little cork fillets which are found in the caps of *Simba* bottles, or else is simply a dress rolled tight round their haunches. So that when they walk, these women make their haunches waggle more than they should, and that, too, is done to seduce you. . . ."

All this is common and painful enough, although M. Bolongo and his friends are perhaps inclined to exaggerate its relative importance. Certainly it is endemic to African urban life under present conditions. Dr. Busia's survey of the coastal city of Sekondi-Takoradi in the Gold Coast, carried out in 1948, included inquiries of 127 known prostitutes. "Many of them said they had no ties with home, and had changed their names. They neither shared any family obligations, nor were wanted by their kinsmen. Some of them said their relatives did not even know where they were. To make up for this, there is a strong comradeship amongst prostitutes, and their 'union' provides the security of a befitting funeral celebration and burial. Fifty of the 127 interviewed had been to school. . . .

"Some of the girls said they were driven to prostitution through sheer poverty. Their guardians could not provide for them with food and clothing, and they had to leave home to fend for themselves. Some prostitutes make their living by remaining mistresses to Europeans who pay them a fixed salary every month. Nine in our sample lived with the Europeans in their bungalows; others lived in town and slept in the European quarter at night. . . ."

There is plenty of excuse for M. Bolongo's pessimism. The African life of Congo cities is wild, disturbing, extraordinary. Old customs, once meaningful and efficacious, acquire fantastic overtones, become frenzied opportunities for removing other people's money. New customs, Christian customs, suffer the same distortion. Never was the anarchist accent of capitalism more wildly celebrated. Everywhere the link between men and women, cause and effect, the past and the future, appears to reduce itself to one of sheer and simple cash.

Consider various forms of marriage, complains M. Bonaventure Makonga. "For example, the religious marriage celebrated with pomp . . ."—bridegroom in black coat and pin-striped trousers, bride in flowing white dress fussily stitched with lace, both facing the camera with stolid faces, aggressively "civilized," deliberately "aping their betters." . . . "It's the copy of the European conception. And it is followed by festivities which profit those who organize them. If Jules gets married this morning, he invites everyone in a cabaret that evening to pay fifty or sixty francs for the 'right of entry.' . . . The number of guests has no limit. . . ."

Everyone comes, apparently, who can. "It matters nothing to the host if he should have a hundred, two hundred, or three hundred guests, provided there be enough for him to see a profit for himself of five or six thousand francs. . . . He invites them for four o'clock in the afternoon next day, but he is careful not to begin the feast until nine o'clock. Like that, he can calculate his profit. If he sees that his hopes are being realized, he tries to put off his guests with immensely long speeches. Do not forget that closing time is midnight. He begins handing out beer at half past nine. But hardly have his guests started drinking than they are called on to dance. Midnight comes before they have had time to empty the bottles that are due to them. But now the owner of the bar is afraid to remain open after closing time . . . so he turns out the light as a signal for everyone to go. Often enough the beer remains untouched and will be sold on the morrow to the profit of the organizer of the feast. . . ."

Alongside this kind of high finance, elementary devices for helping money to go further, such as *likilimba,* seem quite beneath notice. *Likilimba* (*Chilimba* in Northern Rhodesia) is a common practice all over Africa, and is typical of the associative tendencies of tribal Africans beginning to live an urban life: it consists in several men or women grouping themselves together so that one of their number may receive the sum of all their tiny wages for any one pay period—and therewith may buy a sewing machine, or a bicycle, or a wireless set, or a new dress, or something of the kind. M. Bongolo would recognize the essentially tribal origins of *likilimba,* which is always a means of making very low wages seem to go a little further. Admittedly, it is difficult for him to recognize ancestral burial feasts in the *matanga* that is practised in town.

Matanga is a wake feast. Tribally, it is an appropriate propitiation of the spirits of ancestors on the fresh arrival among them of the latest addition to their number. In Elisabethville, however, it is the occasion of a grand set-to and a shindy without parallel. According to M. Makonga—and M. Mons and other authorities would agree with him—the customary period of "active ceremonial" is now lengthened to two or three weeks, and during this time as much may be spent on beer and music as can possibly be mustered by everyone involved. It will end with another big party at someone's favourite bar. "Like the marriage celebrated with pomp, the end of mourning takes place in a bar for everyone who can afford it. Entry is by special invitation after payment. . . . The relatives of the dead person profit from this at the expense of others, the occasion is marked by traditional dances and songs that are often quite scandalous. Nowhere may one find a memory of the deceased on the faces of relatives staggering noisily out of the bar. . . ."

It is natural and understandable that M. Bongolo and his friends should doubt whether this kind of civilization can be worth having: isn't this perhaps another occasion of Africans asking for bread and being given a stone? M. Bongolo and his friends tend to see their past, which they are now learning to evaluate in new terms, in a roseate light. What is more, reacting against European chauvinism (present all around them all the time, whether in the kicks of the farming settler, the contempt and trickery of the trader and storekeeper, or the suave denial of responsibility that is returned to African demands by the administration), they begin to see it as a possible future, too.

No doubt this may be one of the germs of African nationalism in the Congo—increasingly, as we shall see, a live force. It carries with it a tendency to see the pre-European past as pure, noble, and independent; and the disintegration of tribal life as the entirely negative consequence of European presence. This romantic attitude has had obvious European parallels. It lies at the root of much of the obscurantism which is now at work within the nationalist movements of central and southern Africa.

In this there is evidently much delusion. Yet it is not difficult to see why the delusion exists. Instead of the higher civilization they are asked to believe in, many Africans see in reality a Stygian mess of disbelief and dishonesty. Instead of something better, they see what is certainly much worse. They see the venerated tribal links of group and kinship loyalties displaced by an arrant individualism which overrides every frontier of decency. All too often the values they are preached and taught become travestied by the lives they are obliged to lead, and the European examples they are given. They observe that the wicked flourish like the green bay tree, while the upright are diligently fleeced.

When M. Bongolo and his friends look around them they see an African reflection of European custom; they see no reflection of the traditional dignity of their tribal milieu— of that milieu in which the tribal chief, celebrating their ancestors, will exhort his people:

> Master your hearts.
>   May each respect his brother:
> Money is nothing,
> Passion is evil. . . .

They know as well as M. Grevisse, careful administrator of Elisabethville, how greatly "certain bar owners prosper," how "their declared earnings may exceed 20,000 francs a month (over $400), and there is no trick they scorn in making them larger still. Most Native associations are promoted by them. They patronize the bands, all the festivals, all the dances, everything that calls for heavy and pointless expenditure in clothes and that sweeps off the African world in a torment as bad for its health as it is for its future. . . ."

And is it not M. Grevisse himself who calculates that as much as 55 per cent of the tax-produced revenue of the African townships of Elisabethville "derives directly or indirectly from the social malaise"? What is one to make of a civilization which not only appears to foster mass prostitution, but even makes an institution of it by taxing women known to follow that trade?

The anger of M. Bongolo and his friends is understandable; it is shared by many decent Europeans. They observe the disintegration of tribal life, obvious and many-sided; that the emancipation of women leads to mass concubinage and prostitution; that women's associations such as the *Jeunesse Malade-Monnaie*—Youth Sick-for-Cash, and was ever the acquisitive society more festively named?—the Opera, the Diamond and the rest play on what M. Bongolo calls the "well-known vanity of women."

Seldom do they see this as a liberating step towards a new social synthesis more capable of matching the African woman (and hence the African man) to the struggle for equality in the modern world. They do not see that there is evidently no other way for our capitalist society—for the civilization which colonialism reflects in Africa—to make this liberating step. In a word, M. Bongolo and his friends see the collapse of the past, but they do not see the signs of a different future. They see the trees, but not the wood.

For an understanding of this positive side to the disintegration and decay of tribalism, one needs to turn in another direction. And then, for all its initial hesitance, its half-formed consciousness, its immaturity, the reply becomes strikingly clear. The real beneficiaries of momentous change over the past ten or fifteen years—of the possibility for Africans to sell their one great possession, their power of labour, on a more or less open market—are not the *evolués,* the privileged clerks and teachers and others whom the European has tried to "bring over to his side." The real beneficiaries, in spite of very high levels of profit-making by Europeans and very low wage levels for Africans, are the wage workers of a growing industrialism. It is at this point that the story takes on its fuller meaning, the skylines widen and retreat, and much is possible that was inconceivable before.

MISTER JOHNSON

JOYCE CARY

Here Joyce Cary gives us a look at the ragged edges of the contact between people of the bush and the somewhat citified, condescending subalterns of white men's enterprise in colonial Nigeria. Mister Johnson, the mission-educated clerk who conceives himself as an important man of affairs, bemuses and bewilders his "country cousins" with his breezy airs, and scandalizes their old-fashioned decencies. The irrepressible Mr. Johnson is, as the author says, "a young clerk who turns his life into a romance, a poet who creates for himself a glorious destiny." In these first pages of the novel, *Mr. Johnson,* we have intimations of that romance and that destiny. Joyce Cary's comic art does not reduce the stature of his characters, whether they are European or African, because at bottom he loves them, without sentimentality, and with a respect that goes beyond special pleading or covert spite.

THE YOUNG WOMEN OF Fada, in Nigeria, are well known for beauty. They have small, neat features and their backs are not too hollow.

One day at the ferry over Fada River, a young clerk called Johnson came to take passage. The ferryman's daughter, Bamu, was a local beauty, with a skin as pale and glistening as milk chocolate, high, firm breasts, round, strong arms. She could throw a twenty-foot pole with that perfect grace which was necessary to the act, if the pole was not to throw her. Johnson sat admiring her with a grin of pleasure and called out compliments, "What a pretty girl you are."

Bamu said nothing. She saw that Johnson was a stranger.

Strangers are still rare in Fada bush and they are received with doubt. This is not surprising, because in Fada history all strangers have brought trouble; war, disease, or bad magic. Johnson is not only a stranger by accent, but by color. He is as black as a stove, almost a pure Negro, with short nose and full, soft lips. He is young, perhaps seventeen, and seems half-grown. His neck, legs, and arms are much too long and thin for his small body, as narrow as a skinned rabbit's. He is loose-jointed like a boy, and sits with his knees up to his nose, grinning at Bamu over the stretched white cotton of his trousers. He smiles with the delighted expression of a child looking at a birthday table and says, "Oh, you are too pretty—a beautiful girl."

Bamu pays no attention. She throws the pole, places the top between her breasts against her crossed palms and walks down the narrow craft.

"What pretty breasts—God bless you with them."

Bamu recovers the pole and goes back for another throw. When Johnson lands, he walks backward up the bank, laughing at her. But she does not even look at him. The next day he comes again. Bamu is not working the ferry. But he lies in wait for her in the yam fields and follows her as she carries home her load from the field store, admiring her and saying, "You are the most beautiful girl in Fada."

He comes again to the yam field and asks her to marry him. He tells her that he is a government clerk, rich and powerful. He will make her a great lady. She shall be loaded with bangles; wear white women's dress, sit in a chair at table with him and eat off a plate.

"Oh, Bamu, you are only a savage girl here—you do not know how happy I will make you. I will teach you to be a civilized lady and you shall do no work at all."

Bamu says nothing. She is slightly annoyed by his following her, but doesn't listen to his words. She marches forward, balancing her load of yams.

Two days later he finds her again in the ferry with her short cloth tucked up between her strong thighs. He gives her a three-penny piece instead of a penny; and she carefully puts it in her mouth before taking up the pole.

"Oh, Bamu, you are a foolish girl. You don't know how a Christian man lives. You don't know how nice it is to be a government lady."

The dugout touches the bank, and Bamu strikes the pole into the mud to hold firm. Johnson gets up and balances himself awkwardly. Bamu stretches out her small hard hand and catches his fingers to guide him ashore. When he comes opposite her and the dugout ceases to tremble under him, he suddenly stops, laughs and kisses her. "You are so beautiful you make me laugh."

Bamu pays no attention whatever. She doesn't understand the kiss and supposes it to be some kind of foreign joke. But when Johnson tries to put his arms round her she steps quickly ashore and leaves him in the dugout, which drifts down the river, rocking violently. Johnson, terrified, sits down and grasps the sides with his hands. He shouts, "Help! Help! I'm drowning!"

Bamu gives a loud, vibrating cry across the river; two men come dawdling out from a hut, gaze at Johnson, leisurely descend and launch another dugout. They pursue Johnson and bring him to land. Bamu, hidden in the bush, explains the situation in a series of loud, shrill cries. One of the boatmen, a tall, powerful man of about thirty, stands over Johnson and says, "What did you want with my sister, stranger?"

"I want to marry her, of course. I'm clerk Johnson. I'm an important man, and rich. I'll pay you a large sum. What's your name?"

"My name is Aliu."

The man scratches his ear and reflects deeply, frowning sideways at Johnson. He can't make out whether the boy is mad or only a stranger with unusual customs.

"It wouldn't do today," he says at last.

"Why?"

Aliu makes no answer.

"When shall I come? How much money shall I bring?"

"Money? M'm. She's a good girl, that one."

"Anything you like—ten pounds, twelve pounds."

The two men are visibly startled. Their eyebrows go up. They gaze at Johnson with deep suspicion. These are high prices for girls in Fada.

"Fifteen pounds!" Johnson cries. "She's worth it. I never saw such a girl."

The two men, as if by one impulse, turn to their boat. As they push off, Bamu darts out of the bush and jumps in amidships. Neither looks at her. She sits down and gazes at Johnson with a blank stare. Aliu says over his shoulder, "Another day, clerk."

Bamu continues to stare. The two men give a powerful impatient thrust which carries the dugout far out across the water.

Johnson goes on shouting for some time but no one can make out what he says. The village children come and stare. The general opinion is that he is mad. Finally, he disappears into the bush.

Johnson, with his morocco bag of letters under his arm and his patent-leather shoes in his hand, travels at high speed, at a pace between a trot and a lope. In his loose-jointed action, it resembles a dance. He jumps over roots and holes like a ballet dancer, as if he enjoyed the exercise. But, in fact, his mind is full of marriage and the ferry girl. He imagines her in a blouse and skirt, shoes and silk stockings, with a little felt hat full of feathers, and makes a jump of two yards. All the advertisements of stays, camisoles, nightgowns in the store catalogues pass through his imagination, and he dresses up the brown girl first in one and then in another. Then he sees himself introducing her to his friends: "Missus Johnson— Mister Ajali."

The idea makes him laugh and he gives another spring over a root. How he will be envied for that beautiful girl. But he will not only make her a civilized wife; he will love her. He will teach her how to attend parties with him; and how to receive his guests, how to lie down in one bed with a husband, how to kiss, and how to love. Johnson's idea of a civilized marriage, founded on the store catalogues, their fashion notes, the observation of missionaries at his mission school, and a few novels approved by the S.P.C.K., is a compound of romantic sentiment and embroidered underclothes.

Bamu has spoken of the mad stranger once or twice to the other women. Aliu now tells his mother that a clerk has offered a large sum for Bamu. The mother says nothing. She is busy. But the next day she speaks of it to a brother and gradually the whole family find out one detail or another. Then they all talk of it and so it comes to be felt that something important has happened. About four o'clock one afternoon the old mother exclaims, "So a rich man wants Bamu?"

Everyone ponders this for a while; at last Aliu says, "Yes, that's about it."

About an hour later it is agreed that Aliu shall go into Fada and ask if there be really a government clerk called Johnson.

Aliu inquires first in the market, where he learns that there is certainly a new government clerk. But nobody knows any name for him except the "new clerk."

"Go to the hamfiss," an old market woman says. "Hamfiss," "hamfish" or "haffice" is the Fada translation for office.

Aliu goes to the station. He has lived within six miles of it for thirty years, but he has never seen it before. Fada natives avoid the station as English villagers avoid a haunted manor. It seems to them a supernatural place, full of strange and probably dangerous spirits.

Fada station has been on a temporary site for twenty years, because nobody has had time or interest to move it. It stands in the thin scrub which covers two-thirds of the Emirate; that is, all but the river valleys and swamps, where high jungle and tsetse fly are still more discouraging to progress of any kind.

The station has no bungalows. It consists of six old bush houses, with blackened thatch reaching almost to the ground, a fort, and a police barracks, scattered at random, far apart from each other, on bare patches in the scrub.

It is as if some giant had tossed down a few scraps of old rotten hay on a mangy lion skin, tufted with moth-eaten fragments of the hair and scarred with long, white seams. These are the marks of temporary water-courses or drains.

The fort, on a slight hill which represents the flattened headskin of the lion, is a square of earth rampart which has been leveled by time almost to the ground, so that the guard-room just inside it, a mud hut with a porch of corrugated iron, stands up like a miniature cracker hat, a kepi, stuck there, on one side of the lion's battered head, in derision. The tin porch is slightly crooked over the gaping door, like a broken peak pulled down over a black, vacant eye. The gateway of the fort is merely a gap in which dogs like to sleep.

The barracks, across the parade ground from the fort, are four rows of neat huts, like nursery counters arranged for a game. The Union Jack, just outside the guard-room, hangs upon a crooked stick, shaped like one of those old gig whips with a right-angled crank-turn in the middle.

The office, Aliu's mark, the center of Fada government, lies beyond the parade ground in a bare patch of its own, like a small wart of mange grown out of a huge, dried scar, polished brown. It is a two-roomed mud hut with a mud stoop and half a new roof. On the mud stoop between the two door holes a messenger and an orderly are asleep. The orderly's blue fez has fallen off.

Aliu, a brave and stout fellow nearly six feet high, who has hunted lions with a spear, stares at the office, and the office stares at him under its shelving eaves, as with a dark suspicion.

He looks round at the huge bush houses, each alone and unprotected in the scrub, like sulky and dangerous beasts, at the guard-room with its crooked white eyelash, at the rag of pink and blue hanging over it, at the mysterious pattern of the barracks, and his flesh shivers. He steals away from the incomprehensible, terrifying place as from devils. This brings him again to the town road and the store.

The Fada Company store, a tin-and-wood shack with the usual laborers' compound behind, stands on the river close to the town gate. Since it is almost part of the town, natives do not fear it like the station in the bush, with its bush devils. Since it belongs to a white man and has an English-speaking clerk in a cotton suit, it is regarded as part of the government.

Aliu, nevertheless, approaches with care and peeps through the door to spy out his ground. Even when he has been re-assured by the familiar store smell of half-cured hides, mixed with the bitter tiny stink of cheap cotton, which blasts out of the dark twilight within like the fumes of a slaughter-house boiler, he takes five minutes to stiffen his nerve. Finally, he goes in sideways, bowing with his neck at every step, like a hen.

Ajali, the store clerk, is alone behind the broad counter. He is a light-colored southerner with a long jaw, a thin mouth, small, round eyes and a flat, yellow skull. Cut off at the waist by the counter, on which he rests his fingers, he seems to lurk in the hot, stinking twilight of the shed like a scorpion in a crack, ready to spring on some prey. But Ajali does not move at all and his insect face wears a most human expression of boredom.

He is obviously as bored as a reasonable creature can be; not to desperation, but exhaustion. He turns his eyes toward Aliu with weary disgust and, making a great effort, says slowly, "What do you want, you?"

Aliu pulls in his neck and then shoots it out.

"Master, lord."

"Hurry up, clodhopper,"

"Pardon, it's about Johnson."

"Johnson."

"He's rich, isn't he? He's a great one here?"

"Rich? Great? Who told you so?"

"He did." Aliu explains that Johnson has offered a large sum for his sister. Ajali roars with laughter. He is full of excitement and delight.

The fact is that Johnson is a temporary clerk, still on probation, called up on emergency from a mission school. He has been in Fada six months and is already much in debt. He gives parties almost every night, and he seems to think that a man in his important position, a third-class government clerk, is obliged to entertain on the grandest scale, with drums and smuggled gin.

To Ajali, perishing of boredom, the follies of the new clerk are as exciting as scandal in any country village. They fill his empty mind with ideas and his empty time with a purpose.

"Oh, it's too good!" he cries. "Rich and great? Dat fool child, Johnson?" He rushes to the door and screams at an old woman passing along the road. "Has Johnson paid you that debt?"

"No, master."

"That's funny, because he's rich now. He's marrying a wife for fifteen pounds."

"But he owes us all money for a long time. What a rascal. And he really has money, has he?" She goes off in indignation. Ajali, roaring with laughter, shouts after her, "Tell it to the whole market—Johnson is rich now."

Aliu says, "What shall I do?"

"Do, pagan lump? Go home. You smell."

Aliu salutes him and goes with grave dignity and a thoughtful expression. In fact, he is not thinking. He does not know what to think. But he is not surprised at his failure to find out what to think in Fada town. His experience has taught him already how difficult and unusual it is to get any sensible explanation or advice, anywhere.

Authority, as he knows it, is always dangerous, selfish, inexplicable. It looks after its own mysterious affairs in a dark privacy. It never explains. Its servants, even the most approachable, like store clerks, resent nothing so much as a request for explanation. Even when they do give it, it is generally false.

But he feels no grievance, because he fully understands that this is the way things and people are. All things are stubborn and dangerous; all men, except one's own family, find their chief pleasure in tormenting the helpless stranger. After all, what else could anyone do with a stranger except fleece him?

Chapter 7

Roots of the Future:
Aspects of the Cultural Heritage

CREATIVE IMPULSES IN DAHOMEAN POETRY

MELVILLE AND FRANCES HERSKOVITS

Traditional oral literature is not the result of some mysterious, anonymous process. Its makers are known in their time and place although they rarely become known elsewhere. They are always individuals—gifted or more ordinary—working within a tradition. In Dahomey, for example, there is much original verse composition and improvisation, as our authors make clear, on all sorts of occasions, sacred or secular.

Dahomean Narrative, from which the following pages were taken, is a rich collection of stories as well as an analysis of the functions of the narratives in Dahomean life. The book was written by this husband and wife team as a result of their field trip to Dahomey in 1931. They have also jointly produced studies of the Afro-American cultures of Dutch Guiana, Haiti, Trinidad, and Brazil. Melville J. Herskovits' trailblazing book, *The Myth of the Negro Past,* demonstrated the resilience and tenacity of African cultural patterns in the new world.

Dr. Herskovits, director of the Program of African Studies at Northwestern University, initiated that program in 1947, where it was the first such program in an American university. He has been a leader in this field as well as in the general field of anthropology for over three decades.

(See other note on page 60.)

IT IS NOT STRANGE that a culture as specialized as that of Dahomey has professional verse-makers. These are chiefly the originators of new songs in praise of the ancestors of important families, or of songs that celebrate the deeds of men of position, such as chiefs. Verse-makers are classed as *nolodoto* (literally, "good-memory-say-person"), and *ayisumo* ("heart-much-understand"). Since new songs are patterned after old, and proverbs are used to weave any number of variations on any theme, the person of good memory is valued for his usefulness and for his facility. In other words, he is an artificer, in contradistinction to the creative maker of verse, who, to use the Dahomean idiom, has a heart that understands much.

Not all new songs, however, are composed by professionals. It can be said confidently that the greater part are not. To understand this, and its implication for the encouragement and exercise of the creative process, we must examine the occasions that call for improvisation in song.

During the various cycles of sacred and commemorative rites, there are many ceremonies that call for new songs. For example, the deities of the Earth pantheon, Sagbata, have the special prerogative of improvisation, whereas all other gods are worshipped with traditional songs. The new songs may comment on the hard times that have come since the country was "broken" (that is, conquered) by strangers; or they may mock a convert who had not fared well at the hands of destiny; or they may relate, by allusion, how the King of the Earth deities, Dada Zodji, who punishes by giving smallpox to a serious offender against the moral code, had scourged an evil-doer. Such songs "come into the heads" of initiates in a state of possession, and are interpreted as the voice of the deity himself.

The gods of other pantheons also, on occasion, have their specially composed topical songs, even though they are of the traditionally non-improvising group, but this occurs only exceptionally. A song of this sort will be sung when a deity who is worshipped at a regional shrine has performed, let us say, a spectacular cure that other gods could not achieve; or that the same deity has been unable to achieve at other shrines of his own. This calls for new praise-names, phrased as these are in song or spoken as recitative. And when one Dahomean, realistically commenting on these names, said,

"We call it *mlamla,* 'praise,' but most of the time it is flattery." he was alluding to the imagery that goes into shaping them.

In this context, it is important to call attention to the distinction that is to be drawn between the improvisation which is called for in the worship of the gods, and the set formulae which are employed to actuate magic. The *gbo* (the magic cure, the spell, the amulet) works by fixed formula. "But the *vodun* enjoy all the things human beings enjoy. They like praise," said a priest of the Sky Pantheon.

The royal ancestors, as human rulers of the Earth, have the same prerogative of improvisation as the Earth gods, but here it is not at the whim and inspiration of the deities. When ancestral rites are held, it is essential to the prestige of the head of the royal clan and the sons of the royal sons that new songs be sung. A professional singer is called in to compose the new songs for such rites, and they will be sung either by members of the family or by the composer-singer himself. These composers are paid to praise the royal dead, and to hurl defiance at the enemies of the living royal descendants. The number of verses will vary with the theme chosen, and especially with the patron's reputation for generosity.

Yet another form of composition in verse, which is put to music, serves the utilitarian purpose of committing to memory a sequence of events. Here the emphasis is not on elegance of style—the metaphor may be evocative or not—since what is important is the simple statement and refrain that punctuate the listing of deeds, or events, or names that need to be remembered. The king's "remembrancer" who, as we have stated, chanted at daybreak the genealogy of the living monarch, called upon this mechanism; and the records of the wars were kept the same way, as were the genealogies of the clans. We were impressed how often, when we were getting ethnographic information, our informants stopped to sing a long recitative when a chronological series of names or events was needed. One such genealogical recitative that we took down, that of the royal abnormally born, is a song based on the response-and-call pattern of West African music. The leader names directly, or under a praise name, each of these beings, called *tohosu,* in chronological order. The chorus responds after each name with an elliptical allusion to an old man who went to bed hungry, this being the sharpest image of poverty, neglect, and misery that the Dahomean can evoke, concluding,

> And he said to the woman Bodo Buiye
> You see, sleep denies me;
> Come, crush some peppers, even if coarsely,
> And this old man will eat.

Naming ceremonies also provide opportunities for creative expression. A wife receives a new name from her husband when she comes to live in his compound. A man of imagination makes of this name an elaborate tribute to his father, who helped him with the marriage fees; or to his ancestors, who had helped him to prosper so that he could add to the number of his wives; or to the family of his new wife, who may count men of position; or to the bride herself, for her beauty or other qualities. And though she will henceforth be called only by a single word, or at most a phrase from this tribute, it is a matter of prestige that this naming be well phrased, with many allusions in proverb form and rich imagery. The man of no expressive gifts will, if he has the means, call in a professional to help him, though if he is a person neither of substance nor pretensions he will call his new wife by a name that refers to her village, or to the quarters of the city from which she came.

Any special achievement, or any ritual that celebrates new status calls for the pronouncement of new praise names, and for important occasions these are rhapsodies in verse, declaimed and sung. The translation of this custom into the present scene in Dahomey has been achieved with no difficulty. We witnessed two instances of this when sons of chiefs returned from military service in France, and the ancestors were felicitated in their new names for having seen to the safe return of the young men from the war.

An important opportunity for improvisation, especially for the young men and women of Abomey, is the monthly dance held in the principal market of the city, when the people of a given quarter satirize those of another in songs which serve to accompany a social dance, known as *avogan.* Since each quarter gets its turn, this is an effective device to develop new talent. Much prestige goes to those who live in the same quarter as the composers whose songs bite deepest into the shortcomings of their rivals, and thereby become the popular "hits" of the city at large. And such composers are thereafter treated with great tact. "You walk softly with a man like that," friends confided to us about one member of our own household, who was an acknowledged master of the satirical song.

New verses may originate while humble, everyday tasks are being performed. A woman, for example, who is provoked by a co-wife, sings to the rhythm of her pestle while pounding millet. Her lines name no names, but by indirection and metaphor, she weaves a song of reproach, protest, or threat. Or when the cooperative work groups of young men, known as *dokpwe,* are called together, many songs are sung commenting on the generosity of their last host, or on his scant hospitality, and recounting current gossip about people in high places and low. Those who can find new words to an old melody, or know how to reword felicitously or pointedly the lines of well known songs to suit a special incident will enjoy much popularity.

In the days of the kings, during the annual rites dedicated to the worship of the king's head, his subjects were not only encouraged but exhorted to invent songs and parables mocking their ruler, and even naming the injustices they had suffered. The short interlude of license to criticize was set aside ritually so that any repressed ill-will for abuse at the hands of the king's agents might find release, and thereby cease to oppress the king's subjects and "infect their souls." For repressed grievances were felt to have the power to harm the king's soul, as well, and bring evil on the kingdom. It is evident from the songs of this genre still sung that uncensored self-expression was, nevertheless, held in check by the stylistic device of indirection, and the use of the proverb.

A concluding instance of original composition serving in an institutionalized context, being, like so much in Dahomey, neither sporadic nor at the whim of chance inspiration, concerns the annual meeting of the hunters to choose their *degã,* the chief of the hunt, for the ensuing year. To the Dahomean, it is a rite of contesting for office. This time it is narrative improvisation, with or without song sequences. Each candidate recounts to his fellow hunters of a village or a region the adventures that come to any great hunter. The rite is held under a sacred tree, at whose base stands a large pottery jar filled with millet beer. Each hunter, as he is summoned by the incumbent *degã,* comes forward and, dipping his hand in the jar, declares that he will speak the truth before drinking from his cupped hand. He then proceeds to tell his experiences of the past year in the bush—the animals that charged him as he stalked them; the magic he called on to save him; his encounters with the helpful little people of the forest, the *aziza,* or with the giants, sorcerers, or thirty-horned monsters that breathe fire, the *yehwe,* under whatever guises they may have appeared; and the trees or animals turned human who addressed him. When each ends his recital, he makes way for the next, and the one who has most vividly described the happenings that demonstrate the greatest control over supernatural dangers is chosen as chief for the year ahead.

At this point, we may examine some of the imagery that, though present in all forms of Dahomean oral literature, has its most striking examples in verse. Thus, in an ancestral cult song, hope for the future prominence of the clan is expressed in these terms:

Obscurity knows Nature will light the lamps.

A man invoking his important ancestors, sings:

This river and that river,
It is the Sea who is their king.

A funeral song laments a succession of deaths in the family and, obliquely, the fate of Dahomey:

Sadness came to us, and you laughed,
    Your day will come;
Sadness came to the trees, and the lianas laughed,
    The day of the lianas will come;

The water had grief, and the fish laughed,
The day of the fish will come.

A worshipper of the serpent-deity, *Dã,* sings:

He who seeks a favor
Uses a low voice;
Dã says, "You who come entreating,
Give me a low voice."

A secular song, counselling prudence, ends with a well-known
proverb:

When I am on the river
I whisper and say,
"Flow softly."
And for that my two feet
Know the earth of the farther bank.
One who is in a boat at sea
Does not quarrel with the boatman.

A man lamenting his fate cries out to Destiny to make him
invisible to misfortune:

Life has been evil,
Take black clay and paint my soul!

Here a famous singer is addressed:

Ayobo, my song commiserates the hunter who comes on no
    game;
A hunter's wife does not whistle into the horn of his prey.

Ayobo, my song commiserates the man who trips;
A flat shard cannot hold water.

In this invocation to the Thunder god, Sogbo, we again see
how the imagery of a proverb in general use, found in the
third line, is seen to reinforce the theme of the poem:

It is true our Warrior God
Holds man in his grip of fire

War lies in wait on a narrow path,
And seizes us like this,
Holding us fast,
Holding us.

A series of single images taken from the larger forms may
be given to show the range of Dahomean poetic expression in
wisdom and cynicism:
There is no enjoying beyond death.
That which your senses taste of the world goes with you.
The sun does not go in hiding in the season of drought.
The serpent does not measure its shadow against the rainbow.
You do not bridle a horse with thread.
The great sun lights the entire Universe.
Oh, small, small fire, who takes the great and devours them.
When a woman takes up a hoe, man will find no place to
     cultivate.

Or, in allusion to the God of Thunder, whose sacred animal
is the ram,

Ram pounding the earth with hooves of fire.

We give below the words to two songs from our collection
that even in translation give something of the artistry of
Dahomean verse. These songs are traditional cult songs, said
to be of great antiquity. The first is an ancestral song; the
second an invocation to Destiny or *Fa*.

1.

The Giver of Life
Placed the sun in great space,
And said: No hand
Shall be the length to reach it;
Though clouds disappear,

And we become a mountain
Immovable and high,
It will not be that the hand obeys not.

The Giver of Life
Placed the sun in the heavens,
And said: No eye
Shall have the cunning to see within,
Though clouds disappear,
And we become a mountain
Invisible and high,
It will not be that the eye obeys not.

2.

I accept you, O my Destiny,
And I say to you, say,
Let poverty be a stranger in my household;
For if I have no wife, then I am poor;
If no children are born to me, then I am poor;
If I lack possessions, then I am poor;
If my cloth is torn, then I am poor.
O vodun, who creates life and its mysteries,
Let poverty be a stranger
In my household.

The next two are secular songs. The first is said to have been composed by King Behanzin while he was a prisoner in Whydah waiting to be sent into exile. At the time of this field work, this song was heard in Abomey, in Allada, and in Whydah on many secular occasions and was also often sung by the cooperative work groups (*dokpwe*).

What will he do to me,
The stranger?
He can do nothing.

In life, the fish trap that finds no fish
Is brought back to the house;
The elephant will come back
To his father's house.

They are in the land
And they trouble me;
The townspeople insult me.
But if they greet me, I do not care,
If they do not greet me, I do not care.

In life, the fish trap that finds no fish
Is brought back to the house;
The elephant will come back
To his father's house.

The final song, which satirizes foreign rule, was one of the most popular in Abomey at the time of this study. The burden of the song has to do with the judging of a thief at the "residence," before the court presided over by a colonial official. Thieving, a serious crime, was punishable by death or enslavement under the rule of the kings, so that for the official first to send word to the chief who had the thief in custody that it was not a court day, and then, when the chief presented himself on the day named, to order him to return that afternoon with his prisoner, contravenes basic patterns of Dahomean procedure.

The white man says,
"Day after tomorrow."
Eight hundred eighty-five,
Or is it eight hundred eighty-nine?

If this is not theft,
There is no thieving;
But the white man says,
"In the afternoon."

CONCEPTS OF WICKEDNESS IN BANTU PHILOSOPHY

Placied Tempels

In his book, *Bantu Philosophy,* Father Tempels rejected the notion that Africans were "big children." On the contrary, he said, they displayed "an adult humanity, conscious of its own wisdom, penetrated by its own universal philosophy."

One of the concepts in this philosophy is that good will or ill will, even when unconscious, is a vital force that radiates its influence throughout the community. Sometimes, the Bantu believe, an evil influence emanates not only from an unconscious state of mind, but even from a physical defect or an accidental misfortune that the individual has sustained.

Modern psychology has given us a scientific basis for taking into account the influence of unconscious hostility, but in western law this could never in itself be the basis for a juridical finding of guilt as to overt behavior. Yet, as Father Tempels shows, an African can break down and accept responsibility for something which as far as he knows he did not do. We are here going to the roots of a culture: the patterns of moral responsibility, the degree of concern about a moral order.

The word *muntu* as used in this selection is a generic term for man not as a mere physical entity but as a person. In African thought, *muntu* includes the dead with the living, since the dead also have personal or spiritual power that can be used for or against the living.

Placied Tempels spent many years as a Franciscan missionary among the Baluba in the Belgian Congo, but he uses the more general term, *Bantu,* because he believes that the Baluba share their ways of thinking with Bantu peoples in other parts of Africa.

WE MUST CONSIDER the Bantu notions of duty, conscience, guilt, and responsibility. When and why does the *muntu* know and feel himself to be good or evil? When and why does the clan or political society pin the label good or wicked on one of its members? What are the degrees of human goodness or human wickedness? What, in the eyes of the Bantu community, are the aggravating or extenuating circumstances to be considered in relation to such assessment?

According to the Bantu there is unforgivable wickedness in some people: total, superlative wickedness. In all branches of the Bantu family, the *muntu* testifies to an appalling terror, an intense repulsion, in respect of this diabolical form of evil. It is the *buloji* (Kiluba) which, for a Bantu, is as it were a perversion, the corruption of his being, a putrefaction from

which emanates contagion to his relationships, a truly ontological contagion.

The pervert or destroyer ("muloji," "mfwisi," "ndoki")

According to the Bantu, the most degraded crime, the most
cynical prostitution of the sacred laws of nature, is the volun-
tary and conscious crime of destruction by the *buloji,* or by
sorcery. Our ontological study has shown us already that it is
not necessary to effect such destruction that there should be
recourse to magical practices or manipulations, nor even to
any external instrument. The perverted vital force by itself
suffices to realise these destroying effects. This corrosive force
can annihilate directly, by itself. The Baluba call this wilfully
sacrilegious influence, which wreaks mischief against that
sublime divine gift, life, by the name *nsikani,* perverted will.
It is impossible for there to be any reason adequate to justify
or to excuse such action of forces against nature.

All enmity, hatred, envy, jealousy, evil speaking, even false
praise or lying eulogy, are severely condemned by the Bantu.
To anyone who allows his envy or hatred to rise, the reproach
is addressed "Do you want to kill me? Have you *bufwisi* or
buloji in your heart?" Every premeditated act directed towards the destruction of the life of others is called *nsikani;*
and true *nsikani,* that which wickedly brings harm upon the
vital force of another, is the synonym of *bufwisi* or of *buloji.*
Such a *muloji* is held to be in the highest degree blameworthy
by the Bantu. It is reprehensible in the sight of God, the
giver and preserver of all life. Since the *muloji* brings harm
to the natural order, to natural law, and consequently to
human law, the community has the right of defence against
such an evil doer, who spreads destruction and death, who
brings about the annihilation of being.

The evil will excited or provoked

The Bantu recognize lower forms of wickedness. They
admit especially that a man may be provoked or incited by
others to a point at which his good will in respect of life
becomes a will to annihilate. A man may be caused to submit
to such vexations at the hands of his neighbour that he is
impelled in spite of himself to utter imprecations and to will
the diminution of the vital force of another. In such cases, a
man becomes blinded by transports of passion, his eye is no

longer clear, the man so injured has black in front of his eyes. *"Mu meso mufita fututu* (darkness comes before my eyes),"* the Baluba say. *"Bulobo bwamukwata* (excitement seized him)."* *"Nakwatwa nsungu* (I am seized by anger),"* they say again. Excitement, anger, darkening of the eye are not faults: these states of the soul do not constitute a moral evil and consequently they may not be classified juridically as criminal. These attitudes, these human feelings are not in themselves wicked vital influences, although they may lead thereto. Such states, the Bantu say, are in fact determined by external circumstances, things going awry, or misfortunes, evil will, or the injustice of other parties, etc.

Nevertheless, although it is admitted that man finds himself carried away into such states by circumstances foreign to him, it nonetheless holds that anger, even though involuntary, exercises a negative and wicked vital influence when it turns against other people. A man so excited no longer finds within himself a disposition of reverence towards life. He lives in an abnormal condition, in a state contrary to nature; and this abnormal state, in conjunction with a will that despite itself has become destructive is enough to exercise a harmful influence upon those human beings who come into vital relationships with him; and upon all the minor forms of life (of existence) against which his evilly excited will stands on edge.

Although their pernicious effects can be identical, there remains a fundamental difference between the wickedness of the sorcerer and the evil will of the man excited to evil. It would not be said of the sorcerer that his wickedness has taken possession of him, it would be said of him that he is wicked and that his will is totally bad. But of the man possessed it would be said that he was provoked by difficult circumstances and that he was seized by anger. So long as the man acts under the sway of anger, so long as darkness remains before his eyes, the deeds which he may commit will not be reckoned as faults against him. This must be quite understood as a gust of passing anger, since the choleric nature producing continual explosions, or a permanent condition, will be considered as an expression of the wickedness of the pervert, the destroyer. When the excited man recovers his calmness, when his anger leaves him and when he begins

to give an account of what he may have said and done under
the sway of his transport, he is obliged to correct his involuntary destructive influence in order to return to an attitude of
respect for life and to strengthening it. As this anger caused
by an external agent is, by its nature, thus exteriorised, he is
similarly obliged publicly to recant his imprecations and
maledictions and to give evidence of his goodwill, as soon as
his eyes see clearly again. If, on the other hand, he is obsti-
nate after he has become free from the transport of his anger,
he is at fault. There is an evil will in him which may be
imputed to him and which extenuating circumstances can no
longer excuse.

It is useless to say that many Africans are still impressed
by the anger of Whites. The people of a certain village, in
spite of an order given by their Chief, had neglected to prepare a lodging in which I was to stay. My reaction was anger,
recriminations and reproaches. The Chief, far from associat-
ing himself with my diatribes, begged me to withdraw my
hasty and untimely words, *"Kokilo kosyana, Tata!"* lest the
village should suffer on account of them after my departure.

In another village in which I allowed myself to be carried
away by anger the people said: "No, he is not bad; it is we
who are." The only answer was to acquiesce in what their
Father had said.

During revolts, the insurgents and many others have been
in the habit of saying, "The Whites are bad men, they will be
our death." This was simple truth, in that colonizers merely
exploited them, systematically ignoring the human worth and
the rightness of the people. The idea, peculiarly Bantu, is
understandable only in relation to their own conceptions.

The visible proof of the fact that one has dissociated one-
self from all wilful pernicious influence is given by spitting
out saliva. This is done especially when two friends are recon-
ciled after a quarrel. It is used likewise when those who have
injured a third party offer reparation: after the so-called
confessio parturientis,[1] or again, after the farewells of a father

---

[1] When a woman has difficulty in childbirth, the reason is supposed to be that she is withholding the name of the real father,
which must be disclosed so that the child can be born to him.
(Note supplied by Mr. J. L. Pretorius to Colin King, the translator.)

to his departing son if he has previously opposed his going. We shall have to return later on to these particular applications of the custom.

The unconscious evil vital influence

Those who have lived among Bantu have often given striking illustrations of cases in which a man finds himself accused of exercising a pernicious influence and is condemned by reason of the illness or death of another, without his being convicted of fault, or even of any wicked intention. Often the elements of proof are entirely lacking and the miscarriage of justice is palpable to a European witness. And yet it is said that the accused, after making a feeble defense, submits to the declarations and decisions of diviners and ordeals, or to the sentence of elders and wise men; and he accepts the penalties which are inflicted. Such facts are incomprehensible to the minds of European jurists. I believe that I have found an adequate explanation in Bantu philosophy.

The vital forces are under the governance of God, without human intervention. The hierarchy of forces is an ontological order, founded in the nature of being, not depending only on external agreements and on external meddling. All forces are in relationships of intimate interdependence: vital influence is possible from being to being without recourse to external intermediaries. The vital forces, moreover, are not quantitative, mathematical values; nor are they static qualitative values definable by philosophy. They are active forces not distinct from the being itself, which function not only in themselves and on themselves, but forces whose actions can pulsate through the whole universe of forces, to whatever extent they are in vital relationships with them.

In a Baluba village, I happened to see a kid, all deformed. The people of the village said to me that the owner of that kid would be wiser to kill the creature, for it would bring misfortune on all the herds of the village. Many authors have noted that formerly Africans threw misbegotten infants into the river at birth. It is well known that the Bantu carry their sick outside the villages to care for them in the bush or in the forest and bring them back only when they are healed.

I may be allowed to tell of an African in the Stanleyville district who committed suicide because he had lifted his hand against his mother. The reactions aroused in certain tribes by the birth of twins are well known. Such an event, if not considered abnormal, is at least extraordinary, requiring appropriate rites. In the Milambwe region, north of Kamina, two years ago, some hunters killed a five-legged antelope. Nobody dared taste the game and it was taken whole, as it was to the Protestant mission in the district.

These examples show that Africans admit vital influences that are absolutely unconscious. Every unusual phenomenon, every abnormal being is called by the Baluba *"bya malwa,"* and these eccentricities they hold to be disturbances in the natural order, forces out of the ordinary, bizarre. Besides, if all forces find themselves in relationships of influence according to their vital rank, it is but a step to the conclusion that a force, abnormal in itself, will usually if not necessarily have a disordering influence upon the forces upon which it exercises its action. A monstrosity does not constitute, any more than any other being, an autonomous force; but, like every other force, it will have a vital influence and this influence will be logically monstrous.

In some cases the Bantu seem to see a certain automatism in the reciprocal influences of vital forces, nearly as we see a necessary relationship between the cog wheels of a piece of machinery. It is enough if one pinion is out of truth to upset the whole working.

The Bantu accept this unconscious influence, not only between inanimate beings, plants, or animals, but also from *muntu* to *muntu.* They are convinced, as it seems to me, that the man animated with the best of feelings, the best vital intentions, may nevertheless exercise a pernicious influence. Who, in fact, can boast that he knows the vital system to its ultimate ramifications? The general laws of causality are known by every *muntu,* in the same way as the knowledge of the elementary laws of Bantu physics belongs to the common patrimony. These especially are the criteria whereby the vital forces can be discerned. Nevertheless, particular and concrete knowledge remains ever contingent. It belongs to the realm of approximation and hypothesis. Seers alone have the faculty of knowing particular things certainly and yet . . . how often it happens that diviners are deceived: *"lubuko lutupile,"* as the Baluba say. The soothsayer's error has miscarried, has "missed the mark" as a hunter misses his prey. But a failure in divination does not necessarily lead the African to conclude that this means of knowledge is vain. In their minds these errors seem entirely natural, proceeding from the very nature of things and conforming to the nature and possibilities of our human power to know beings.

From that the Bantu admit—and they are thoroughly convinced—that man can by an act, an attitude, or by his mere manner of being, of which he remains entirely unconscious, bring harm upon the ontological order of forces and consequently do harm in this way to his neighbour. I see no other explanation, founded in Bantu philosophy, to explain how Africans bow before an accusation when they know very well, in their inmost conscience, that they have not consciously willed any destructive influence against life. It seems to me that they find themselves in the position of the man who was learning to be a chauffeur. He was convinced that he had followed his theoretical teaching in every detail, that he had in no way been guilty of an error in driving, and yet, confronted with the cuts and bruises and the wrecked car, he dares not deny that he had caused the accident.

Nobody, moreover, would deny that the Bantu community recognizes the right to defend itself against this kind of injury to its vital order. The "not-life," the force destructive to life, cannot possess rights, it is anti-ontological.

What, to the Bantu mind, are conscience, obligation, fault and responsibility?

Bantu conscience: The moral conscience of the Bantu, their consciousness of being good or bad, of acting rightly or wrongly, likewise conforms to their philosophical views, to their wisdom. The idea of an universal moral order, of the ordering of forces, of a vital hierarchy, is very clear to all Bantu. They are aware that, by divine decree, this order of forces, this mechanism of interaction among beings, ought to be respected. They know that the action of forces follows immanent laws, that these rules are not to be played with, that the influences of forces cannot be employed arbitrarily. They distinguish use from abuse. They have a notion of what we may call immanent justice, which they would translate to mean that to violate nature incurs her vengeance and that misfortune springs from her. They know that he who does not respect the laws of nature becomes *wa malwa,* as the Baluba would express it; that is to say, he is a man whose inmost being is pregnant with misfortune and whose vital power is vitiated as a result, while his influence on others is therefore equally injurious. This ethical conscience of theirs is at once philosophical, moral and juridical.

The notion of duty: The individual knows what his moral and legal obligations are and that they are to be honoured on pain of losing his vital force. He knows that to carry out his duty will enhance the quality of his being. As a member of the clan, the *muntu* knows that by living in accordance with his vital rank in the clan, he can and should contribute to the maintenance and increase of the clan by the normal exercise of his favourable vital influence. He knows his clan duties. He knows, too, his duties towards other clans. However hostile in practice intertribal relations may be, Bantu know and say that it is forbidden to kill an outsider without a reason. Outsiders, in fact, are equally God's people and their vital force has a right to be respected. The diminution and destruction of an outsider's life involves a disturbance of the ontological order and will be visited upon him who disturbs it.

The *muntu's* obligations increase in accordance with his vital rank. The elder, the chief, the king know very well that their doings do not involve their own personal vital force only. They and their subjects fully realise that their deeds will have repercussions upon the whole community subject to them. From that proceeds the scrupulous care that can be observed among all primitive peoples to protect the Chief, the strengthener of life, against every injury to his vital force, by means of a bundle of vetoes and prohibitions. These are designed to maintain intact his ontological power, his vital force, the source of the inviolability of all his subjects.

THE TRIBAL ARTIST

WILLIAM FAGG

William Fagg is one of the world's foremost authorities on the traditional art of African peoples. He is deputy keeper of the Department of Ethnography at the British Museum, and edits *Man*, the monthly publication of the Royal Anthropological Institute in London.

"The tribal artist," says Mr. Fagg, "is a distinguishable and original personality, just as much as Cellini or Turner or Matisse." Here again, as in the case of the Dahomean oral poetry, we have to dismiss the myth of the anonymity of tribal art. Mr. Fagg speaks of the dilemma facing African art: lucrative European patronage for African carving tends to destroy all artistic qualities of the work—its great emotional power and stylistic range of uniquely African character.

THE STUDY OF tribal art has fallen sadly between two stools. On the one hand, the artists, who have admired it for nearly half a century, usually insist that any knowledge of the circumstances in which tribal sculptures are produced is entirely irrelevant to their appreciation. On the other hand, ethnologists, though they began to see merit in them at a much earlier date and collected them with discrimination, did not fully appreciate the light which they could throw on tribal life. In the early days of social anthropology the emphasis was on analysis, on classifying ethnographical facts about each tribe under a number of well established headings such as birth, marriage and death customs, initiation, religion, industry, warfare; art did not qualify for a place. After the first world war the pendulum swung with a vengeance; the old ethnology was replaced by the theory that societies should be studied as dynamic, functioning entities; study of the different parts or aspects of a culture was regarded as of little value except in relation to the functioning of the organism.

This again was an unpromising climate for the study of art, which being an activity of the spirit, does not lend itself to deterministic treatment. But now that "functionalism" has been largely assimilated in the main stream of anthropological development, there are signs of the growth of a dual approach. Tribal art may one day be studied both for its own sake and for its place in culture and society, each approach constantly complementing and cross-fertilising the other. In the meantime, we must regretfully note that an enormous amount of cant has been written about "primitive art" in the past forty years, and that most writers have given us far more insight, by implication, into themselves than into the subject.

If we wish to pass through the veil which stands between our attitudes to life and art and those of the tribal peoples, we must first consider how our own artistic preconceptions arose. The whole fabric of our modern civilisation stems from the revolution of ideas which took place in the Aegean during the middle centuries of the first millennium B.C., in the time of the Seven Sages, when science was born on the Ionian coast of Asia Minor, and when man became, or thought he became, self-sufficient. Philosophical systems were brought into being whose purpose was to explain the whole universe in rational terms; where nothing remained inexplicable there was no need of symbolism. Art gradually felt the effects of these great changes: not only was its philosophical basis transformed, but its methods and techniques were affected even more directly by the development of geometry and the possibility of accurate measurement. It became possible, and therefore it seemed desirable, to reproduce the human form, or any other subject, accurately in stone. This revolution, like most others, was by no means free from iconoclasm: the incomparably stylised archaic figures were cast down and broken up as rubble for the foundations of the new Acropolis. Later, the pragmatic Romans made the art of the straight line their own and carried it to every part of the known world, from Watling Street to Meroë. The Renaissance, the Industrial Revolution, and the scientific and technological achievements of our own day are logical developments; so is the tendency of European art, challenged only in the Middle Ages and to some extent in the twentieth century, to keep close to the single norm of naturalism instead of developing in countless different directions.

What I have been saying may seem to be a digression, but it is really an attempt to define what social anthropologists would call our "observational bias." In talking about tribal art I am going to confine myself for the sake of simplicity to Africa, although I believe that much the same things could be said about the tribal areas of Asia, Oceania, America, and Europe. African sculpture is almost entirely confined to the vast area of the Niger and Congo basins, for reasons which are far from clear. The Niger basin is inhabited mainly by Sudanese Negroes, the Congo by the Bantu, who are Negroes with a greater admixture of Hamitic and other strains. Both great divisions are thought to have reached their present habitat thousands of years ago from centres somewhere near the upper Nile Valley, but little is known of these movements or of the ultimate origins of these peoples. The origins of African social and material culture, and more particularly of art, are equally obscure. We do not even know whether sculpture was introduced from the Near East via Egypt, or whether it was already flourishing in central Africa before the first Egyptian dynasties, for in Africa wood carvings decay or are eaten by ants in a very few years.

This perishability of the artist's material has no doubt been one of the main conditioning factors in the growth of African art. The art of tropical Africa is at the opposite pole from Egyptian art. The indestructible stone colossi of Egypt served by their very existence to petrify the Egyptian style and to preserve its essentials through several millennia. In the tropics, the turnover is very rapid: wooden figures may have to be replaced after anything from five to fifty years, very few ever reaching a full century of life. Since variations may be introduced at each replacement, the tempo of evolution may be very quick; a style might become quite unrecognisable in two to three centuries. The pace is stepped up still more with dance masks, which are usually of soft wood and subject to very hard wear; perhaps this accounts for the fact that masks are on the whole far more stylised than figures.

Apart from the masks used by the semi-secret societies all over West Africa in their dances for the promotion of the increase and well-being of the community, sculpture takes the form mainly of figures carved either in honour of the ancestors or as a means of bringing pressure to bear on spirits or on abstract forces. In some parts large doors, furniture, and wooden utensils are also elaborately carved. In West Africa, too, there is a strong tradition of brass-casting, the earliest examples—from about the thirteenth century—being the magnificent brass heads of Ife, which are exceptional in being almost completely naturalistic. The earliest datable finds are the fine pottery figurines of Northern Nigeria, from the first millennium B.C., which demonstrate that stylisation is no new development.

Tribal art did not have the benefit as Europe did of the concentration of the whole artistic talent of a continent within the narrow mould of naturalism, but it did retain the great compensating advantage of freedom to develop in an infinity of different directions. So we find a far greater range of stylistic variation in African art than has obtained in Europe at any period; artistic discipline is exerted at the level of the tribe, the sub-tribe, or the village rather than at the continental level. But most important of all, the element of symbolism and mysticism has always maintained its place in tribal art, and has tended to condition sculptural forms. Art, like music, "begins where words leave off": forms intended to convey symbolic meanings, and therefore by their nature poetic, are likely to be a more congenial and stimulating medium for the creative artist than the more prosaic forms of a purely realistic and descriptive artistic idiom. Therefore, I would argue, the tribal artist is in a sense at one with his medium, whereas the European artist of the Renaissance tradition is rather in opposition to his, seeking to transcend and transfigure it, as the greatest European masters have always done.

Moreover, this poetic character is seen not only in tribal art, but in tribal life in general. Categories of thought tend to rely more on analogy and metaphor than on inductive reasoning. Straight lines seem to be instinctively avoided as inartistic if not sacrilegious; in the making of a path or the building of a house, straightness is not considered desirable in itself, but is sought only so far as is absolutely necessary. Similarly, a craftsman making a complex and symmetrical decorative pattern will often introduce a deliberate imperfection, as though to avert the evil eye.

In a recent article on tribal sculpture, Henry Moore stated his opinion that the tribal artist never transcends the religious or magical basis of his work to the point of producing art for art's sake; but he went on to say that he thought no real or deeply moving art could ever be purely for art's sake. He was thus equating tribal art with all the other great art traditions in which the artist responds to an inextricable complex of motives, which it is profitless and naive to label functional in one case or purely aesthetic in another. Tribal art is no simpler than any other, and its human—and therefore its aesthetic—values should be considered on no less high a plane. This is why I prefer to speak in terms of the tribal artist rather than of that vague abstraction, primitive art, which is too often thought of as a kind of impersonal pool of inspirational material for our modern artists.

The tribal artist is, in reality, a distinguishable and original personality, just as much as Cellini or Turner or Matisse, even though in most cases we know him only through his works. [In 1950] I was fortunate enough to be able to make an all too brief reconnaissance for the British Museum of some of the chief art producing areas of Nigeria, as well as of Dahomey and the Belgian Congo; I was constantly surprised at the individuality of the work of different traditional carvers, and soon found that nearly all the books I had read on African art had greatly overstressed the part played by the force of tradition in conditioning the artist's actions. The impression had been created that the artist must conform so closely to certain fixed patterns handed down by his ancestors as to leave little or no scope for creative originality. It is quite true that tradition usually prescribes the general nature of the work and also certain details and conventions (such as the form of a mouth or the posture of an arm), by which we recognise the style as that of a particular tribe or district. But these traditional influences are in effect the framework within which the artist must work and create; he will certainly take account of them (for he must not get out of touch with his patrons), and if he is a poor artist he will be completely dominated by them, but I should doubt whether

they are any more restrictive of genius than were the conventions of religious art in Renaissance Italy.

One of the districts of Nigeria where traditional carving
can still be said to flourish on a limited scale is in the northeastern part of the Yoruba country, about the towns of Illa
and Omu and Otun. I spent a week travelling round the area,
visiting the houses of chiefs and other men of substance and
photographing many fine sculptures in their possession. They
were all carved during the past half-century by such acknowledged masters as Ajiguna of Iloffa, Bamgboye of Odo-Owa,
Areogun and his half-brother Osamuku of Osi, and Ayantola
of Odo-Ehin. Although these villages are all close together,
and each carver served the whole area, it is quite impossible
to confuse the work of any one of them with that of any
other (except perhaps in the case of Areogun and Osamuku,
who worked together and sometimes carried out each other's
contracts). After seeing a house post, or a door carved in
relief, or a great mask with a superstructure of figures in the
round by one of these men, I found that one could afterwards
recognise instantaneously another work by the same hand.
The mental processes by which one recognises them are
essentially similar to those by which the European art expert
identifies a Giorgione or a Rubens; he will probably form an
intuitive judgment at first sight, before he makes a scientific
analysis. So the slender grace of a Bamgboye sets it apart at
once from the more massive but admirably co-ordinated
volumes of an Areogun.

In that district also one may readily refute the common
idea that there is little or no conscious and articulate aesthetic
appreciation, as such, among Africans. The sculptors I have
mentioned competed for patronage over a wide area; one
minor chief at Illa commissioned Bamgboye, twenty miles
away, to carve two large masks, and Areogun of Osi, thirty
miles away, to make some small figures carved in memory
of dead twins. Again, some owners of early works by Bamgboye apologised to me for their quality, as they were done
"before he became perfect."

The career of Bamgboye aptly illustrates the dilemma
which faces African art and those Europeans who are inter-

ested in encouraging it. He is now about sixty-five years old and respected as an *oluawo,* or priest of the tribal religion. In the surrounding villages may be found many carvings done in his early days as a carver about forty-five years ago and throughout his prime up to about 1935. The best of them show a fine feeling and an unusually high degree of finish compared with the work of other carvers in the district. No doubt it was these qualities which led enlightened British educationalists to recognise his skill by appointing him a teacher of woodcarving at the excellent Government School at Omu not far from his home, and also by obtaining many commissions for him from Europeans. Seldom have good intentions been so frustrated; whether the necessity of passing on his technique to school pupils rather than through the traditional apprenticeship system brought on self-consciousness, or whether the change of patronage, from his own people to Europeans, was the only cause, the fact was that all feeling disappeared from him work, it became "slick" and stereotyped and repetitive, and he ceased to carve the masks and house posts which had been his greatest achievements. I asked him why he was content nowadays to carve innumerable coffee tables and wooden paper knives, all of identical design, for the Europeans, and whether he did not regret the days when every work was a new creation. He answered, very simply, that the Europeans paid him and wished him to do it this way, so why should he wish to do otherwise? Certainly his recent work is not the true African art, but something hybrid and utterly sterile. The tribal carver knows his patrons; they are members of his own community, and his sure and instinctive relationship with them has been built up during his whole working life, or perhaps by his father before him. He knows just how far he can go with them, and within these well-understood limits he is free to create. But divert him from serving his own people to serving the European birds of passage, and how is he to judge what will sell except by the criterion of what has already sold?

There is one more question that we may ask. Are we to class these tribal sculptures as fine art or as folk art? We Europeans, following in the excellent footsteps of Socrates and his fellow dialecticians, tend almost by second nature to pose our questions in some such analytical form as this. So we may well be taken aback when we come up against a philosophy of synthesis such as seems to me to underlie African life and art. Things which seem mutually exclusive in terms of our categories of thought are not necessarily so in terms of a quite different set of categories—which may be just as valid in their way as ours. For example, European writers on West African religion have often been at cross purposes with each other and with the facts through not realising that a deity of the Yoruba or the Ashanti may have both sexes, or neither; or that two supposedly separate gods may be complementary aspects of a single being; such mystical conceptions may be seen, expressed with a superb directness, in some of their finest works of art.

To our question, then, about tribal sculptures only one answer can be given: that they are both art and folk art. The best of these carvings are masterpieces fit to rank with the fine arts of Europe and Asia; yet if you call unannounced at the home of one of their carvers, you are as likely as not to be told that he is away at his farm and will not be back for three days. It is a synthesis that would have delighted Eric Gill. Both fine art and folk art may, then, be a literally correct answer to the questions as we so innocently framed it; but its real value is in superseding that imperfect question and clearing the way for more important ones, which may lead us to a deeper understanding of the nature of creative art.

THE AFRICAN RENAISSANCE

Thomas L. Hodgkin

An important vehicle of African culture is the magazine *Présence Africaine,* published in Paris since 1947. Founded by African intellectuals and other writers and artists of African descent, supported by French cultural leaders, it soon became much more than a magazine, for it has published many books by Negroes from all over the world and has organized international conferences of Negro scholars. The first conference of this kind held under its auspices was in 1956. We give here an engrossing report on that conference by an Englishman who attended as a "privileged eavesdropper." The discussions summarized by Mr. Hodgkin can serve as an excellent finis to *African Heritage,* because they touch again and again on the central concerns of this volume.

Mr. Hodgkin is the author of *Nationalism in Colonial Africa* and edited *Nigerian Perspectives: an Historical Anthology.* He has been a lecturer at many universities and is now Director of the new African Institute at the University of Ghana.

EVEN WELL-DISPOSED Europeans sometimes have residual doubts about Africans. "Yes," they say, "we agree that Africans are not eternal children. We know there is no reason to suppose that pigmentation has anything to do with intelligence. We recognise that, given adequate opportunities, Africans are likely to produce as many capable doctors, engineers, historians, physicists, as any other branch of humanity— indeed, they have already begun to produce them. Yet the fact remains (this argument continues) that Africans have not so far bred a Shakespeare, a Dante, or an Aristotle. They have never built a Parthenon or a Chartres. Surely, therefore, there is some justification for regarding Africans as in a sense 'on probation'— until they have shown that they can match our standards of achievement?"

This still fairly widespread assumption of the superiority of European culture, the demand that Africans should prove themselves according to criteria which we determine, is part of the background to the First International Congress of Negro Writers and Artists, held in Paris in September, 1956, under the auspices of that enterprising French-African institution, *Présence Africaine.* One purpose of this conference, whose proceedings have recently been published, was to challenge that assumption: to ask the questions: What are the essential qualities of the Negro-African inheritance? How best can it be developed and renewed?

This was only part of the problem which occupied the conference. Those who took part in it were also conscious, as I suppose we all are, that the African stage is now set for an

accelerated movement towards independence: Ghana yesterday; Nigeria, French West Africa, the Cameroons, tomorrow;
Uganda, the Belgian Congo, a little way behind. In actual
years the colonial epoch has been relatively short; scarcely
the life-span of a man since the hey-day of partition in the
last quarter of the nineteenth century. An old Hausaman, or
an old Muganda, can remember the days of the pre-European
kingdoms.

But enormous transformations, obviously, have been packed
into this short historical period. At the moment I am concerned only with one kind of transformation—the export of
European culture, and the process known as assimilation.
Whether they have preached assimilation as a theory or not,
all the European colonising Powers have practised it in some
degree. The African élite has been taught in schools organised
on the model of British public schools or French *lycées*. It
has sat for its Senior Cambridge or its *Baccalauréat*. It has
been compelled to learn a little Latin and less Greek. It has
been taught to reason in the style of Hume and Ayer, or
Descartes and Gilson. It wears academic dress, or drinks
vermouth in cafés. When it succeeds in winning a measure of
self-government, its institutions take the form of a parliament
on the British model (complete with Speaker and mace), or
a territorial assembly derived from the French *Conseil-
Général*. When this élite wants to write poetry, or do scientific research, or run a business, or make political speeches,
or philosophise, it is obliged as a rule to use a European language. Friendship, family relationships, love-making, can be
handled in the vernacular, but little else. Naturally, in this
situation, the African élite is confronted with the question:
"How can we be ourselves? How can we make use of European ideas, institutions, and techniques, without becoming
their prisoner—without ceasing to be African?" This is a
question which political independence by itself does not solve.

This is not a purely African question, nor a purely modern
one. And the sharpness with which it is felt seems to vary.
It is surely not an accident that the focus of the African
renaissance should be Paris; or that so many of those who are
most actively concerned in their writings with the revolt
against "cultural colonisation" should be Senegalese and

French West Indians—Léopold-Sédar Senghor, Alioune Diop,
Aimé Césaire. For they have been exposed to assimilation in
its most uncompromising form, to the dogma that there is
only one civilisation, and that civilisation is French.

British colonisers, on the other hand, have always had a
more take-it-or-leave-it attitude to their culture. We do not
really like the word, to begin with. When it comes to the
thing, we are diffident about our contemporary poets; we
have grave doubts about our educational system; we know
our cooking is terrible. Hence, at least in West Africa, Africans have never felt the same sort of need to assert bellig-
erently their values, styles, traditions, against a barrier of
European contempt. They have asserted them more as a
matter of course. In his opening statement to the conference,
M. Alioune Diop insisted that every serious African writer or
artist is bound to be "committed," to "bear witness against
the racialism and imperialism of the West." Later, Dr. Davidson Nicol (a biochemist and writer from Sierra Leone, now
a Fellow of Christ's College, Cambridge) explained that, as
a matter of fact, British West African writers have not hitherto found it necessary to think of themselves as "committed"
in quite the same way as French Africans:

> In British West African writing there is a lack of the
> motive power of burning racial injustice which carries
> through in the writing of other peoples of African descent.
> . . . The distressing but stimulating convenience of a setting
> of Afro-European conflict is fortunately or unfortunately de-
> nied them. They have to seek other verities and tensions.

However, in Paris, the British West Africans, though something of a special case, certainly accepted the chief presup-
position of the conference—that Negro Africans have made,
and can make, their own particular valuable contribution to
humanity, if once they are free to contribute. Within this very
broad framework of agreement there was naturally room for
all kinds of opposition to emerge: between Marxists and
Liberals; between Christians and secular humanists; between
the American Negro's interest in total equality and the African nationalist's interest in total independence. But more profound, I think, than any of these was the opposition between

what you might call Africanophiles and Westernisers. The outstanding representative of the Africanophile standpoint is M. Senghor, which is interesting, since superficially it might seem that he was totally integrated into French civilisation: a former prisoner-of-awr and member of the resistance; for the last ten years deputy for Senegal, and a junior Minister in M. Faure's cabinet; Professor of African languages at the Sorbonne; and a distinguished French poet in his own right. Yet no one is a more passionate exponent of the ideas of negritude. Senghor's reply to the "why have the Africans never produced a Shakespeare?" type of attitude is, put simply, "Why should they?" The Negro-African genius is essentially different from the European, and has produced different sorts of fruits. (Only Europeans, with their itch to act as the world's schoolmasters, or the world's examiners, would attempt the absurdity of judging between fruits—giving an A to Shakespeare and a B ++ to the Benin bronzes.) African culture is what it is because Africans are what they are— rational, but in a different way from Europeans, understanding through insight and sympathy rather than through discursive thought. As Césaire described them, in a poem that has become familiar in French Africa:

Hurrah for those who have invented nothing
for those who have never discovered
for those who have never conquered
but abandon themselves to the essence of all things
ignorant of surfaces, but seized by the very movement of
    things
not caring to conquer, but playing the game of the world
truly the elder sons of the world
porous to all the breaths of the world

African metaphysic—the typical African metaphysic, Senghor might say—conceives of the world as a hierarchy of forces. African social systems order men in a hierarchy of groups. African culture is the complex of activities, symbols, rhythms, through which African man expresses his understanding of the world and society and his sense of unity with them. African art is essentially a collective art, done for everyone with the participation of everyone. It is a practical art: Senghor quotes as an example an episode from Camara Laye's novel, *The Dark Child*, in which the forging of the golden jewel, the recitation of a poem about the jewel, the dance to celebrate the completion of the jewel, are all parts of a single process. It is a committed art: the artist mirrors his people, his time, his history, but he mirrors them from a definite personal point of view. And it is an art which virtually goes on all the time. As Senghor puts it:

> Literature and art do not simply occupy people on Sundays, or "theatrical evenings," but continue through the eight months of the dry season. Man is all the time absorbed in his relations with Others: spirits, ancestors, members of his family, of his tribe, of his kingdom—even foreigners. These relationships are expressed in feasts, and death itself is the occasion for a feast—for the supreme feast. There are the feasts of harvest and the feasts of sowing; of births, initiations, weddings, funerals. There are the feasts of corporations and the feasts of fraternities.

Senghor's rhetoric is so persuasive, in French at any rate, that it is hard to summarize his argument without emasculating it. But his main thesis is the need for Negro writers to return to their sources, to the African classics, where they can find as rich a variety of myth and story, poetry and drama, sculpture and decoration, as any man could desire—based on a kind of grasp of man's essential nature that Europe has lost.

This thesis of Senghor's was disputed from two points of view. M. Alexis, a Haitian doctor and poet, attacked what he regarded as one of Senghor's underlying assumptions—the notion of a single archetypal African culture, perhaps an idealised portrait of Senghor's own local Serere culture, about which valid generalisations could be made; whereas in fact Negro Africa contains a great diversity of cultures. The answer given to M. Alexis by M. Senghor's supporters was that while, certainly, every African culture was unique, there was a real kinship, or "cousinship," between them. It made as much sense to talk in a general way about African culture as about European culture. Just as Frenchmen and Italians have a common European-ness, so Wolof and Fulani have a common African-ness. As one down-to-earth speaker put it: "Why on earth should we all be gathered here if there were not some common Negro-African culture?"

A much more profound question was raised by Mr. Richard Wright, the American Negro writer who [before his death] lived in Paris. These traditional cultures, which Senghor described so movingly, might they not simply be, in the contemporary context, a beautiful dream? Had they any relevance, really, to the needs of contemporary African man? [Said Mr. Wright:]

> The ancestor-cult religion with all of its manifold poetic richness, that created a sense of self-sufficiency—did not that religion, when the European guns came in, act as a sort of aid to those guns? Did that religion help people to resist fiercely and hardily and hurl the Europeans out? I question the value of that culture in relationship to our future. I do not condemn it. But how can we use it?

At times the conference became a kind of dialogue—with Senghor, the Africanophile, saying in effect: "We are very old, and all our future achievement depends upon grasping and using this ancient African inheritance"; and Richard Wright, the Westerniser, replying: "We are very young; and while we can admire this ancient culture, we must recognise that, where it survives, it is the reflection of a moribund medieval metaphysic; the ideas which we can use are secular, scientific, western." Richard Wright was just as positive as Senghor in his rejection of "cultural imperialism," but from a totally different standpoint. The argument that Milton and Descartes justify the British and French claim to some kind of superiority in relation to Africans is absurd—not primarily because of the uniqueness and rich resources of African culture, but because Milton and Descartes are in no sense British and French "possessions." Africans possess them also, perhaps in a more fundamental sense. Descartes "belongs" in a truer sense to the black African who attacks the irrationality of color prejudice than to the French *petit blanc* who defends it. (Symbolically the conference met in the Salle de Descartes at the Sorbonne.) Milton "belongs" to the Bantu engaged in a struggle for civil liberties rather than to those Englishmen who assert the Divine Right of Europeans.

I hope I have interpreted Richard Wright fairly. He thought aloud so much, and added so many footnotes to himself, that it is not always easy to be sure of his meaning. But I think that the burden of his paper on "Tradition and Industrialisation" is that he, as an American Negro, stood firmly rooted in what are generally called "western" values: the secular state; the free circulation of ideas; the right of protest; the autonomy of art; science as a liberating force; human persons as ends in themselves, and so forth. These values, though constantly denied by the West in its dealings with Asia and Africa, have now been taken over by the new Asian and African elites, and are beginning to be applied to their own local situations. Thus they are ceasing to be "western" values, and becoming simply human.

What follows? Is the intellect of African man forced to choose—as Césaire puts it: "either to discard our inherited civilisation as childish, inadequate, historically out-of-date, or, in order to preserve our cultural inheritance, to barricade ouselves against European civilisation and reject it . . . to choose either loyalty and backwardness or progress and betrayal?" M. Césaire—a Marxist deputy from Martinique, and a remarkable poet—regards the idea of such a choice as unreal. The present situation of African culture, as he depicts it, is depressing: colonisation has shattered beyond repair the beautiful equilibrium described by M. Senghor, and left in its train a new barbarism—islands of bogus traditionalism, occasional human "zoos," to divert the tourist or interest the anthropologist, among a waste of pseudo-westernised men, the new *cocacolanisés* (a nice French expression), living in a "cultural undergrowth" that has grown up among the ruins of the old civilisation.

The solution, for M. Césaire, lies in Africans refusing to say "no" either to inherited ideas and attitudes or to acquired European values, but to draw selectively upon both. But before Africans can set about this task of reconstruction, they must recover the historical initiative. Subject peoples cannot perform the needed act of synthesis. An African renaissance presupposes the political liberation of Africans.

I want to end by making three comments—comments which occurred to me, a European, a privileged eavesdropper, after listening to these Africans, West Indians, and American Negroes discussing their own absorbing problems among themselves. First, I find myself wanting to ask: "What is it likely to involve, this new synthesis, when you have recovered the historical initiative and set about making it?" I know the correct answer: that it is not for writers and artists to try to predict the future culture of Negro Africa: this is a question which can be answered only in practice. But I doubt if it is the whole answer. Most of those present at the conference would, I think, agree that they wished to retain, though in a new form, this strongly developed African sense of community, expressed in dance, in age-sets, in village democracy.

What, on the other hand, about traditional religion— animism—which has provided the sanctions for this sense of community? M. Paul Hazoumé of Dahomey, who is a specialist in these matters, when questioned had no doubts: "The future of animism?" he said, "What will happen will be what has happened already in western Christianised Europe. Part will disappear. Part will survive as magic. And that is all." On the question of language, too, there are ideas in circulation: not only the point that certain African languages should be given special attention, and developed as national languages; but also the interesting suggestion, thrown out by M. Senghor, that the historical relationship between ancient Egypt and the peoples of Africa might well justify substituting ancient Egyptian for Latin and Greek as a classical language. It seems to me inevitable and right that such questions should be raised, even if they cannot yet be answered.

Second, I find myself asking: How relevant is this kind of very sophisticated discussion to the interests of ordinary Africans, or, if you like, ordinary educated Africans? Naturally those who, like Senghor, Césaire or Alioune Diop, have sucked in French techniques of thought almost with their mothers' milk, have a marvellous gift for impassioned philosophising. British West Africans, brought up in a quite different intellectual discipline, tend to react to it rather as Hume reacted to Rousseau. But, beneath the obvious differences of style and language, there is, I am sure, an important common interest in the central questions raised at this conference: What is there of enduring value in our African traditions? What do we need to take over from Europe and adapt to our purposes? What can we afford to discard? For many Africans these are much more pressing issues than some of the rather dusty questions that are often posed over here, such as: Can these people run a rural district council efficiently? Can they maintain a nonpolitical Civil Service? Can they play the parliamentary game according to our rules? Questions of this kind tend to make the mistake of assuming that free Africans will want to go on imitating us. On the evidence of this conference, that is not the case.

Finally, what are the implications for us of the conference, and of all the ferment that produced it and that it has produced? I think it is one sign, among many others, of the new, much more interesting, phase which relations between Europeans and Africans are now entering. For centuries we lived in virtual isolation from one another; occasionally a remarkable character from the one world would penetrate the other. Then came the period of European domination—first through the slave trader, later through the colonial system—with the curious twisted racial ideas which were its intellectual counterpart. Only recently we have begun to enjoy the stimulus of Africa, principally through its music, its dances, its plastic arts. How much we will gain when this diversity of gifted peoples—the Wolof and the Bambara, the Yoruba and the Fulani, the Bakuba and the Baluba, the Banyarwanda and the Baganda—with their diversity of insights and capacities, and their common negritude, cease altogether to be regarded as the inhabitants of an ethnological museum and are free to live and operate and speak in the same world as ourselves. I find it an exciting prospect.

Epilogue

FUTURAFRIQUE

M. B. Tolson

The Futurafrique, the chef d'oeuvre of Liberian
    Motors slips through the traffic
    swirl of axial Parsifal-Feirefiz
    Square, slithers past the golden
    statues of the half-brothers as
    brothers, with *cest prace*.[1] . . .
The Futurafrique, the accent on youth and speed
    and beauty, escalades the Mount
    Sinai of Tubman University, the
    vistas of which bloom with co-
    eds from seven times seven lands. . . .
The Futurafrique, windows periscopic, idles past
    the entrance to the 70A subway
    station, volplanes into the aria
    of Swynnerton Avenue, zooms
    by the Zorzor Monument,[2] zigzags
    between the factory hierarchies,
    rockets upcountry and backcoun-
    try, arcs the ad-libbing soapy
    blue harbor crossroads of Wal-
    dorf Astorias at anchor, atom-
    fueled and burnished in ports
    of the six seagirt worlds. . . .

[1] "All honor to labor."
[2] The Zorzor twins were miracle workers in iron.

284

The Futurafrique strokes the thigh of Mount Bar-
    clay and skis toward the Good-
    lowe Straightaway, whose colo-
    ratura sunset is the alpenglow
    of cultures in the Shovelhead Era
    of the Common Man. . . .
The Futurafrique glitters past bronze Chomolungma, odic
    memorial to Maltilda Newport—
    on and on and on, outracing the
    supercoach of the Momolu Bu-
    kere Black-Hound winging along
    the seven-lane Equatorial High-
    way toward Khopiru.[3] . . .
The Futurafrique, flight-furbished ebony astride
    velvet-paved miles, vies with the
    sunflower magnificence of the
    Oriens, challenges the snow-lily
    diadem of the Europa. . . .
The Futurafrique, with but a scintilla of its Niagara
    power, slices Laubach Park,
    eclipses the Silver Age Gibbet
    of Shikata-gai-nai,[4] beyond the
    ars of Phidias;[5] on and on, herds
    only blears of rotor masts roulet-
    ting, estates only rococo decks
    and sails swirling, the Futur-
    afrique, the Oriens, the Auster,
    the Americus, the Europa, rend
    space, gut time, arrowing past
    tiering Nidaba,[6] glissading side

[3] "To be." The concept embraces the eternity of Thence, which free from blind necessity contains the good life.

[4] "It cannot be helped." This is the stoicism with which Japanese villagers meet the earth convulsions of sacred Fujiyama.

[5] *cf.* Rodin: "Beyond Phidias sculpture will never advance." Also Shakespeare, *Troilus and Cressida:*
        The baby figure of the giant mass
        Of things to come.

[6] Dr. Samuel Noah Kramer's translation of a Sumerian tablet in the Museum of the Ancient Orient: "You have exalted Nidaba, the queen of the places of learning."

by side, into the cosmopolis of
Höhere—the bygone habitat of
mumbo jumbo and blue tongue,
of sasswood-bark jury and tsetse
fly, aeons and aeons before the
Unhappie Wight of the Question Mark[7] crossed the Al Sirat!

[7] The Question Mark: refers to the cartographic and also symbolic shape of Africa.